Michal Wimmer

The Complete Guide to Children's Drawings

Accessing Children's Emotional World through their Artwork

Michal Wimmer

THE COMPLETE GUIDE TO CHILDREN'S DRAWINGS

Accessing Children's Emotional World
through their Artwork

Bibliographic information published by the Deutsche Nationalbibliothek
Die Deutsche Nationalbibliothek lists this publication in the Deutsche
Nationalbibliografie; detailed bibliographic data are available in the Internet at
http://dnb.d-nb.de.

Bibliografische Information der Deutschen Nationalbibliothek
Die Deutsche Nationalbibliothek verzeichnet diese Publikation in der Deutschen Nationalbibliografie;
detaillierte bibliografische Daten sind im Internet über http://dnb.d-nb.de abrufbar.

First edition copyright © 2012; licensed from eBookPro Publishing (www.ebook-pro.com).

Please visit Michal Wimmer's website: http://childrendrawingcenter.com/

∞
Printed on acid-free paper
Gedruckt auf alterungsbeständigem, säurefreien Papier

ISBN-13: 978-3-8382-1245-6
© *ibidem*-Verlag / *ibidem*-Press, Stuttgart 2019

Printed in the United States of America

Content

Content

About the Author

Michal Wimmer, M.A, is an art therapist and an international expert on children's drawings analysis. She has years of experience supporting families with children (aged 2–18) with emotional and social difficulties using their drawings. Michal is also the founder of an advanced studies program, introducing social workers, psychologists and art therapists, as well as elementary and preschool teachers to the world of children's drawings analysis. The program includes a two-year graduate study on children's drawings analysis, based on practical exercises, various psychological theories and parental guidance.

A popular speaker, Michal has given hundreds of workshops and keynotes about children's drawings analysis in Universities, Colleges and private events. She is often interviewed in TV shows, magazines and newspapers for insights about parenting through children's drawings. Michal manages a national forum about children's drawings analysis, providing parental guidance based on drawings. Finally, she also provides written expertise to courts of law, based on analysis of children's drawings, mainly in the context of family abuse and children at risk.

Michal runs a private clinic for treating children, adolescents and adults. She also works as an art therapist in psychiatric hospitals and mental health clinics. Recently, she has founded the Roshida website. Her therapeutic strategy is deeply influenced by the classic psychoanalytic approaches of Sigmund Freud and Jacques Lacan.

PREFACE

One of the most charming moments in parenting is when your child shares a new and fascinating discovery with you. Together with the child, you too are excited to see a tiny beetle resting on a green leaf, sand dunes that have instantly become giant slides, and an entire world of scents, tastes, colors and shapes we have all but forgotten over the years.

Children's drawings reveal similar experiences. Each drawing is the starting point of a voyage led by the child explorer. In this book, you – educators, therapists and above all parents – are offered the opportunity to join this unique voyage and understand the child's world from his distinct perspective.

Parenting in today's world is far from straightforward. Parents who may be successful in other areas in their lives are often unconfident and even helpless when facing parenting tasks. The parental role involves dealing with fundamental questions, such as: Have I set the appropriate boundaries? Have I understood my child properly? Have I given him the right behavioral reinforcements? Have I correctly interpreted his signals? Today's parents are anxious to understand their child and be more involved in his emotional world, so as to be able to provide the right answers when he'll need them.

In this context, children's drawings offer a kind of map enabling you to navigate in the child's inner emotional world. Through the drawings, the child expresses his difficulties, as well as the solutions he requires. Informed observation of the child's artwork may provide parents, therapists and educators with a reliable compass for understanding the child's present needs.

My approach to interpreting children's drawings and to diagnosing children in general is positive and optimistic. The drawings shed light on the child's world, enabling us to understand his difficulties but also the strengths which enable him to grow towards solutions that are appropriate for his personality. All children want to develop and experience the world around them, but they require proper encouragement and guidance to support them on their way to realizing their potential. Interpreting children's drawings enables the parent to avoid forcing standardized, one-size-fits-all solutions that have been offered to different families under different circumstances, and instead assess what is most appropriate for his child at a given moment in his life. Just as many children can have fever, but each for a different reason, children's drawings allow us to better understand the various reasons for the same behavioral manifestation.

This book presents hundreds of fascinating examples of children's drawings that I have collected from various places around the world. Most of these drawings have been made by children whose parents had been referred for emotional counseling and therapy, in the course of which multiple drawings have been analyzed. The conclusions presented next to the drawings are based on comparisons with other drawings by the same child in different periods of his life and on a personal interview with his parents, which add an important dimension to understanding the child's world in the family system. Drawings selected to illustrate various phenomena usually include one manifestation of the given phenomenon (sometimes the most common and sometimes a particularly rare one). Naturally, every interpretation is based on recurring manifestations of the same phenomena, together with graphic indicators supporting my conclusions. Note that one may never reach any final conclusions based on a single feature in the drawing – such features are offered only as illustrations of broader phenomena.

The last few years were dedicated to a thorough research, which included reviewing findings of studies conducted in the best universities in the world as well as conducting my own groundbreaking studies on 100–300 children each in order to obtain statistically significant results. It is an honor and privilege to present the fruits of this labor to you, in this book. Throughout the book, I have sought to enable all readers to understand the significance of the various research findings and to integrate them with my professional knowledge and experience as an expressive art therapist.

I sincerely hope that the resulting book will enhance public awareness of how the child's inner world is reflected in his drawings and open an additional channel of communication between the parent, educator or therapist on the one hand, and the child on the other – a channel that will enrich and reinforce their relationship.

Note: All drawings in this book have been published with both parents' informed consent. Wherever necessary, identifying details of the child or family have been changed or removed.

Right after this page begins a magical and colorful journey in the world of children's drawings. I hope the book will give you tools to gain a new perspective of your child's drawings, your child's world and even the child within you…

Michal Wimmer

1   INTRODUCTION

Developmental Stages in Children's Drawings

When you observe a child's drawings over an extended time period, you will notice trends of change and development. Without any deliberate adult intervention, the child advances from stage to stage and develops his abilities. Nevertheless, despite evidence of clear and general developmental stages, I do not recommend analyzing a child's artwork in strict terms of how it matches a certain population norm. When I interpret a child's drawings, I do not compare them to his friends' drawings but to his own developmental trajectory. Therefore, the ages noted in the titles below are suggestive only and should be treated with caution.

Age norms are important. However, if your 4 year-old child still scribbles – unlike his friends who are already drawing human figures – this does not necessarily attest to any developmental lag. The ages appearing below indicate developmental periods and their general characteristics, but you must bear in mind that each child has his own combination of such characteristics, some enhanced, and others nonexistent, etc. Moreover, the developmental trajectory and the transitions between stages are individual. Some children may skip a certain stage or regress to a previous one before moving forward again.

Stage 1: Spontaneous Scribbling – Ages 1½–2½

The first times a child holds a pencil and discovers what it can do are highly significant to his development. In families with several older children, you can see babies as young as 9 months imitate their brothers by using drawing tools and admiring their own work.

In many senses, these occasions are similar to the moments a child realizes he can produce sounds and begins to speak. Scribbling is thus akin to the infantile muttering. In both cases, the child begins a prolonged learning process by way of trial and error. He moves the drawing tool (changes his voice) in different directions and observes the different results on the page. Moreover, just as infantile murmuring or crying expresses a certain need or emotion (hunger, anger, boredom, etc.) scribbling is intentional, albeit pre-schematic.

To the untrained eye, drawings made at this stage would seem like senseless doodling. However, a closer look reveals that children definitely develop distinctive scribbling styles.

At this stage, the child attaches great importance to the dynamic aspect of drawing, and delights in the sensory experience of moving the drawing tool across the page. Lines start and end at random, and if there are any geometric shapes in the drawings, they are usually drawn inconsistently and disproportionately. Given these factors, I recommend checking that at least three months have passed since the child had first began to experience drawing before his artwork can be analyzed for emotional meanings.

Figure 1-1:   Inconsistent and unstructured lines

In the following drawing by a 22-month old girl, you can see lines that extend beyond the page's boundaries, lines with different lengths and directions, without any consistency or personal preference. You can also see asymmetric loops, lines drawn erratically across the pate, cyclical circular scribbles and insertions of the drawing tool into the page, whether vertically or diagonally, to create a "point map" (children enjoy doing this very much, and tend to imitate one another around the drawing table at kindergarten).

In terms of psychological development, Sigmund Freud (1954) calls this age span the oral stage, a period characterized by children's tendency to taste paints and crayons, to check what sounds they produce and to explore them tactually as an integral part of the creation process.

Stage 2: Structured Scribbling – Ages 2½–3½

At this stage, the child begins to plan the drawing in advance. Basic geometric shapes begin to appear on the page, including circles (or quasi-circles), and squares (or lines that cross to form a square area). This time, they do not appear accidentally; on the contrary, the child would often use up entire pages in recurring attempts to draw the same shape. Finally, at this stage we begin to see children who critically observe their artwork as it unfolds, or even stare fixedly at the page before they even start.

Usually, children at the structured scribbling stage are happy to talk about what they have drawn, and will explain about the various elements on the page.

Figure 1-2:   Drawing accompanied by the sound of a motor

Although the drawing still looks like a mess, the child sees it in a completely different light. For example, a 34 month-old boy made the sound of a motor while drawing this example and when he finished, exclaimed: "I drew a car!"

Figure 1-3:   Drawing accompanied by a barking sound

Similarly, a 31 month-old girl drew the following disarray of short and disjointed lines, and while drawing, she said: "This is a barking dog, woof, woof".

Figure 1-4:   Initial attempt at formal structuring: drawing a circle

Drawing a circle requires meticulous planning. The child has to start at a certain point, move the drawing tool around a central axis (this requires optical control) and arrive at the starting point. At this stage, you can see children go past the starting point because they get carried away with the movement and find it difficult to stop. You can see the opposite phenomenon in the following drawing by a 38 month-old. This boy took great care to structure the circle appropriately, and although he didn't manage to draw it accurately at the endpoint, he returned there until a closed and well-structure circle was drawn. You can also see various snail-like shapes, which also belong to the circle family and require careful planning and executive control.

Figure 1-5: Tadpole figures

Once the child has become adept at drawing circles, human figures begin to appear (at this preliminary stage, they are called "tadpoles"). To draw a tadpole, the child uses lines acquired in the previous stage to represent the four limbs. These are attached directly to a large, round head. Children with the same level of skill also draw suns with linear rays.

In terms of cognitive development, this stage marks the beginning of symbolic cognition: the child can now use his drawings to represent events along a temporal sequence, distinguishing between past and future events. The child free-play style and the stories related to the drawing will be more and more clearly related to actual experiences during the day, and at the same time the child's verbal skills will develop significantly.

Freud identifies this age span as the transition from the oral to the anal stage, marked by improved motor control and brain-eye-hand coordination. The child internalizes cause-and-effect processes and therefore examines his drawing at the end of the process, rather than just enjoys making it. Piaget defines this period as the beginning of the pre-conceptual (pre-operational) stage, in which the child solves problems by trial and error, his thought is concrete and reality is perceived as a static image. The child uses objects around him and his own drawings as internal representations of events he has experienced, and adopts an animistic perspective, whereby inanimate objects are humanized. Examples of this tendency may be seen in Figures 1-2 and 1-3, which represented an interesting occurrence experienced by the children, with the disarray of lines animated at will.

According to Erik Erikson (1993), in this period the child develops willpower and confidence as well as doubts in his abilities. The latter are usually dependent on the environment's critical response to the child's inquisitive behavior. In his drawings, the child directs his curiosity to every drawing tool and surface which could enable him to express himself. This is why drawing on walls is most common at this age. From his point of view, the child expresses himself confidently and autonomously, while the environment criticizes him and demands that he exhibit control and understands the boundaries set for him.

Stage 3: Pre-Schematic Stage – Ages 3½–5

At this stage the child begins to plan his artwork, which usually also receives a name at the end. We begin to see features that are recognizable to adults: flower, house, tree, car, etc. However, the child still does not attach any importance to the relationships among the various figures in the drawing. Now that he is interested in depicting reality as it is, he carefully draws every element by itself, with all the items he can recall from his daily reality.

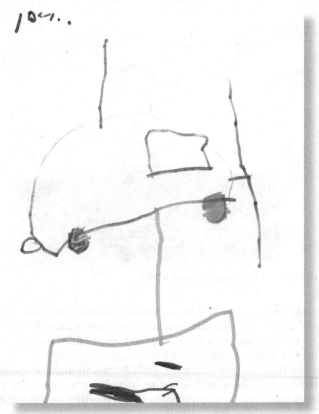

Figure 1-6: Three-wheeled car

In fact, the child draws everything he "knows" about the drawn object, rather than the object as it really looks.

The resulting images often do not make visual sense, but they are accurate as far as the child is concerned because they document the characteristics and functions of the object in question. Thus, this 45 month-old draws a three-wheeled car, despite the fact that it is not a common sight in daily life.

Figure 1-7:   Two-dimensional limbs

Human figure drawings also become more sophisticated at this stage. Usually, we begin to see two-dimensional limbs (rather than the lines typical of the previous stage), and some children begin to draw bellies as well, the forerunners of future torso drawings.

In addition, the pre-schematic child begins to acquire the ability of drawing diagonal lines, and later also triangles. The previously rounded roofs now take their typical triangular shape, together with skirts, cypresses, high-heeled shoes, hair ribbons, etc.).

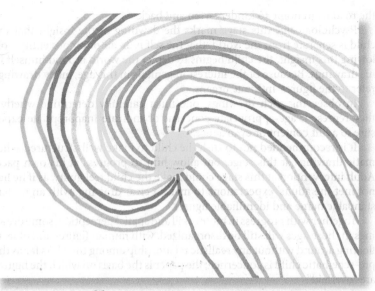

Figure 1-8: **Sun-like ray structure**

Beside meaningful schematic drawings, this stage also marks the appearance of schematically structured graphic diagrams, such as sun-like ray structures, symmetrical constructions crossed by a line in the middle, balanced square structures and cyclical lines.

Figure 1-9: **Square and cyclical linear structure**

The child begins to give meaning and names to all these diagrams and drawings (graphic drawing naming). He describes the act of drawing as if he is "inside" the drawing. Closed forms are described as closed elements familiar from daily life, such as door or window. Finally, the child uses a minimalistic, single line to describe a daily movement experience, such as the road from home to kindergarten and back.

Psychologically, this stage marks the dawning of the insight that the child is separate from the world, that the self is an autonomous entity. Following this insight, the child begins to depict the world around himself in his drawings. Because of the interest in genitals in this age, many drawings refer to the figures' intimate organs.

In observing such drawings, one must carefully determine whether they represent age-appropriate concerns or indicate inappropriate exposure to adult content or even abuse.

It is recommended not to rush the child to make well-structured schematic drawings at this stage, but allow him to progress at his own pace. Adult intervention at this stage could make the child feel guilty, as if he has not met the adults' expectations to make a clear drawing, with an understandable name and identifiable figures.

Together with progress in motor skill and spatial perception, some drawings in those ages will still be disorganized, with human figures and objects floating around without any realistic relationship among them. As far as the pre-schematic child is concerned, the paper is the basis on which the figures are "overlaid".

Stage 4: Schematic Stage – Ages 5–8

By this stage, the child begins to be aware of the logic behind laws and rules of conduct, develops his own rituals, and judges the world according to his inner feelings. He also begins to treat the world of colors more realistically (brown earth, blue sky, etc.).

Figure 1-10: Realistic approach to colors

The child already knows the drawing scheme by now. He doesn't have to observe a tree to be able to draw it. However, through drawing he reprocesses his impressions of reality, so that his documentation skill improves each time. Freud identifies these ages with the onset of the latency period, in which children show greater interest in their peers and other people around them.

Consequently, human figures assume a central role in their artwork. Technically, children are now able to add more organs to the basic human form, as well as articles of clothing. The figure becomes more elongated, and children begin attending to differential proportions within it: elongated legs, belly, outstretched arms, and so on.

Drawings by 5–8 year-olds focus increasingly on the family and begin to show tendencies of accuracy to the point of perfectionism (reflecting the conflict between industry and inferiority).

In the drawings, you can see the objects are rendered complete with their identifying characteristics, as part of the adult conceptual world: a simple square becomes a window; a straight line with circles on top becomes a flower, and so on. Piaget also characterizes perception at these ages as polarized between good and evil, with inflexible and one-dimensional approach to rules. Indeed, in their drawings, children at the schematic stage begin focusing on evil characters (monsters and witches) and good characters (knights and princesses).

Cognitive development enables the schematic children to abstract and separate the wheat from the chaff:

The child will often neglect many details (although he may be fully aware of their existence) and emphasize only those perceived to be critical to functioning: legs that walk, arms that reach out, a mouth that talks or expresses some emotion, and so on.

Figure 1-11:   Legless human figures

This emphasis can make the drawing seem surreal, as in the following drawing by a 5 years and 2 months-old girl. For this girl, the most important thing is to draw the figures holding balloons or each other's hands. Therefore, she allowed herself to ignore their legs (which is not typical of her other drawings).

Another example is children who draw a human figure on one side of the page, and the figure's behind on the other, "because it is behind".

Drawings at this stage are concise: the children focus on the common denominators of all houses/trees/flowers, rather than on the characteristics which differentiate them. Only after formulating general schemes can these children document the exceptions to the rule.

Figure 1-12: Connecting elements in the drawing

Schematic children begin to attach importance to the relations among the various objects in their drawing. In the following drawing by a 5½ year-old, for instance, you can see a child, a dog and a line (leash) connecting them. The schematic children's spatial perception also improves, and they often begin the drawing by marking the ground and the sky at the lower and upper edges of the page.

Moreover, this period is also characterized by drawing multiple land lines (for example, one at the bottom of the page to designate nearby objects, and another nearer the top to designate distant object) or rounded baselines (to indicate sitting around the table, for example). Usually, the child will refer to the bottom of the page as a baseline, and not turn the page while drawing. In terms of perspective, objects will be drawn in their complete form, and it is rare to see objects hidden by others.

Figure 1-13:   Drawing by a Tibetan child with multiple land lines

Multiple land lines are a fascinating phenomenon in drawings by Tibetan children. Despite being in the midst of the schematic stage, well aware of the locations and colors of earth and sky, these children choose to revert to drawing row after row over imaginary land lines.

This style may be affected by the Tibetan prayer wheels, set in a row one next to the other, which represent balance and recurrence which are part of their religious worldview.

At this stage, children still find it difficult to draw figures in profile or in motion, because doing so requires them to ignore schematic characteristics and omit some of the organs (such as a hidden eye, or an arm that is only partly visible while the figure is walking). Instead, they draw "everything that has to be there" by making some organs transparent. Use of colors is also schematic, as children tend to use basic colors rather than shades and combinations. Finally, schematic children attach central importance to the drawing's subject, and can even engage in a deep conversation about its meanings and the story hidden in the drawing.

Stage 5: Pre-Realistic Stage – Ages 8–11

Pre-realistic children acquire motor skills which enable them to refine their depiction of reality and differentiate objects more accurately. Thus, we see attention to various types of cars or trees, local animals, etc.

Figure 1-14: Yaks in a typical Tibetan pre-realistic drawing

By this stage, each human figure receives individual attention, with its own typical details and accessories: glasses, buttons, bag, hat, and so on.

In each human figure drawing, the pre-realistic child tries to resolve graphic difficulties such as: How to draw a person lying down? Should I draw all the table legs or only those visible from this angle? How to draw the house interior and exterior at the same time? In most cases, the difficulty is resolved by flattening the image: for example, houses will be drawn as seen in figure 1-15.

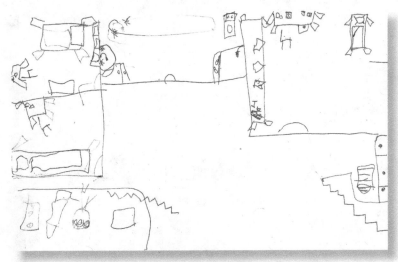

Figure 1-15:   Typical flattened house drawing

As abstract cognition develops, this flattening tendency will disappear.

Since the pre-realistic child wishes above all to document reality, he is careful to maintain the proportions among the various objects in the drawing.

His subjects combine figures from his intimate world (family drawings) with imaginary and historical drawings (Bible stories), as well as current affairs (war scenes, etc.).

In terms of psychological development, Piaget calls this period the operational stage, in which the child can grasp concepts of preservation (of quantity and weight) and to organize items in groups according to common denominators. Problem solving no longer relies exclusively on trial and error, but also on social rules of conduct, as well as the opinions and emotions of others. The child's understanding of reversibility (every change in location, form, or order may be reversed) and of hierarchic relations refines his family drawings, to which other groups are added, such as sports teams. Moreover, the child begins to attach several drawings together to represent a continuous plot.

Figure 1-16:   Family drawings advance to group drawings

The pre-realistic drawing represents an overall improvement in quality: the child refines his composition and landscaping skills. He draws the same subject repeatedly with improving skills, particularly in terms of his ability to render graphic elements that are unique to specific human figures.

At this stage, children begin to view their drawings as an expression of their self-efficacy. This is why they tend to compare their drawing abilities at these ages.

Stage 6: Realistic Stage – Ages 11–14

At the realistic stage, the child/adolescent is fully aware of his environment and has advanced graphic abilities that enable him to start dealing with depictive difficulties by refining his technical skills, such as games of light and shadow, three dimensions, complex scenarios, shades of color, perspectives, etc.

Figure 1-17: Combined techniques indicating improved spatial perception

The subjects become more realistic and less fantastic. The realistic pre-adolescent attaches greater importance to proportions among the various elements, to the point of depicting different shades of color to emphasize their relative locations.

As opposed to drawings made in earlier ages, by this point the child will deemphasize his own image and assume the reference point of an observer.

According to Erikson, the most significant social group at this age is the peer group, which also explains why (unless otherwise directed) realistic children will tend to draw peer groups rather than families.

Figure 1-18:   Advanced drawing of facial organs

The drawings typically depict complex situations, including copies of diagrams, illustrations and cartoon figures. We see more faces in profile and detached organs (eyes, mouths). The interest in the human body which is typical of these ages will also be seen in the drawings, with methodical attempts to produce accurate anatomic sketches.

Nevertheless, the young realistic artist is often dissatisfied with the final result, seen as a distorted, inaccurate rendering of the landscape, building or human figures. Since there is no clear educational requirement to continue drawing on a daily basis (unlike other skills, such as writing), many children stop drawing at this age and remain at this level as adults, with bad memories from their difficult and exhausting drawing lessons at school.

The Scribbling Stage – More than Meets the Eye

Simple comparison of scribbles made by several children from the same kindergarten will show that they do have some distinct characteristics: some children prefer certain colors and refuse to use all crayons. Some children apply strong pressure, while others do not. Some scribbles are composed mainly of round and spiral movements spread over the entire page area, while others are dominated by broken lines in a limited area.

In order to properly interpret a scribble and explore how the child translates from the sensory modality to the drawing modality, you must gather a considerable amount of information about the child's graphic language. Most studies on emotional interpretation of children's drawings begin from that starting point. When we study graphic language we focus on the quality of the pressure produced by the child on the drawing tool and the way the child conducts it on the surface. For example, weak pressure that is not the result of physiological problem may indicate certain inhibitions. Other indicators include the style of the lines (fragile, disjointed, thin or wavy lines, etc.) and the way they cross each other; the general planning of the page; the child's ability to compose and combine various geometric forms; how he colors and fills in the forms; his attention to detail, etc. The key point of graphic expression is that the pattern of the drawing on the page is affected by the muscular pressure applied to the drawing tool, which is in turn affected by cerebral activity and the child's inner emotional world.

Scribbling is the first step in the graphic expression process, and in that it is akin to the babbling which precedes speech among infants. Although scribbling is a preliminary experience, children who scribble soon begin to develop personal preferences and show a clear desire to produce diverse and interesting artwork. Some children start scribbling already at age one, and soon proceed to draw familiar geometric forms, followed by realistic objects (house, tree, etc.). At school age you will still find evidence of scribbling, for example beside the written lines in the notebook. Writing letters, of course, requires prior knowledge in scribbling and drawing.

During this stage, the child begins to develop his spatial orientation and ability to experience the world kinesthetically as well as through the senses. The scribbling process also provides sensory stimulation, and children at this tender age often taste their crayons. At this stage, children understand the world actively and creatively, so that they affect the information rather than receive it passively. In my opinion, older children will also do well to understand the world in this active approach. During this period, it is important to allow the child to experience a broad range of nontoxic materials such as gouache, markers, finger paints, and pastel crayons, as well as a broad range of surfaces such as rough paper, papers of various sizes and colors, wooden boards, Bristol papers and newspapers.

Some children actively seek these surfaces, ignoring the fact that the surfaces may already be written over. It is also important for children to experience a wide variety of kneading materials: dough and other foodstuffs, modeling clay, etc. to stimulate their senses.

At this stage, the edges of the surface are not absolute boundaries for the child, who tends to "stray" to nearby surfaces. When the child first starts to draw, he does it accidentally and admires the product. His fascination and that of others around him challenge him to continue exploring this dimension. However, only when you begin identifying recurring trends in the drawing will you be able to start talking about deliberate drawing that represents conscious intervention by the child.

Drawing is fundamentally a muscular activity and as such, it attests to the child's temperament and adjustment to his environment.

When the child draws, he is required to balance between movements away from the body (executed by relieving pressure, as you can see in Figure 23) and movements towards the body (executed by contraction and applying pressure, as you can see in Figure 22). Internalizing this pressure is evidence to the maturation of certain brain and nervous system mechanisms and helps the child refine his equilibrium system. By way of drawing, the child enhances his control over various bodily organs and adjusts his bodily posture to the type of drawing he wishes to produce.

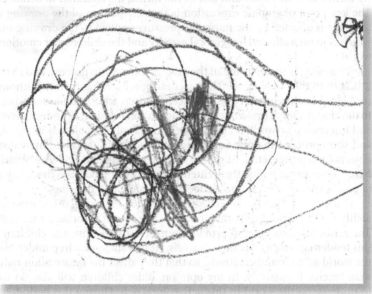

Figure 1-19: Example of a scribble from the circular sub-stage

A student of creative education, Victor Lowenfeld (1947) saw drawings as reflecting the child's view of reality. His studies led to the identification of fours scribbling sub-stages: (1) Disordered or lacking control over motor activity; (2) Longitudinal or controlled repetitions of motions; (3) Circular – further exploring of control motions demonstrating the ability to produce more complex forms; and (4) Naming, where the child tells stories about the scribble, gives it a title and demonstrates symbolic condition.

In other words, according to Lowenfeld the child acquires skills as he practices drawing, wherein lies the importance of recurring drawing elements. Recurrence is also stressed by Rhoda Kellogg (1969), who compiled a list of 20 basic scribbles that represent the foundations of graphic development. Kellogg proceeded to identify 17 compositions which suggest certain regularity in the scribble's location on the page.

Kellogg argued that scribbling has nothing to do with the child's present psychological development, but that it is evidence of collective hereditary memory.

Namely, the various scribbling variations are not acquired from the environment but inherent to the human organism from birth, indicating the drawer's uniform sequence of graphic development and nothing more.

Kellogg's studies are considered controversial. Many of her critics argued that the basic patterns she identified appear in only some of the scribbles in her record, so that they cannot be considered indicative of a universal graphic development sequence.

Likewise, while Kellogg argued that the motive for scribbling is an innate urge to build and to create, that has more to do with the collective unconscious than with the desire to depict external objects, her critics (e.g. Matthews 1988) presented a large number of drawings by children who accompanied their artwork by statements of their desire to document reality, notwithstanding the jumble of lines on the page. Personally, I believe children are affected by a primary urge to create while at the same time being affected by the need to communicate with the environment by way of borrowing existing concepts (archetypes such as the recurring house pattern).

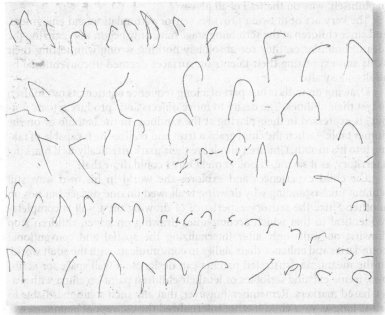

Figure 1-21: Letter-like symbols

The scribbling stage is also when mandalas begin to appear in children's drawings. These are rounded forms, from which lines extend in various directions, or forms crossed by lines). By drawing mandalas, children acquire the ability to later draw suns with rays, or tadpole figures (human figures without torsos).

Between the ages of 1½ and 3½ you can also find scribbles reminiscent of letters, which are called «letter-like symbols».Such shapes cannot be found in all drawings, but when they are found they do seem to resemble handwriting, including careful attention to lines and spaces.

Such writing attests to the development of fine motor skills, as well as to enhanced brain-eye-hand coordination and spatial orientation. It does not, however, suggest the child is ready to learn how to read and write. Rather this is a passing fad which will return, in some children, around age 4. At this age, many children start writing their names and often use mirror writing, suggestive of internal development processes related to hemispheric dominance.

In art therapy, scribbling is considered a nonthreatening and even soothing technique in that it is completely purposeless. Scribbling is not oriented towards a final outcome and not committed to produce a pretty and accurate picture, but promotes an experiential process free of any rules or inhibitions (Kramer 1975).

Another phenomenon typical of this stage is drawing on walls. Almost every parent is familiar with this situation, facing the masterpiece and asking himself, why on the wall of all places?

The very act of drawing provides sensory stimulation and enjoyment, and since children at the scribbling stage have only begun internalizing the idea of boundaries, they see absolutely nothing wrong with testing their skills and expressing their talents on surfaces deemed unconventional by adults, like walls.

Drawing on walls is just part of a long sequence of attempts by children to test their abilities. The desire to move objects and "produce artistic output" is expressed in their playing at the sandbox, in the bathtub or on the dinner table – when the child grabs a fruit and realizes he is capable of taking it to his mouth. Children also leave their mark artistically, as if marking a territory, as if saying, "Look at me! Only I could draw that!"

The child experiences and explores the world in his own way, still without understanding why drawing is allowed on one surface but not on another. Since the sensory experience of drawing on a wall is completely identical to that which accompanies drawing on paper, children stop drawing on walls only after internalizing the spatial and conventional boundaries and enhance their ability to communicate with the adult world. In the meantime, frustrated parents can designate a wall space for scribbles, frame existing scribbles or let their children paint on china with water-based markers. Remember, however, that any such solution is liable to fail as long as your child has not internalized the concept of boundaries.

The parents of the 2 years and 9 months-old girl who made the following two drawings told me that recently, her behavior changed. Since they had been collecting drawings for a year, I could compare them and identify the differences. In her scribbles, I could see evidence of her willfulness and resistance. She wants to do everything herself and relishes in dictating her rules to the environment.

Figure 1-22:   Shrunk and highly pressurized scribble

Among other things, this is evident in the strong pressure she applies to the drawing surface. In her scribbles, you could clearly see when everything began to shrink and she showed a withdrawal tendency that concerned her parents tremendously.

Figure 1-23: Unconstrained scribbling with balanced pressure

Her more recent drawings indicated that she was more attentive to external demands than to her own desires and acted quickly to please the environment. I could also see signs of the extraordinary fears which caused sleeping disorders, constipation and irregular eating patterns. Socially, she began to evidence adjustment difficulties and at home she kept clinging to her parents. After the parents were advised to move her to a kindergarten with fewer children, her scribbles showed a change for the better.

To conclude, the graphic complexity of every scribble (which makes it appear senseless) requires thorough scrutiny of a large number of drawings before any comparisons can be made. Such comparisons can offer important insights into the child's temperament, behavior patterns, difficulties and fears he may be experiencing.

The Emotional Significance of Drawing: Process and Drawing Tool

The artistic experience is basically a sensory experience combining multiple modalities. Through this experience, the child structures his worldview. For the child, drawing is friendlier and more comprehensive than verbal expression; through drawing the child can create something out of nothing. This is in fact the starting point of the creative experience in art therapy: through creative experience, the child undergoes a process of trial and error which enables him to discover and express his inner world. Children "use" drawings as a way of sublimating aggressive drives and relieving stress. They let their imagination run wild and draw the world as they see it, rather than as an accurate copy of reality.

Sitting Position

At first, you must pay attention to the child's sitting position: it is important for the child to feel comfortable, with the table and chair adjusted to his size. Don't be upset if you see your child drawing lying down, because this position enables him to place more of their body's surface on the floor, and often helps them concentrate on their drawing. Some children will prefer this position also in older ages and you will find them doing their homework on the floor, but in most cases this is a fleeting phenomenon.

For some children, lying down is preferred because their shoulder muscles are too weak for them to draw while sitting or because they have difficulty focusing their eyes and thus want to draw as close as possible to the page.

Page Size

The size of the page is also significant for the child. Above all, it should fit his physical size and experience in drawing. At the scribbling stage, it is recommended to use large pages. At this stage, the child is unaware of the page's boundaries and it is important for him to delve into the experience of drawing. When the child begins to develop his drawing skill, he can use smaller pages and even let him try small notes that will encourage him to concentrate and develop fine motor skills.

Naturally, there is no mandatory age-to-page-size ratio, and it is always recommended to combine various page sizes so as to allow the child to hone his skills in drawing small details as well as to draw in a more uninhibited way. However, you should observe the degree of confidence and satisfaction experienced by the child: when an unconfident child is asked to draw on a large page, he might give up before even starting. Thus, make sure the child is exposed gradually to various stimulations and let him pick the page size that is best for him.

Drawing Tool

Drawing tools also play an important role in the process, and each exposes the child to a different experience. First, the way the drawing tool is held can indicated disabilities that could become manifested in a later age. For instance, children with low muscle tone will grasp the tool tightly within a fisted hand. Note, however, that you must be wary of rushing into conclusions, because children undergo multiple change processes at this age.

In any case, if drawing requires the child to apply too much force, which wears him down and prevents him from drawing as much as he would have liked to, you are advised to seek professional diagnosis.

Markers are quite mechanic in nature, particularly the thinner markers that emit a screeching sound when applied to the paper. Usually, children aged 4–5 prefer markers, as you can see in figure 1-24. It is important for them to be precise when coloring the house drapes or the monster's eyes.

Figure 1-24: Drawing with markers

Some children who prefer markers overwhelmingly and consistently will become children who need certainty and control over events, and will often express anger (at themselves and at the page) if they haven't managed to draw as accurately as they had intended.

Using markers requires greater manipulative skill, and stresses color variety over working deep into the page. Therefore, they will be preferred by children with a strong need for neatness as an integral part of the creative process.

Pastel crayons introduce the child to a completely different experience. Using pastels requires greater muscular effort since the crayon has to be pressed down on the page to produce results. The child's active contribution to the creative process makes him an integral part of the artwork. Some children pay the utmost attention to painting with pastel crayons, devoting effort and concentration to the task, while others treat the final result with indifference, show no interest in the painting and paint with low manual pressure and without attention to detail so as to "get it over with".

Essentially, pastel crayons produce less accurate paintings, such as the example in figure 1-25, and challenge the child to resolve this issue or simply enjoy the strengths of this medium.

Figure 1-25: Drawing with pastel crayons

Pastel crayons invite the child to get dirty as part of the creative process, and provide an experience of depth in addition to the color variety. Thus, children who prefer pastel will work in several layers and explore this tool's potential to conceal and reveal.

Gouache paints, like all types of finger paints, offer the perfect sensory experience. Whether the child uses a brush or his fingers, the soft sense of paint flowing over the page offers a combined sensory-kinesthetic-emotional sensation. Naturally, painting in gouache requires the child to cope with neatness issues. Some children will refuse to use these paints at all, because they don't want to be messy.

When working with these children, it is important to give them the protections they need (for example, by giving them a towel to wipe their hands), but it is also important to invite them to continue exploring the sensory experience, which in many cases can also lead to behavioral change.

Children who show clear preference for gouache could use this experience to learn how to effortlessly take control of the entire page area, but also to maintain its boundaries and improve their gross motor skills.

What to Look for in Children's Drawings?

For the child, drawing is a daily language and additional medium of communication. The child has never been taught how to draw before, and he advances through the developmental stages freely and intuitively. As in any language, the language of art combines social codes that make it understandable and "spoken", together with private codes borrowed from the child's inner world which mark his artwork as unique.

In order to gain a broad perspective on the child's inner world and self-image based on his drawings, I recommend analyzing at least 25 samples drawn in various techniques (gouache, pastel, markers, pencils, etc.). Analyzing fewer drawings will provide limited indications, representing passing moods rather than broad trends. Accordingly, it is also important to analyze drawings made over a period of at least six months, so as to provide a clear picture of the child's emotional world and enable comparison to earlier periods.

Interpreting the drawing requires assessing a wide variety of phenomenon, from the way the drawing has been executed and the child's various artistic choices, through his use of the page area, line pressure and color selection, to analysis of the child's verbalizations during and after the drawing.

The drawing environment is also significant to the diagnosis: children draw in different styles and with different materials at home and at kindergarten. Drawing at kindergarten next to other children is naturally different than drawing at home, alone or with a parent. Bear in mind that kindergarten drawings are not always spontaneous, and that the teacher often invites the child to the table and focuses him on a particular subject (such as a holiday or a season). In these cases, it is important to compare such artwork to spontaneous drawings made by the child at home.

Free choice is essential to the success of our interpretation. It is important for the child to choose the page size, drawing tools and colors. This will contribute to his free and authentic expression, and paint a more reliable picture of his subjective emotional world.

Having met these conditions, you must check whether the child uses a dominant hand or whether he is still switching hands. You must also check whether he prefers a certain position (lying, standing and even walking). The answers to those questions have direct bearing to the degree of pressure applied to the drawing tool and the angles from which the various elements on the page are drawn.

Finally, you must know the child's exact age (in months) in order to assess his developmental level. In younger ages, children may achieve developmental leaps every month, so that frequent analysis of their artwork combined with awareness of their precise age will provide clearer indications as to their emotional state.

The drawings shed light not only on the child's inner world, but also on his social environment and the various influences of the adults in his life –

from his parents and wider family, through his teachers to people he met on the street or saw on TV; all of them shape the child's worldview and all will leave their mark on his art.

How to Respond to Children's Drawings?

As you pick up your child from kindergarten at the end of the day, you see him bursting enthusiasm as he presents you with his most recent masterpiece. You look at the drawing and don't know how to react. At first (as well as second) glance, it simply looks like a senseless doodle. And yet, since you want to encourage your child, you mumble things like, "Wow! This is the most beautiful drawing I've ever seen!" In most cases, that's all there is to it: the child seems pleased, and the parent is happy, having succeeded in the positive reinforcement task.

This triple encounter – parent, child and drawing – offers a splendid opportunity to conduct a meaningful conversation about the child's inner world. But first of all, the parent has to be truly available to attend to the child's artwork.

As in other parenting situations, this is the first question you need to ask yourselves: "Do I have the energy and patience to totally be with my children?" Granted, it is important to teach our child that we cannot be available to them around the clock; as adults, we have desires, needs and occupations that are independent of his existence. On the other hand, as parents, we are aware of the child's needs and willing to channel them to other times when we are more available. It is essential to fulfill the promise and "reconvene the meeting" at a later time, instead of just blurting "this is so beautiful", without even gazing at the drawing.

When you first look at the drawing, it is important that you refer to what you can see – even if it's just a scribble consisting of seemingly random blots of paint. You can say things like: "I see you drew over the entire page… pressed hard on the marker… used lots of colors/only two colors… drew many lines". These specific references indicate to the child that the parent is indeed observing his drawing and noticing every little detail he made such an effort to produce.

Naturally, you can also ask the child to explain what he drew, but it's just as important to respect his answer, rather than badger him with questions such as "Why this way and not otherwise", or suggest ideas for additional elements. Thus, when your child paints the sky green or red, there is no need to correct him out of fear his perception may be flawed. The drawing is a window onto his inner world, and there is no reason to assume that he is confused about the world outside.

When observing the drawing, bear in mind that it is also a product of his motor development. As such, it is not always pregnant with symbolic meaning. Sometimes your child simply enjoys the process of creating by way of manipulating objects in the world and leaving his mark.

Next, you should wait before complimenting the child, and try to hold a real conversation about the drawing. More often than not, your child will be happy to talk about it. In the conversation, you can mediate between the child's world and the world of art, and draw his attention to the fact that he loves a particular color that appears time and again both in his drawings and in his room, for example. Invite the child to tell you what he drew, whether verbally or simply by showing your interest through body language and curious eyes.

During the schematic stage (ages 5–8) when human figures tend to appear more frequently in drawings you can broaden the dialogue and talk about the figures' character. If one character looks angry, for example, you can ask the child why and start a conversation about anger in daily life, about real-life events that may have inspired him to draw that figure, just as you would talk to an artist about his artwork and its emotional underpinnings.

Figure 1-27:   Asking questions about the drawing: What grows on the tree? Why is that man sad?

In older ages, you can ask your child about what is hidden in the drawing, and not only about what is clearly visible. For instance, if he drew a house with windows, you can ask him who lives in the room the window's in. This will start a fascinating and imaginative conversation. You can also use the drawing as a stepping stone to the world of knowledge and riddles: How do clouds form? Why can't we fly? How do we know the fruits on the tree are ready to eat?

You will not always get answers to your questions – some children will prefer philosophical questions while others will prefer concrete ones, all in accordance with their age and character.

Nevertheless, note that questions such as, why didn't you draw daddy, or why are you big and mommy small, are unnecessary, and will usually not produce an informative reply. In general, you should avoid overwhelming your child with questions so as not to pressure him.

When you want to give your child a compliment, say things you really mean. Saying things like "this is the most beautiful drawing in the world" is clearly problematic in that sense – it is too demanding. It is better to say, "this is a wonderful gift... this is the most beautiful gift I have ever received". You can also refer to emotions related to the act of drawing: "I'm so happy that you drew for me... I love it when you give me your drawings... I've noticed you enjoy drawing very much..."

When you give a compliment, it is important to encourage the creative process and experience, rather than the final outcome. You can be proud of the drawing and show it to the entire family, but at the same time you must be attentive to your child's reactions and make sure your pride does not make him feel under pressure to perform. Sometimes the best compliment is to keep the drawing near your bed or in your briefcase.

When lots of drawings fill the house and there is no room for new one, you can ask your child how he would like to distribute them among relatives, as special, personal gifts. Grandpa and grandma will surely be happy to receive a decorated album of drawings. Another option is to put several drawings one next to the other (on the table or on the fridge) and photograph your child as he presents them. You can then place the photos in an album, so that the drawings will not be forgotten.

In different periods of his life, every child needs a different approach to his artwork. Sometimes he likes a kind word or expects a profound conversation, and sometimes he would prefer a dramatic reaction and applause. When there are several children in the house, it is important to attend to each child's drawings individually, without comparisons. If you use the same compliment with everyone, it is liable to be perceived inauthentic.

Intervention in Children's Drawings

"Daddy, draw me a castle with knights and fire breathing dragons!" The child asks, and daddy complies. He does his best to draw the most lavish castle, with the mightiest forts and bravest knights, spending time and effort on sketching the wall and windows. Finally, he presents the drawing proudly to his child. The child smiles, hangs it in his room and... stops drawing! From now on, he prefers doing anything but drawing. After a while, whey you ask him in passing why he's not drawing anymore, he answers with quiet frustration: "Because I can't draw as nice as you..."

Parents often find themselves sitting next to their child while he's drawing. The child is completely engrossed with the task: his tongue protrudes, his eyes are open wide and all his muscles are geared to a single objective – his masterpiece. He has been doing it from the moment he learned how to grab the drawing tool, and beyond the sensory experience involved this artwork is a reflection of his rich inner world. Therefore, no intervention in the drawing process can be considered minor; by necessity, it will have a profound impact on inner psychological processes.

There are ways of intervening other than drawing the castle for the child. Some parents start intervening already early in the scribbling stage, in order to help their children advance to the structured scribbling stage, in which the "doodles" become familiar geometric forms such as circle, triangle or square. However, when the children are not mature enough to move on to this stage, they will try imitating forms that are beyond their skill level or worse, give up and stop drawing.

Children will stop drawing for other reasons as well. For example, when they are not only forced to wear an apron but also have to listen to lectures about neatness and orderliness, or when they can only draw during certain hours of the day, the natural process is obstructed and they no longer express themselves freely.

The drawing surface and tools can also deter children. Some dislike drawing on large pages, while others have sensitive skin and avoid rough surfaces. Broken crayons are not necessarily a problem, because often it is easier for children to manipulate the smaller pieces. However, markers that no longer draw or pastel crayons that require strong pressure could tire out children and make them abandon drawing altogether.

It is also important to notice the supply of artistic materials available to the child. If there are plenty of coloring books at home, or if the kindergarten teachers spend considerable time with the children on coloring decorations (for holidays, or whenever the teacher draws a certain shape and invites the children to color it), the child could overemphasize the need to color within the boundaries. He will be busy with the figures and shapes available to him, at the expense of creating original drawings.

The drawing subject may also be significant in cases of refusal to draw. For example, when a child grows in a difficult family reality, he will tend to avoid family drawings or consistently omit one of the family members. In such a case, there is of course no point in asking about the omission.

Another example for intervention has to do with the adults' attitude to the finished product. For example, when you ask the child, "What is this drawing? Why is the sky all red?", or when you artificially identify familiar objects in what is clearly an unrecognizable scribble ("this looks like a flower, and this looks like a heart). Such an attitude communicates to the child that he has to draw recognizable elements that mimic reality. Next time he draws, he might "force" the drawing to be more realistic, and when asked about it, he will try to explain what he drew in a way that would please the adults around him.

Finally, when you talk with the kindergarten teacher you have to remember that the child is also listening. Saying things like, "She's already four years old and still doesn't draw houses!", can make the child feel frustrated and stop drawing altogether.

Why, then, do adults intervene?

Some adults intervene because they fear their child is not drawing at an age-appropriate level, because of some developmental problem. By intervening, they "teach" the child to mimic age-appropriate patterns and abilities. Note, however, that just like copying from other children, it is easy to identify children who "fake" when they draw, using similar indicators used to identify fake handwritings. Namely, when children use elements that are out of sync with their inner development, their drawings will have a hesitant and inconsistent quality. Thus, studying an adult design and mimicking it could help the child produce a drawing that may look impressive, but a professional observer will easily identify it as fake.

Figure 1-28: Intervention drawing, with adult contours

Others intervene when they want to correct mistakes, to teach the child to draw "correctly". In art, however, there is no such thing as "correct" or "incorrect". The drawing is designed to mirror the child's inner world and as such there are no correct or incorrect ways to go about it. Moreover, children who paint red skies are usually perfectly aware of their real color, but choose to draw them red for other reasons.

This attempt to "teach" the child how to draw correctly will fail in most cases. An interesting study (Cox 1996) on children at the "tadpole" stage (age 3) found that they become attached to their tadpole figure and are slow to abandon it even after observing college students drawing conventional human figures. In fact, the reason for the intervention – be it fear of developmental lag or any other reason – does not matter. The drawing mirrors the child's inner world and "fixing" it will change nothing. Worse, as you have seen, it could disrupt the natural process. Note that when discussing adult interventions I do not refer to therapeutic interventions, as in occupational or art therapy.

When the girl who made the following drawing was 5½ years old, her mother contacted me in order to understand why she omitted the arms in her human figure drawings. At first, she told me that she had tried to intervene and check whether she was aware of all the body parts the arm is composed of (such as forearm, palm and fingers). When the child demonstrated her awareness, the mother continued to explain how important it was to actually draw all these body parts. Her daughter agreed with her, and yet, after several days, she returned to draw armless figures.

Figure 1-29: Armless human figure

My analysis of her drawings, including figure 1-29, indicated that she was a creative girl with a strong desire to control her environment. She made an effort to seem perfect on the outside, and her coloring was particularly meticulous. Despite her relatively developed emotional side, she preferred to set clear boundaries for herself when it came to sharing.

Nonetheless, she continued to draw armless figures because this is an age-appropriate phenomenon! Many children at her age draw complete figures and even dedicate considerable attention to drawing the fingers, and yet many others ignore the arms completely. This is highly typical of children aged 5–7 and there is no point persuading them to draw otherwise, mainly because they will do so in due time.

Naturally, most adult interventions are motivated by good intentions, without awareness of any negative effect they may have, such as refusal to draw. Many adults treat painting just like any other motor skill acquired with adult guidance, such as cooking, and are simply unaware of how important it is for the drawing child to experience and explore on his own.

Still, what can you do when the child refuses to draw?

First, you must make sure the reason for his refusal is not any physiological disorder (motor problem, visual disability, low muscle tone, learning disability, etc.). Once this possibility has been rejected, there are several courses of action available to you. If your child feels his drawings are not "good enough" because they are graphically inaccurate, take him to the museum and show him the wide range of "inaccurate" artworks. If your child asks you to draw for him, use your non-dominant hand to make a "bad" drawing on purpose. Another possibility is for you to draw with your eyes shut and ask your child to guide your hand.

Next, you can ask your child to turn your scribble into a recognizable drawing and then switch parts (Winnicott 1971). Finally, you can designate a special drawing notebook. This way, your child will have a sense of continuity from one drawing to the next and will be able to show his drawings around. In addition, the notebook will encourage him to make up a serial story around the drawings.

If you've tried several approaches and your child still refuses to draw, and assuming the possibility of physiological issues has been rejected, you should remember that drawing is a hobby and that there are plenty of other creative avenues still open to your child.

Boys versus Girls

Society tends to treat boys and girls differently. One study (Huston 1983), for example, explored adult attitudes towards infants at the age when their sex is hard to distinguish. It was found that when the infant wore blue cloths, adults used to hold it high and throw it in the air. When it wore pink, however, they treated it gently, held it close to their chest and avoided rough play.

This is just one of many examples proving the social influence that molds boys and girls into gendered roles. On the other hand, many believe that gender identity is primarily innate. For instance, little boys independently choose "boyish" games (cars, superheroes), even when they have "girlish" toys (dolls, kitchen) at easy reach, and vice versa (Hoffman, 1964).

Figure 1-30: Typical painting by a girl

Just like playing with dolls, drawing also gives children the opportunity to create an imaginary world and draw themselves as superheroes or delicate princesses. Everything is possible on the drawing page and children relish this absolute freedom. Beyond themes that are popular among all children regardless of gender, such as family or holiday drawings, most boys tend to draw superheroes combined with various angular shapes, while girls prefer princesses combined with hearts, flowers, jewelry and similar details.

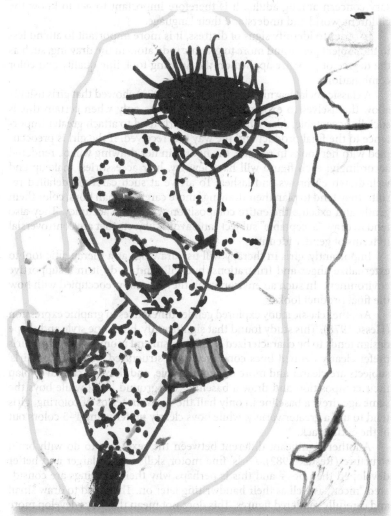

Figure 1-31: Monster drawing as a normative tendency

Unless there are indications to the contrary, drawings of monsters and violent heroes are considered normative among boys, and are usually not considered as evidence of any internal distress or anxiety experienced by the child. Sometimes they lead to precisely the opposite conclusion: the child who draws monsters is socially integrated and understands the social codes of the community, and accordingly has interests that are shared with his peers.

The drawing subject can thus be misleading and even cause unnecessary concern among adults. It is therefore important to get to know the children's world and understand their language.

In order to identify signs of distress, it is more important to attend less to the subject per se and more to graphic indicators in the drawing, such as the degree of pressure applied on the drawing tool, line quality and color combinations.

A classic social learning study (Bandura 1971) showed that girls usually allow themselves to express negative emotions only when certain this is socially acceptable. Also when drawing, girls tend to attach greater importance to the final product and the way it is received. If the girl is preoccupied with her looks in real life, the figures in her drawing will be rendered accordingly: each figure will have jewelry, hair accessories, makeup and well-drawn eyebrows and lashes. To arrive at such carefully detailed results, they tend to plan their drawings more carefully than boys, color them gently and execute the entire composition with great accuracy. They also tend to draw "acceptable" subjects and avoid subjects that are controversial in terms of gender identity.

Importantly, girls in therapy will use drawings as a therapeutic tool to externalize anger and frustrations, but will tend to do it in a supportive environment. In such an environment, they are less preoccupied with how the final product looks.

Another classic study explored gender differences in graphic expression (Hesse 1978). This study found that significantly, boys' line style and shape design tends to be characterized by dynamism and momentum, while girls prefer clearly defined lines combined with structured static forms. Girls' subjects are clearer and more understandable, and they are careful to plan their composition and draw a baseline (the ground line), while boys the same age drew a baseline in only half the cases. In terms of coloring, girls tend to use a greater variety, while boys clearly prefer using 1–3 colors out of the entire pack.

Another significant different between the sexes has to do with brain structure (Restak 1982). Girls' fine motor skills area is larger and better developed than boys' and this is perhaps why their drawings are considered "nicer", as well as their handwriting later on. They tend to draw small and carefully rendered figures. This does not mean that boys develop more slowly, but simply that the developmental trajectory used to judge their drawings is different than that of girls. Another difference that may have to do with brain structure is that girls seem to be better in reading facial expressions. This contributes to their developing social skills and also explains their preference to draw human figures and depict the relationships between them.

Indeed, one of the first studies in this area (Goodenough 1926) found significant gender differences in human figure drawings. Boys tend to draw figures in profile with long, dominant limbs, while girls draw small palms and feet. Goodenough attributed these differences to society's tendency to emphasize girls' appearance and encourage boys to be more physically active, a tendency that has changed considerably since her studies.

Physiological differences and differential tendencies to have certain disabilities are central to assessing gender differences in drawings. For example, the dominance of their right hemisphere, combined with other physiological factors, mean that learning disabilities are more common among boys. Thus, many cases of refusal to draw or difficulties in drawing and writing are later discovered to be related to dysgraphia or another disability. Particularly in the disabilities area, however, it is very important to avoid jumping into conclusions and test the child's skills using other diagnostic methods, in addition to drawings.

Figure 1-32: A typically "boyish" drawing

This right hemispheric dominance also means that boys have better spatial perception. They study mazes and love drawing maps and diagrams. They also love drawing vehicles such as airplanes, tanks and cars. The following drawing by a 12½ year-old is a typically "boyish" drawing that emphasizes structure and space, as well as demonstrating considerable effort to reach the required level of accuracy.

To conclude, the objective in interpreting boys' versus girls' drawings is not to arrive at generalized conclusions supporting statistical findings about gender differences, but to identify differences that simply mean that the child in question is a typical boy or girl. Children of both genders have always experimented with gender atypical behaviors, a phenomenon that seems to be more acceptable nowadays. When interpreting children's drawings, you must be keenly aware of such social developments.

Copying

A group of children is seated around the table and everyone is busy drawing. A pair of inquisitive eyes checks neighboring drawings and sees that one girl drew a sun, while one boy drew a red car. The eyes return to their own page and want to draw like that as well. When our children return from kindergarten with a stack of drawings held in their little hands, how can we know which are really their own? Did somebody help them out? Did they copy from others?

Copying is prevalent since early age. Learning by observation is the basic way of acquiring language, for example, and indeed adults also tend to imitate others' speak, clothing, style and even opinions and ideologies. Given these universal truths, you need to ask, what made the child copy? Is the final product exactly identical to the source or has it been adjusted in some way? Finally, did copying help the child improve his drawing skills and enable him to continue on his own, at a higher level?

Copying has many positive aspects. First, it means the child is aware of his environment. He is curious to learn from older and more experienced children – by studying their behavior he reaches conclusions that are relevant to his future behavior. Second, copying introduces the child to peer society – now he's just like all the boys (girls): everyone draws spaceships (mermaids) and now he does as well. Copying is often a way of belonging and advancing socially. Clearly, the very act of observing other children's behavior, regardless of whether it leads to copying, promotes the child as it exposes him to diverse approaches to the same issue and thus sharpens his social perception.

Figure 1-33: Original drawing

Figure 1-34: Copy by a second child displaying unimaginative, stereotypical elements

There are other reasons for copying and imitating, however. Western culture encourages children to develop quickly and be achievers. Children who lag behind will obviously notice this and may copy out of fear of seeming less intelligent. This trend continues and even intensifies during the school years: the fact that all classmates study together and receive grades for the same assignments encourages many children to constantly compare themselves to others, and even copy from them.

Observing a variety of drawings by the same child enables experts to identify atypical, "fake" elements. For example, you would find figures or styles that are age appropriate, but rendered in a rigid and stereotypical manner, with no personal touch.

By the way, the pressure to perform does not always originate at kindergarten. It is often the parents who insist on teaching the preschooler math and English in order to turn him into a genius that pressure the child, or older siblings whose achievements are a source of envy. In such cases as well, when the atmosphere at home is so demanding, children are liable to copy for the wrong reasons.

Remember always that even when children copy from others, their natural human tendency is to leave their own mark, so that the copying child changes the drawing and eventually produces a unique work of art.

7 tips on how to respond to children's drawing:

- Look at his drawing when you are available for it

- State clearly what you *can* see in the drawing

- Ask him if he wants to explain his drawing and respect his answer

- Try not to give him remarks on "mistakes" in his drawing

- Avoid overwhelming him with questions so as not to pressure him

- When you give compliments, do it fairly and meaningfully

- Encourage his creativity rather than the final outcome

2 COLORS

Introduction

In 1777 the German philosopher Goethe climbed Mount Brocken in the Harz Mountains, where he noticed how the color shades changed on the snow: "Over the yellowish background of the snow, the shadows looked purple... while during sunset, everything around was filled with magnificent magenta and the shadows became beautifully green. Later on, following the sunset, the magical harmony vanished, replaced by a gray starry night". The sunset which Goethe describes appears in countless other songs, stories, legends and drawings and one cannot remain indifferent to its powerful color combinations.

Colors and Science

Scientifically, colors were studied in terms of wavelength and frequency. It appears that the order of colors in the spectrum matches wave characteristics. For example, the color red which appears at one end of the spectrum has the longest (visible) wavelength and the lowest frequency. Purple, on the other hand, appears at the other end of the spectrum, with the shortest wavelength and highest. These characteristics, discussed in depth later on, affect children's energy levels, as can be observed in their drawings.

Colors have also been studied from a physiological perspective, and it was found that they have a clear effect on our bodies (Fisher & Zelanski, 2009). Adding the clear physiological relationship between colors and our body to the mind-self relationship explains why children who are exposed to a certain color project it from their inner world to the outside by behaving in a certain manner. It is no coincident that we relax when we look at green mountains or blue oceans, and yet become more aroused when we see red. These insights are used for marketing purposes, but can also be relevant to our effort to understand our children's world through their drawings.

When you compare children's drawings to their personality traits, you see a significant relationship between them. Years of research have proven to us that using a certain color or color combination may project on emotional meanings that will be detailed further on. However, what is the reason for the strong influence colors have on our lives and drawings?

Observing nature and our long evolution process may provide the answer to this question. In prehistory, and in fact almost throughout human history, people were busy raising crops, domesticating animals and barter trading. These activities often included spending long hours outside, close to nature. As a result, people have developed various insights regarding nature and the way it operates.

These insights were subsequently used for survival or comfort. Their intensive contact with nature also caused our forefathers to unconsciously internalize the meanings of colors – they understood that green meant growth, new beginnings and abundance, brown meant a solid ground, black meant danger, and blue meant that the rain had stopped and they could resume work, and so on.

Analysis of children's drawings and the meanings of colors used in them will show striking resemblance to our forefathers' perception of colors. In other words, current color perception is a product of human cultural evolution. So, similarly to our instinctual perception of snakes as dangerous, we see in yellow (sunlight) as a source of joy.

This idea is reinforced by other phenomena in children's drawing, which also show a connection between physical and mental aspects of decisions children make while drawing. Two such examples are the stages of development in drawings and the way objects such as houses are drawn in various cultures. In these cases, studies clearly show that children from all over the world follow the same general artistic path, most probably dictated by our inborn perception and collective unconscious.

Colors and Psychology

Colors form a universal language. Psychological theories, like Jung's, about the meanings of signs, concluded that signs in dreams, stories and drawings are part of our collective unconscious. Accordingly, colors were also shown to have collective meanings. This means that even if a certain color has a specific meaning in a certain culture and different meanings in others, the internal, profoundly symbolic influence on individual choices will nevertheless be homogenous and universal.

The first psychological studies of the emotional meanings of colors were conducted by Goethe. In 1810, he began attributing positive significance to warm colors and negative significance to cold colors. He was followed by artists such as Kandisnsky and psychologists who studied color preferences at kindergarten age, among schoolchildren, among adults and among children hospitalized for cancer.

Colors in the Child's World

Colors fascinate children ever since they are a few months old. The cerebral cortex is responsible for the complex interpretation of sensory input, enabling children to identify and name certain colors. When babies develop eyesight, they are able to distinguish between dark and light colors and show greater interest in shiny colorful toys. Later on, they will develop the ability to differentiate shapes and patterns.

Colors arouse various feelings among children – for example, some will like red, but others will hate it because it reminds them of medicine. Some colors rouse children to action, others calm them down, and still others will cause disquiet and stress. Similarly, it seems the choice of colors in the child's bedroom affects his mood and general functioning.

Most children enjoy using colors in their drawings. The exposure to colors develops their sensory mechanisms, so that the sense of sight integrates with the sense of touch, improving the child's perception and functioning.

However, some children are color blind. These children process colors differently, and find it particularly difficult to distinguish between red and green and between blue and yellow. The problem is usually diagnosed around ages 4–5, after the children have acquired the ability to name colors. In the case of color blind children, no personality conclusions may be drawn based exclusively on the colors in their drawings; other elements and graphic indicators must be used instead.

Figure 2-1:   Using color simply to depict reality

The key to diagnosing through colors is to look beyond the drawing. That is, ignore the drawing's structure and elements such as house or tree, and focus on the dominant color. Nevertheless, you must beware of attributing far-reaching personality or behavioral meanings to the colors without cross-checking additional indicators. For example, the color green in figure 2-1 must not be ascribed emotional meanings because the use of green in this case is natural when drawing the ninja turtle figure.

In addition to the cross-checking of additional indicators in a child's drawing, another important prerequisite is the amount of drawings analyzed – 25–30 will provide a good basis for a comprehensive analysis. If you observe recurring and dominant use of the same color in many of the child's drawings, you may reach conclusions about his personality and difficulties based on the meaning of this color.

Furthermore, when you see a dominant color in the child's drawings check with his parents whether this color was the only color available for drawing at the time. If the child had no other alternative, I don't recommend reaching any conclusion about his inner world based on the meaning of colors.

This chapter explains the meaning of colors in children's drawings and their relationship with various personality traits. The choice or overuse of a certain color can help us arrive at conclusions about the child's life.

In the following review of the various colors used in children's drawings, I offer various examples of overuse. On the other hand, the two drawings below are examples for balanced color use. When color use is balanced as opposed to imbalanced, the emotional meanings detected through the colors will tend to be positive. Nevertheless, such tendencies alone cannot support emotional conclusions unless backed by other graphic indicators.

Figures 2-2 & 2-3: Examples for balanced use of colors in different ages

Red

This is one of children's favorite colors. In fact, in most cases, it is the first color which comes to our mind when discussing colors. Because of its dominancy and attractiveness, you may find it in traffic lights and life-saving vehicles, but also in fast food restaurants. As red refers to guilt and sin, you may see examples of it in fairy tales like Little Red Riding Hood, who paid a heavy price for her "red" curiosity.

In history, red was used as a symbol of courage and bravery; hence it was included, even in ancient Rome, in warfare-related objects. In ancient Egypt, people used to paint their body red to demonstrate their power. In

India, red symbolized lust for power and materialism.

In China, red has a positive connotation and is a symbol of luck. Therefore it is used in celebrations and wedding ceremonies, where brides traditionally wear red dresses. In addition, the ceremony in which a newborn is named is called Red Egg.

Red has a stimulating effect on our nervous system and exposure to it increases the breathing rate and blood pressure (Ritberger, 2009). This is why red is associated with aggressiveness and competition.

In nature, it was found that red causes seagull nestlings to excessively search for food. It was also found that among European robins red triggers aggressive behavior.

Red has other meanings in our life, such as the power of life and inner energy, as well as survival. Max Lüscher – Inventor of the Lüscher Color Test – referred to red as symbolic of activity and leadership, as well as life's pleasures and success motivation. Goethe referred to red as a noble and graceful color, which symbolizes monarchy and sanctity, but when used in an exaggerated proportion might cause anxiety. Kandinsky agreed with him and thought of red as a color which is in constant movement and therefore causes restlessness.

Following its historic and cultural meanings, in children's drawings red is considered dominant and impressive. It is related to activity and doing. Children who constantly use red are often characterized as dominant and extrovert. These children like to be at the center of social attention. They like competition and challenges and prefer, of course, to be the winners. They are willing to invest great effort and energy to become leaders. Socially, they are direct and willful, so they know how to get what they need, without giving up to other children. Excessive use of red is common among aggressive children.

In the following drawing, it is possible to see excessive use of red. The girl who made this drawing did not try to document reality, but preferred red over other colors.

Note that when observing colors in drawings I recommend focusing on the amounts of color used, in order to differentiate between balanced and exaggerated amounts of color.

Figure 2-4:   Excessive use of red

In general, when the color is used in a reasonable and balanced way, you may tentatively conclude that the child's is balanced with positive "red meanings" such as active, enthusiastic and having a strong desire to be in the social center. However, when the page is swamped with red, my tentative conclusion would be that the child is attempting to compensate for contents and traits he lacked. Warmth will be replaced by aggression, hastiness by disquiet and the desire to be in the center by an existential need to be popular.

In this case, when the child is not at the center of attention, she behaves as if exposed to an existential threat, and reacts with nervousness and temper tantrums. All this may be concluded from her overuse of red. Nevertheless, as mentioned above, you must cross-check the information gleaned through colors with other graphic indicators in the child's drawings. Some such indicators are pressure, line drawing style, subject, and figure drawing style. These indicators will help you make a comprehensive and quality analysis of the child's drawings and determine whether the use of specific color is balanced or exaggerated.

Orange

Kandinsky liked the power of orange – the combination of red and yellow represented, in his opinion, balanced emotions and closeness between people, each remaining aware of his own powers. Like red, orange belongs to the warm color family and as such symbolizes energy, enthusiasm and doing. Children attracted to this color tend to be creative and optimistic. They are willing to dare and join new adventures, out of curiosity and a desire to experience independently and achieve their goals. A child who likes to draw with orange does not obey rules easily, but demands explanations for most requests. He often exhausts his parents with long verbal discussions, in which he usually prevails.

Figure 2-5:   Excessive use of orange

Nevertheless, the combination of yellow and red which produces orange somewhat moderates the emotional meanings we associate with red. Thus, children who use this color in an exaggerated way will be assertive rather than aggressive, enthusiastic rather than overeager, etc. When orange is used too intensively, it means the child sees pragmatism and creativity as important elements in his existence. Note that as a rule, orange stands for quality and represents ambition, health and also good communication with the environment, even at high doses.

Yellow

Similarly to red, yellow also symbolize caution and thus appears in many warning signs. Yellow is traditionally associated with jaundice and cowardice, as well as with aging, for both people and objects. In ancient Egypt it was used to mark criminals' and traitors' doors. In the Middle Ages, yellow costumes were used as the sign of the dead. In India yellow robes are often worn by Hindu swamis and Buddhist monks in their schools and during the spring festival. In Russia, yellow represents romantic breakup. Finally, we all remember Dorothy's Yellow Brick Road.

For Lüscher, yellow is a sign of lightheartedness, joy and comfort, which are felt after escape from restricted situations. Moreover, it symbolizes diligence which is not stable or consistent. Often, yellow symbolizes a conflict one must resolve. In the positive aspect, it represents a child's ambition with the ability to manage others in order to reach his goals.

Goethe observed that yellow is a complex color and noted that although in its basis yellow is a peaceful and joyful color, which gives a sense of warmth, when it becomes soiled, it gives a sense of nausea and discomfort. Kandinsky referred to yellow as an earthly color without any depth, which gives a feeling of restlessness, anger and jealousy.

When children use yellow in their drawings, it represents sensitivity. These children are well aware of their surrounding and deeply influenced by it. They are characterized by cleverness and patience, as well as joyfulness and mischief, but tend not to be troublemakers like children who use red. In addition, they are connected to their family and do not need many friends to find interest, because they have a rich inner world. They are also characterized by high concentration ability and a desire to experience, while taking the right precautions.

Exaggerated use of yellow represents oversensitivity which makes it difficult for the children to manage outside the inner circle of their loving family. When the child swamps the page with yellow, this also connotes naivety, innocence and empathy with other people's pain.

Figure 2-6:   Excessive use of yellow

This drawing was made by a 5½ year-old girl who desperately needs family closeness. Her family relocated to a new dwelling and she was about to enter first grade in a new school, without any of her old friends. As a result, this period was characterized by dependence, sensitivity and a strong need for support and reinforcements.

Pink

As expected, pink is most commonly used by girls. At a certain age this color dominates their world and they dress in pink clothes, play with pink toys, sleep on pink sheets and dream pink dreams. Although some boys also show interest in this color and add pink to their drawings, this color is commonly identified with femininity. Women who are attracted to stereotypically feminine jobs, and who adopt behaviors considered feminine, such as makeup, body care and fashion, tend to use it.

Many parents look at their girl when she is at this pink stage, smile and say that she is a little lady. This girl imitates dress codes of older women, but does it in an extreme and grotesque way, so some parents cannot bear it anymore. Beside her obsession with her appearance, she also adopts the mannerisms of older women, giving orders and bossing other children. Often she would find a boy who will be willing to kowtow to her every whim.

In children's drawings, pink refers to pleasing. Such behavior is common and normal at ages 5–7, but at older ages, a child who uses pink excessively may be characterized as having a strong need to please others, willfulness and a sense of esthetics.

Blue

Unlike pink, which is associated with femininity, blue is associated with masculinity. Blue is also associated with royalty and divinity. In ancient Egypt blue symbolized protection against evil, with the Pharaohs wearing blue clothes. In India, blue symbolizes the creation of the universe and divine wisdom, and the Buddha's body is often painted blue.

In nature, there is a lizard which can change its head's color to blue during sexual excitation periods. Toads see blue as water and a safe haven, hurrying to reach it in time of danger. Tamed chicks also associate blue with safety, so they tend to follow a blue figure.

In western civilization, especially in the US, brides traditionally wear a blue accessory as a sign of eternal love. On the other hand, blue is also associated with sadness and glumness, as in the blues musical genre.

Blue is also associated in the western world with the working class, as in the term "blue collar" worker. Some experts recommend wearing blue shirts to job interviews, because blue has a good and soothing effect on the interviewer. Blue affects our nervous system and causes a decrease in breathing rate and blood pressure.

Lüscher associated blue with tranquility and content, as well as a need to be physically or emotionally relaxed. Psychologically, blue represents the tendency to be sensitive and easily offended. According to Lüscher, blue symbolizes the relationships a person has with his surroundings and his sense of belonging.

Goethe differentiated between the various blue hues. On one end of the scale, it gives us a cold impression, and on the other reminds us of a pleasant shade. Kandinsky referred to blue as a color which creates a sense of loneliness, melancholy and daydreaming.

In children's drawings blue represents relaxation and calm behavior patterns. Children who tend to use blue in their drawings will search quiet social interactions and will try to achieve harmony and pleasant atmosphere in their relationships with others. In their family relationships these children behave logically, demanding logical explanations and refusing to accept answers such as: "Because I said so...". Children who tend to use blue are also characterized by a rich inner world, and it is important for them to express it.

Exaggerated use of blue represents cold, distant and restrained communication. It may also symbolize the child's lack of confidence, oversensitivity, vulnerability and even his tendency to suppress his feelings.

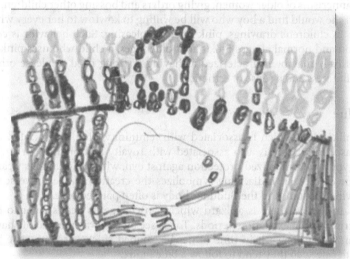

Figure 2-7:   Excessive use of blue

The following example was made by a 4½ year-old child whose parents contacted me because he had social and emotional difficulties. One of the issues that concerned them was that he didn't have many friends at kindergarten because he was offended easily and when he met them in the afternoon, he insisted they meet only at his home. The excessive use of blue in his drawings represented his restrained communication pattern and social difficulties, as well as his low self-confidence and vulnerability.

You should note, however, the amount of blue used in the child's drawing as well as graphic indicators in it. The parents of the child who made the next drawing contacted me because his kindergarten teacher reported that he was having a hard time, which made him nervous and caused him to beat other children.

The boy's decision to use blue in this drawing is very clear, as it is spread over the entire page. In addition, he draws in an angular line, rapid movement and various pressure levels.

Figure 2-8: **Extreme use of blue, combined with rigid, fast line movement and variable pressure level**

Integrating all these factors indicates that this child has some emotional difficulty, which he tries to overcome by using the cold and relaxing blue. In other words, blue was used in this case to compensate for fears and anxieties that the child has but are unspoken, yet causing his unpleasantly distancing behavior, which is expressed either actively (aggression), or passively (withdrawal or detachment).

Purple

Queen Cleopatra of ancient Egypt loved purple. She loved it so much she forced her servants to immerse 20,000 snails for 10 days, so that they would secrete enough purple mucus. In Christianity, the pope and cardinals wear purple – perhaps the most expensive dye in the pre-modern world.

In human color psychology, purple is considered symbolic of royalty, nobility and gift. In one of his letters, Leonardo da Vinci wrote that he found meditation to be ten times more powerful when performed in a purple-colored room or under purple light. Similarly, Wagner used to compose his operas in a purple room which he called "my inspiration room".

Lüscher described studies that associate purple with emotional and mental immaturity. In his opinion, preferring purple represents emotional fears, which cause people to create an imaginary world, while ignoring their surroundings. Such perception of the world as an imaginary place matches children's natural view. In other words, purple is associated with escapism, usually caused by hidden anger or sadness. Another meaning purple has in our culture is the wish to charm others. Kandinsky noted that purple is created when red withdraws into blue. Therefore, purple is more related to blue in its meaning and associates with sadness and distance.

In children's drawings purple is symbolic of imagination and intuitions. These children demand others to be particularly patient with them and are sensitive about managing things in their own pace. They have principles and ideas from an early age and it is important for them to keep them. In addition, children who tend to use purple may be characterized as day-dreamers and generally confused.

Figure 2-9: Excessive use of purple

This drawing is an example for exaggerated use of purple. The excessive use of purple symbolizes the girl's connection to her childhood experience, in the simplest sense of what it means to be a child. Note that although this girl is very in touch with her intuition, this connectedness to her childish side clashes with daily demands by her parents who think she is not grounded enough in reality.

Green

Green often appears in children's drawings as it is also common in nature. Children are aware of the green color of tree and plants, but do not always use it when drawing them.

Historically, green symbolized victory. Green bay leaves were laid on the victor's head in ancient Greece. In ancient Egypt temple floors were painted green as a sign of success and victory. In addition, green was considered symbolic of resurrection and immortality. Nowadays, green is often used symbolically in many African countries to represent natural richness, but also in Islamic countries, because it is considered by Islam to be sacred, as it is symbolic of the lushness of paradise. Green is also associated with prosperity, as in the dollar bills.

Since green is a cold color, it is usually considered calming and harmonizing. For example, green is used in billiard or card games tables, because it creates harmony between the gamblers. In medicine, green is often used in surgery rooms or clinics, to create a relaxing atmosphere.

Culturally, we associate green with envy, as well as with beginnings ("green light"). Politically, green represents environmental activism.

According to Lüscher, green is symbolic of willpower, diligence, stability, self-awareness and self-esteem. Green is characterized by precise, factual and critical assessment. It is also associated with efficiency. In addition, Lüscher sees in green a symbol of one's will to outstand, impress, dominate and receive recognition from others, in order to boost one's self-confidence. Kandinsky and Goethe both share the opinion that green projects peacefulness, stability and quietness.

Figure 2-10:   Excessive use of green

In children's drawings green symbolizes many characteristics of childhood such as fresh start, different and unique view of situations, learning and a need for space. Consequently, green appears more often in drawings of children who like nature and outdoor games.

This drawing was made by a 5 year-old. No need to refer to the grass or stalk which are naturally green. However, it is clear that the child chose not to use any other colors, so that the house is made of green contour lines, as well as green windows and door.

Recall that we must examine a large number of drawings in order to draw conclusions about the child's personality. In this case, as in other drawings by the same child, green is used extensively. Excessive use of this color may indicate compensation, for example, for the child's need to learn, start anew and blossom.

In the case of this particular child, excessive use of green indicates his fears of learning. At the time of this drawing, the child started first grade and was afraid of studying and found it difficult to manage in class, mainly due to motoric difficulties not diagnosed before my analysis of his drawings. This child used to sit next to his classmates in front of the teacher and blackboard but could not compare himself to their capabilities, mainly because he could not copy quickly enough from the board. As already noted, the combination of excessive coloring with graphic indicators, such as the shaky lines representing the house walls and roof, lends further support to my conclusion regarding his emotional difficulty.

Gray

In nature gray is associated with fall and wintery weather. In many languages, a "gray" face is a weary facial expression. Gray life is a meaningless and boring life, and a gray job is similarly boring and lacking in glory. Nevertheless, somewhat ironically, shades of gray represent a balance point of view, as opposed to the sharp dichotomy of black and white.

The brain tissue is called "gray matter", associating the color with thinking. The term "gray market" refers to semi-legal economic activity. Finally, a "gray area" represents territories or activities known to be problematic but that is not dealt with specifically by the law or enforcement authorities.

Lüscher associates gray with neutrality, a wish to "sit on the fence", but also a border. This is why we often observe gray boundaries in drawings, which protect the painter from external threats.

In children's drawings, gray is usually used topically, as in gray clouds. In addition, gray, just as any other color, has a range of qualities – positive and negative. Children tend to use gray mainly in its negative aspects. However, gray may also indicate positive aspects such as the ability to integrate or perform measured steps. Remember that the color analysis must be supported by other indicators, primarily graphic indicators and that it is this combined analysis that will determine the meaning of the color.

Brown

Brown is the most dominant color in nature besides green. It appears in landscapes, plants, animals, as well as in the color of our eyes, skin and hair.

Lüscher refers to brown as a symbol of sensation. Meaning, brown is the reflection of our physical aspect. In addition, it was found that when a person feels uncomfortable with his family, or experience physical insecurity or discomfort, he will tend to choose brown. That is, the choice of brown indicates an increased need for physical and sensory comfort. This could indicate lack of confidence or actual physical illness. The lack of confidence could stem from conflicts or problems the person feels unable to cope with.

In most cases, brown will be used realistically in children's drawings. For example, the earth will often be painted in brown. Exaggerated use of brown indicates difficulty to deal with changes and tendency to prefer the well-known and familiar.

Figure 2-11: Excessive use of brown

The following example represents excessive use of brown. The child draws all figures completely brown, without any distinctions among body organs: eyes, eyelashes, noses, mouths, arms and torsos are all brown. Usually, in drawings by children her age, human figures are more colorful and their organs more distinct.

All shades of brown are characteristic of the human skin. Therefore, it may be that this girl attempted to find a color similar to natural body colors. However, other drawings by the same girls are also characterized by excessive use of brown. This means the girl may have needs associated with using that color, such as groundedness, stability, earthliness and confidence. She needs to know what is going on around her, down to the smallest details, to feel that confidence, otherwise she may suffer anxiety.

Black

One of the most commonly asked questions about children's drawings is about the meaning of black. In western culture black symbolizes mourning, bereavement or depression. However, in other countries and cultures white is used to represent these situations and sentiments. In western society, if a person had a rough day, he would say that he had a black day. Black is also associated with dark and mysterious events – for example, a black cat as a sign of the evil eye, black lists, black humor and black magic.

However, black is also associated in our culture with authority and momentousness, as in "black tie" events. In Japanese culture, black is a symbol of nobility, age, and experience.

According to Lüscher, black negates any other color and as such symbolizes relinquishment, surrender and abandonment. But black also has an ability to emphasize and empower any color drawn next to it. Kandinsky associated black with eternal silence, without hope.

When analyzing drawings, recall that the use of black is not culturally dependent. In that it is similar to many other elements in children's drawings, such as houses, which appear in the majority of children's drawings from diverse cultures in the shape of a triangle placed on top of a square, regardless of the real-life appearance of their lodgings.

Likewise, the use of colors in drawings is not culture-dependent, and when a child draws exclusively in black, it definitely does not mean he is depressed or in mourning. Thus, you can find black drawings even in countries where mourning is represented by other colors, such as red in South Africa, blue in Iran, and the white flags hoisted along the streets of Colombo, Sri Lanka, following the Tsunami disaster.

Figure 2-12: Excessive use of black

Most children use black in their drawings simply because it gives a strong and dramatic effect to the drawing. Figure 2-12 was made by a 3 years and 5 months-old boy, who named it "The world in black". By doing so, he increased his parent's anxieties about his general condition. When I checked other drawings he made, it was found, in addition to other graphic indicators, that black was used sporadically, enabling me to calm his parents.

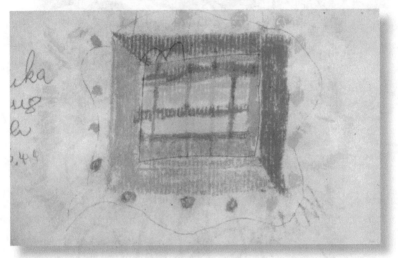

Figure 2-13:   Black-less drawing from the ghetto

On the other hand, the next colorful and joyful-looking drawing was made by a girl who lived in a ghetto during the Holocaust, under severe stress and anxiety, before she was killed in an extermination camp.

There are some issues related to black that you must check. First, find out whether the colors in front of your child included only black, or did not include it at all. This may sound weird, but sometimes children simply draw with the colors in their possession. I once met a kindergarten teacher who consistently withheld black crayons from her children, explaining that she didn't want the children to spoil their drawings by covering them in black. Such behavior could be the source of children's strong attraction to drawing with black at home.

I do not recommend this approach, because colors are rich with personal meanings for children and it is important that they experience drawing freely and intuitively.

The next issue that you should check is the surrounding in which the drawing was made. Does the child draw differently at home, compared to kindergarten? Do drawings made while staying with grandparents include different colors than usual? Does the phenomenon repeat itself or appear in one drawing only?

If the child continues to draw exclusively in black, I advise checking his behavior when other colors are placed in front of him. Does he ignore them, or does he try them out but prefers using black? It is also important to note the length of time in which he chooses to use black exclusively, similarly to the "pink period" or "heart-shape period" common among girls, which passes naturally with age.

Many children who prefer black argue that it is "the most powerful color", since it can erase all colors painted underneath. In addition, it forms a strong contrast with the page's white color. Nevertheless, if the child persists in using black excessively, you must check whether he suffers from some visual problem, perhaps color blindness (if the child's age allows you to make such a diagnosis). Interestingly, a study conducted among children with learning disabilities, perceptual and visual problems found that drawing on black paper made it easier for them to create a wider variety of shapes and details, probably thanks to the strong contrast provided by black (Uhlin 1979).

In any case, even if the use of black is exaggerated, you must refer to the overall drawing level: Does the child draw in an age-appropriate manner? Does he enjoy drawing? How much pressure does he apply while drawing? If the pressure is very intense, to the point of punching holes in the paper, the use of black may indicate emotional inhibition, internalized fears and fear of criticism.

To conclude, the colors in children's drawing paint a fascinating picture. Nevertheless, it is important to beware of attributing far-reaching meanings and spiritual symbolism to little children. The combination of meanings of the colors in children's drawings, combined with the meanings of graphic parameters and the various symbols in other elements, can add a deeper layer of significance to our interpretation of colors and shed light onto the drawing child's subjective emotional world.

The Meaning of Colors in Children's Drawings

Red – A dominant and extroverted child who likes to be at the center of attention. He is active and full of enthusiasm. Like challenges and competitions and strongly needs to be the winner. Usually, his behavior is goal-directed – he can get what he wants and does not easily let other children have their way.

Orange – An energetic, enthusiastic boy who loves doing. Usually, very creative and brimming with optimism. Willing to dare and join new experiences, and showing charming mischievousness. Obeying the rules does not come easy to him and he demands clear explanations for every request.

Yellow – A clever boy, highly sensitive to his environment. He is playful and full of joy of life, but not a "troublemaker" like his red friend. He is strongly connected to his family and does not need "the boys" to find interest. Has a rich inner world and good concentration.

Pink – Usually girls who love to be at the center of attention. They feel older than their age and require the environment to treat them accordingly. They are intensely interested in and curious about their femininity and end to give orders and act like "little mothers".

Blue – An easygoing, calm boy. In his social conduct, he will seek quiet and harmony. He demands logical explanations and refuses to receive answers such as, "Because I said so!" Has a rich and intricate inner world, but it's important for him to express himself and his wishes.

Purple – A boy with well-developed imagination and intuitions. Demands to be treated with exceptional tolerance, but conducts himself at a personal pace that suits him. He has principles and ideals that guide him and lead his thought and action.

Green – Curious with a passion for learning. He likes new beginnings and transition, and can examine situations in his life in a different and refreshing light. The educational approach to him needs to be liberal, with plenty of free space for action.

Brown – A judicious boy, who usually thinks rationally. As such, he demands and needs logical explanations. In his social conduct, he shows confidence and even leadership skills.

Black – A responsible boy with a presence, needs attention, prefers to be the social leader and decide for everyone.

3 FAMILY RELATIONSHIPS

The parent-child relationship can be a challenging and empowering experience, but also a complex and exhausting one. Some may say parenting is one of the most complex and meaningful tasks in our lifetime and as such, it is rife with changes and internal conflicts. Drawings shed light on parent-child dynamics, helping us understand the reasons behind a child's behavior and find unique ways to improve the atmosphere and relationship at home.

Family Coalitions

One of the keys to analyzing family drawings is identifying the common denominator to all family members. In children's drawings this could mean similar colors, drawing style, clothing, accessories and so on. Children draw family members close to each other, even if they are distant in reality. By identifying the common denominator in a family, you will also be able to reach conclusions regarding inner family coalitions that are significant to the entire family dynamic.

Internal family coalitions refer to both overt and covert coalitions between parents and children that form the family power structure. For example, if children, during an argument, often tend to agree with the mother, it will be very hard for the father to stand up to all of them.

Nevertheless, it is important to note that the way a child draws his family does not necessarily reflect the reality he lives in. Children often beautify their lived reality or draw more desirable family power balances. Be that as it may, drawings will enable you to understand how family relationships are perceived by a child and reach conclusions regarding his general behavior.

Most approaches to analyzing family drawings rely on Salvador Minuchin's structural family therapy (1974). Structural family therapy basically assumes that the family is a structure in which a person's identity is shaped.

According to this theory, the family is a living and developing organism. Similarly, the inner dynamics of family drawings also change as the family evolves. Eventually, the goal of drawing analysis is to find family-relevant solutions rather or in addition to particular solutions tailored to each member.

In spontaneous drawings, based on the ambiguous instruction "draw a family", you can clearly see whether a child is aware of his family boundaries. Drawings reveal how a child perceives the subsystems in his family. In other words, drawings will show his attitude towards parents and siblings. Some of the most common ways children use to describe relationships in a family are distance between figures, height and width of family figures, different colors and clothing.

Figure 3-1:   Family coalition

At first glance, the drawing in figure 3-1 does not seem to indicate the existence of any internal family coalition, mainly because all family members are drawn in the same color and all seem to be of the same height. However, the topographical location of the figures on the page (the form of the ground line beneath their legs) indicates the existence of a coalition nevertheless, with the eldest boy standing on the same plain together with his parents, while the 5½ year-old girl who made this drawing and her little brother forced onto a different plain, with added "grass" to compensate for their stature and make them as "tall" as the eldest brother and the parents. In this case, height of course represents dominance in the family system.

The behavioral approach and its view on family therapy (Cordova, 2003) may also be represented in family drawings. This theory focuses on family members' social relationships and level of involvement. When a certain family member is more involved in a life of a child, the latter will tend to draw that member bigger and in a more positive way than other family members. Conversely, when they lack emotional communication, this will be represented by poor quality line and color selection.

Other issues such as criticism, positive evaluation, and trust relationships will also be represented in the way a child draws his family figures. The main focus in this case will be on the distance and relationship between figures: Is one figure distant from the rest? Are the figures holding hands or looking at one another? Do the figures have similar clothing accessories or other things in common? (Spigelman, 1992)

Temper Tantrums Directed at Parents

Most studies on temper tantrums (e.g. Waska 1990) view this as a common or even normative phenomenon at age two. However, as many parents know, reality is a bit different and temper tantrums occur also at older ages (Koch 2003).

Figure 3-2: **Low self-esteem as an antecedent of temper tantrums**

I recommend referring to the two following key aspects of this phenomenon:

1. *Location* – Some children are liable to throw a tantrum anywhere, while others make a clear separation between home and kindergarten. Such separation is important, because you may learn from it about a child's ability to regulate his behavior.

For example, some children will throw a tantrum each time they fail in a task at kindergarten. Their frustration overwhelms them, so they react in rage. In such cases, as you may see in the following drawing, a dominant trend is related to low self-esteem and a weak sense of achievement. The parents of this 6 year-old girl, who started first grade, reported that she bursts in anger every time they point to a spelling error or when she mistakenly messes up the page.

Her drawing style combines trends of weak pressure with a shaky line with trends of drawing body organs such as the legs – drawn with a thin and fragile line, so that the entire figure seems unstable – or the eyes which are drawn without pupils, suggesting difficulty deciphering peer society behavior codes.

Other children will throw tantrums in situations such as social frustration due to unfair treatment by their peer group. For example, they would get angry and say "I didn't get what I wanted… it's not fair…"

2. *Expression style* – There are two basic types of expression: extraverted and introverted. Children with an extraverted expression style will usually react to their environment and beat, scratch or bite their parents or other children. Introverted children, on the other hand, turn their anger into themselves – they will bite their fingernails, smash their head against a wall, have tics or otherwise behave compulsively.

The parents of the 7 year-old girl who made the drawing shown below consulted me because of her temper tantrums, which occur mainly during family gatherings at her relatives' homes. During these events, sometimes things would not go according to her plan – for example, when playing with her cousins, she would claim they are unfair to her and get mad, screaming and running out of the house in anger. In such cases, she finds it hard to relax, despite her parents' attempts to calm her down.

Figure 3-3: **Emotional overload and stress as antecedents of temper tantrums**

My work with her family included the following stages:

3. *Understanding the scope of the phenomenon* – It appeared she would not throw tantrums at school or at home on a regular basis. Most of her temper tantrums occurred at her grandfather's house during family gatherings. Therefore, my first assumption was that the source of her behavior was related to the parental dynamic at her grandfather's house. My discussion with her parents confirmed my suspicion, as it seemed that when she is at her grandfather's place, she is faced with multiple authority figures telling her how to behave. In other words, during such family events, her parents are left aside, letting other family member rebuke her, creating a confusing parental reality for her.

4. *Accepting the phenomenon as natural* – Many parents fear any manifestation of aggressive behavior because they think it's the tip of the iceberg and that they will soon find out something terrible about their child. Despite your need to be politically correct and maintain a pleasant social atmosphere, you must not forget that aggression is a natural instinct. I recommend teaching your child how to behave and how to control his aggression, keeping in mind that it is a natural part of all of us. This point of view facilitates family dialog as it mitigates the fears related to the phenomenon.

5. *Exploring the reasons for the tantrums through drawings* – Among other causes, temper tantrums may be precipitated by

a. Regressed emotional development – In this case, the child did not have temper tantrums until a certain point in time, from which a regression was identified. In general, such behavior indicates stress – the child is stressed and angry outbursts offer the only outlet. Thus, a temper tantrum may also serve a positive emotional purpose for the child (albeit being unpleasant for his environment). In drawings, you will see regression in drawing stages, parallel to the behavioral regression. In this particular case, this possibility was rejected because the girl's drawings were advanced for her age.

b. Temperament types – Parents with several children will be able to confirm that children have different temperaments since birth. A temperament usually does not change and characterizes a child's behavior throughout his life. Temper tantrums will be more frequent in impulsive children with a "warm temper". In such cases, a child's outburst is not a sign of stress, but part of a natural expression style. However, this drawing was not made in an impulsive style – she filled the page areas meticulously, drawing slowly and patiently and attending to the smallest details.

c. Stressors – Based on Freud's theory, we assume that a child's behavior has a reason and that he benefits from his behavior, in this case, temper tantrums. Adler argued that each outburst has a purpose. This could be trying to get attention. The solution will then be to prevent the secondary gain involved. I prefer to focus on the cause for the temper tantrums more than on their purpose. In this case, you can clearly see that the reason for the girl's behavior is her stress. The figure's hair is drawn with a rigid line and dense coloring, which overloads the figure. This overload symbolizes the child's emotional burden, caused by her expectations from herself or others' expectations of her. Whatever the exact cause, it is clearly out there and indicates a real-life difficulty. Once she became less stressful and her parents learned to disregard her negative behavior, her temper tantrums simply disappeared.

To conclude, temper tantrums are a way of expressing anger and usually occur when a child experiences frustration and difficulty finding a better way to cope with his reality. Note that anger and aggression are natural and convey this belief to the child, in addition to having a dialog from which he may learn about other ways of coping with aggression.

Figure 3-4:   Following therapy: emotional relief as indicated by the more spacious hair

A child should understand that socially, there are more effective ways for him to cope with failure or frustration. When parents have difficulty coping with temper tantrums themselves, and these become a recurring pattern, they should consult a therapist or parental guidance expert.

Stubbornness and Power Struggles

The generic term power struggles will be used here to refer to struggles that parents have with their children. Unlike temper tantrums, power struggles might be prolonged and accompany almost every interaction. Power struggles may extend from the age of 1½ years to late adolescence. Often, but not always, power struggles involve temper tantrums.

Children who have adopted a power struggle attitude will be ready to fight over anything as if it were a matter of life and death – they will scream, become stubborn and act aggressively. In other cases they will lie or behave in a domineering way towards their family members (Madigan, 2003).

Parents living in such an atmosphere are exhausted and usually state that "there are shouts, threats and punishments all day long. Without them, nothing works". When parents reach the point of joining in a power struggle, they will tend not to give up on their principles, even if leads to "a severe clash with my child, until he understands who's the boss".

Figure 3-5: **Power struggles indicated by dense painting with intense pressure**

The children's drawings and the children themselves, in this case, react to this harsh treatment. In the drawings, this may be indicated by intense pressure on the drawing tool and the use of multiple and dense paint layers, to the point of tearing the page.

Eventually, despite their militant statements, many parents feel defeated and frustrated. They will often admit that "this is not how I planned on raising my child…" Their child usually shares this exact feeling, although his feelings are not as clear to outsiders.

Figure 3-6: Emphasized shoulders and exaggerated height as a way of indicating desired status in the context of power struggles within the family

He also feels humiliated and beaten, resulting in continued efforts to fight for his place and status at home. His drawings, such as that presented in figure 3-6, often include figures whose legs look like pedestals the figures are mounted on, in a compensatory attempt at enhancing his status and influence at home and stressing the shoulders by drawing with intense pressure, as the emotional meaning of this bodily part is associated with status within the family.

The 4 year-old boy who made the following drawings is charming and lovable. Eight months after his young brother was born he started his power struggles with his parents and never stopped since. He responds to almost every request with "I don't feel like it", even if they offer him something enjoyable in return. In other words, almost every interaction with him leads to a fight.

Figure 3-7:   Spreading over the entire page and circular coloring

His rapid and circular drawing style represents his energy and activeness. The broad deployment of elements on the page represents his tendency to be dominant in social interactions. He knows how to find ways to receive constant quality attention from his family members. Moreover, you may conclude from the gaps in his scribbles that he is outgoing, with a developed sense of humor, which enables him to get applauses and remain at the center of attention.

However, his drawings are below average compared to his age. Such regression, as expressed in the following example, represents his behavior, turning every interaction into a fight. According to his drawings, he experiences his social environment as a battlefield, where one wins or loses.

Figure 3-8:   Regression in drawing level indicating prolonged power struggles

No doubt any parent would be exhausted by such behavior, especially if it lasts long. Due to such behavior many parents report having lost the pleasure of being a parent. Naturally, children such as this boy give their parents many moments of joy and laughter. It's nice to observe him running and playing, but his objection to simple requests makes his parents feel weak and frustrated.

How to improve the family atmosphere?

There are several ways to improve an atmosphere in a family with a child who constantly turns down requests and acts defiantly:

1. *Coping with daily transitions* – Some children have difficulty with changes, which is mainly expressed by filling the entire page with a variety of scribbles, using sharp transitions from circular to angular scribbles. Such difficulty may be expressed in events such as going to trips with friends, going to kindergarten, bathing in the evening, falling asleep, etc. Any transition should be made gradually and slowly while using the opportunity for motor activity in the form of competing to the destination, even if the child only competes with himself.

Figure 3-9: **Sharp transitions between circular and angular scribbling: difficulty with daily transitions**

2. In all such transitions you should first check whether the parents' behavior is consistent – each separately and both together. In this case, the source of the child's difficulty was an unstructured daily schedule. Note that going to kindergarten and dining on regular hours provide children with confidence and emotional calm. Consistency should not be merely technical of course, but accompanied by parental messages and other valued behaviors.

3. *Use movement to reach out* – Most children like to run, but some need to do so more than others. This child, for example, needs to move during most of the day. This is indicated by his rapid and inconsistent scribbling style. Every time you want to talk to such child, it would be better to do it while walking or combined with any other activity. When such a child is in motion, he learns better. When walking is not feasible, try to maintain physical contact with the child during the conversation – even if you just put a hand on his shoulder, it will improve his listening. Note that some children like this one need activity to improve their attitude, rather than long dialogs that tire them.

4. Positive feedback – This method, using words or stickers, can do wonders. The feedback should be gradual – every succeeding stage is rewarded. For example, first a child will get a sticker only for getting up and dressing by himself in the morning. Next, he will

receive a sticker for other activities at home and finally, for outdoor or complex requests. Note that a child may object to some requests along the way, so expect progress to be slow.

All of the above solutions work only if parents have faith in them and truly believe that keeping boundaries and complying with their requests are important for their child, even in adulthood. If the parent's standpoint is "he is only a child…nothing will happen if is late for kindergarten…anyway he will have, as an adult, to get to work on time every day…", then it will be difficult for the child to cope with transitions. Every parent prefers raising his child in a positive and joyful atmosphere, without quarrels or anger, but you must be aware of the thin line separating positive and negative stubbornness. This child's resistance is an example of negative stubbornness. He takes his energies and spends them in a negative ways, doing things on purpose. His parents could teach him how to spend his energies in a positive way, empowering his positive stubbornness, which will later help him achieve goals in life.

Positive feedback messages delivered gradually teach a child to be in contact with his powers even when faced with complex situations. Proper positive feedback must include encouragement by the parent, showing confidence in his child's abilities. The parent's confidence will then increase the child's confidence that he can succeed in the task. It is important to continue and challenge a child, until he himself adopts a behavioral pattern that will make him feel calm and confident in his abilities. In this case, the child's independence is important for him, so it would be wise to reinforce this element in his personality, while weakening his negative stubbornness, which does not make for a healthy relationship.

Delegating responsibilities to children also helps boost their self-confidence and empower them. In my example, following the birth of the child's younger brother, his parents could have asked him how he pictures himself as a big brother and what responsibilities he would like to receive with regards to his little brother. At the same time, it is important to give him the privileges of a big brother. For example, sitting alone with the parents when possible, just like they used to do before his brother was born.

Nevertheless, it is wise to "pick your battles". I recommend not starting to fight with children on all fronts at the same time. It is better to pick a fight and focus your efforts to resolve it first before moving on to other issues. For example, if you first choose to cope with the child's resistance to going to kindergarten in the morning, you had better reach mutual understanding on matters such as sleeping hours, morning rituals, what to do when he resists getting up, who should take him to kindergarten, how to turn the road to the kindergarten to an appropriate activity for the child based on your conclusions from his drawings, etc.. Later on, I recommend sharing the new approach with your child, explaining to him that you expect gradual progress and a pleasant atmosphere at home and that you have complete confidence in him.

To conclude, note that I wrote "battles" in quotation marks, because the goal in parenting is not to "win". There are no winners or losers in a family. The purpose of parenting is to achieve common objectives. In this case, the parents and the child had a common goal, which was for the child to cope independently with transitions. In other words, the goal was to hear him say: "I want to get up in the morning and get ready by myself, so I could go to my kindergarten and meet my friends".

Tips for Coping with Stubbornness, Power Struggles and Tantrums

- When your goal is to defuse a power struggle with your child, first try to calm the general atmosphere down. You will not be able to conduct an effective conversation when both parties are in the middle of a fight.

- Decide that from now on you talk to your child respectfully as if he were older.

- Tell your child that you have decided to act differently and that you are sure that he will agree to take part in the new process.

- Try to simplify the issues that usually cause resistance. Provide two possible solutions and let the child choose between them. Adjust the number of possibilities and their content to the child's age and emotional level, as expressed through his drawings, as well as his behavior.

- Talk clearly and simply when in a power struggle and use cause-and-effect formulas without any personal reference. For example, instead of saying "Don't get up of bed. It annoys me!", say "If you choose to get up of bed, I will take you back to bed, because it's time to sleep".

- Pick your battles – choose certain issues you will be willing to discuss only after establishing trust between the parties and improving the atmosphere.

- Legitimize anger – anger is a natural emotion designed to release negative energy and it basically indicates caring. However, help your child find better ways to express his anger. Drawings can be used as a positive channel to release anger.

- Create moments of quality time and positive feedback. When a relationship is good and a child feels loved, he will go to great lengths not to destroy the special relationship formed with a parent.

- Check for reasons for temper tantrums and try to avoid them. Note that more children lie down in anger on the mall floor than on the ground, during a hike. The mall's environment, which is noisy and hectic, makes many children restless and is the true source of the power struggles.

- Power struggles and temper tantrums cause a child to be afraid of his own anger. Even if you choose to stay away from a child during a fight, do it in short breaks, giving him the message that he is still wanted and loved. If you abandon a child at a time of anger, he might make unrealistic and unspoken assumptions. Hence, adult's presence in such a situation is very important, in order to relieve his anxieties. You may also use his drawings to understand how he perceives his family and reveal his unspoken assumptions.

- Often, the parents' reaction to power struggles is aggressive. Try to avoid such behavior and use fewer threats, showing him a different role model. However, if a child might harm himself or damage to the surrounding, hug him tightly and say, "I love you and I will be here until you relax".

- Keep looking at your child's drawings, while searching for changes in their trends. If the behavioral change you are making at home really works, your child's drawings will also change accordingly – dense drawings will become spaced, heavy pressure will lighten and so on.

- Believe that an improved relationship with your child is like a seatbelt, as it keeps your child safe. A good relationship helps him in many areas in life, enabling him to socialize without needing to constantly fight. To stretch the same metaphor, just like driving a car the improvement in relationships is gradual but eventually pays off and benefits you throughout your entire life.

Positive and negative spoiling

There are cases in which a child's babyish behavior might confuse his parents and be considered as a desire to be spoiled. Therefore, I would like to discuss the meanings of such behavior, while distinguishing between positive and negative spoiling.

I refer to *positive spoiling* as a wide variety of affectionate behaviors between parent and child: hugs, kisses, positive feedback, compliments and gifts. There is nothing wrong with spoiling children, because this is a natural and important part of every parent-child relationship. Spoiling makes a child feel loved and at the center of attention, which is an important emotion for the development of a child's ego in his early years (Ehrensaft, 1999). Therefore, we can determine that positive spoiling is one which is made at a reasonable degree, one that doesn't prevent the child from taking part in age-appropriate activities.

On the other hand, *negative spoiling* may be defined as any activity which eventually is unpleasant for a child or his parent. Usually, such spoiling creates a child who is dependent on his parent and a parent who feels burdened by the need to satisfy his child. The parent's purpose in negative spoiling is to prevent his child from having to undertake challenging tasks which could make him feel frustrated, so he performs these tasks by himself in order to please him. So, negative spoiling is about a parent providing "extra services" for his child, doing things the child can do on his own because they are age appropriate.

I would like to emphasize again that every child definitely deserves to be spoiled, as long as he knows he is capable of doing the specific tasks required of him by himself when he should want to.

In relation to children's drawing, I recommend referring to spoiling as an outcome which obscures the reason for it. In other words, many parents consult me about their children's spoiled behavior, but the actual reason for their behavior often varies. Analyzing drawings helps understand the reason behind each case. Understanding the reason then helps me find the right solution.

The starting point when discussing spoiling is that it serves an unsatisfied need that the child has. Therefore, first and foremost, you must determine whether a specific act of spoiling is due to manipulation or an authentic sense of inefficacy.

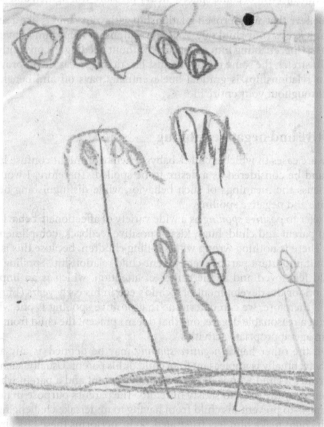

Figure 3-12:   An authentic sense of inefficacy

Figure 3-12, made by a 6½ year-old boy, exemplifies an authentic feeling of inefficacy. You can see that his drawing level is regressive and age inappropriate. In addition, line quality is poor, the tree trunk is thin and fragile and the treetops are sagging. This drawing style represents low self-esteem. Accordingly, my conclusion was that the child behaves in a spoiled manner due to real inefficacy rather than high self-confidence and sense of power in family situations. Analyzing his drawing helped me understand the reason for his behavior and provide the best solution for it.

Figure 3-13:   Regression in drawing quality combined with areas of over-intense coloring

Another example of spoiling, stress and anxiety is presented in figure 3-13. The 6 year-old who made it suffers from multiple fears expressed, among other things, in evacuation. In this drawing you can see regression in drawing level, which is expressed in the poor drawing level of the house and tree, and wide areas drawn with heavy pressure and dense coloring, such as the tree trunk and the treetop's left side, symbolizing her high stress level. In her case, the reason for her spoiling is the sense of protection she gets by remaining close to an adult who protects her against a scary and dangerous world.

The conclusions I derived from her drawings helped her parents find new powers from within to cope with her dependent behavior. Concurrently, I drew up a comprehensive plan for creating a stable atmosphere, which includes moments of closeness and security with her parents. The change in her relationship with her parents enabled her basic needs to be met, without having to act so childishly and dependently.

Figure 3-14:   Schematically advanced drawing by a 3 year-old

My last example in this section is by a 3 year-old. His parents consulted me complaining on his dependent and spoiled behavior, which was age inappropriate. This drawing represents a high drawing level, advanced for his age. A human figure with a torso does not characterize drawings by 3 year-olds, who usually draw "tadpoles" (see Chapter 1). Another (positively) age inappropriate aspect is his wide covering of the page and use of its edges as bases for elements such as the sky or the figure.

Note that drawings by spoiled children usually demonstrate inefficacy. In this case, the child's rich drawing style represents a clear sense of self-efficacy. For this reason, and as an integral part of my analysis, I also looked into drawings by his older brother, who was aged seven at the time. My conversation with his parents seemed to indicate that the older brother set a positive behavioral role model for them. The older brother's drawings were high quality, very organized and advanced for his age, as can be seen in following example.

Figure 3-15:   High-quality drawing: order, organization and slow pace

The precision, esthetic values, symmetry and slow and cautious drawing style all represent significant differences in the brothers' temperament. In this case, analysis of the children's drawings helped their parents to see the younger brother as he really was and not as compared to his older brother. Note that as a result of his parents' new perspective the younger brother gradually became independent.

Tips for Coping with Spoiled Behavior

Look for a reason. Children who ask their parents' attention do not always do it to gain control, but rather to fulfill a genuine need for intimacy and reassurance. Drawings often indicate the child's genuine reasons, so observe them carefully and look for signs indicative of the child's needs.

After finding the reason for a child's spoiled behavior, make a plan which will enable him to gradually find his powers and abilities. You may use his drawings for two purposes: first, to discover his talents and second, to compliment him on his artwork.

Check for other family members who complain about inefficacy in their lives. Such an atmosphere of inefficacy might affect a child's worldview, and be manifested in his behavior.

Empower your child when he makes it on his own, even in minor tasks.

Legitimize your child's feelings of frustration, sadness and anger. These emotions are an integral part of his personality and your purpose as parents is not to prevent your child from expressing them, but rather to help him talk about them as part of his life.

Spoiled behavior usually leads to sharp dichotomous relationship between a spoiled child and a responsible adult. Try to break this dichotomy by reversing the dynamics – play a game called "up-side-down day", in which your child spoils you. Show your child that you also like to be spoiled and that sometimes you are also weak and need help from someone.

Search for signs of stress and low self-esteem in your child's drawings, because these are common reasons for dependent and spoiled behavior.

Discipline and Boundaries

Boundaries, consequences, admonishments, threats, agreements, discussions, contracts... all represent honest attempts by parents to discipline their children. Many parents feel overwhelmed with guilt for trying to deny their children certain pleasures and asking them to show some restraint. However, the truth is quite the opposite.

Setting boundaries

The parents of the 4 year-old who made the following drawings consulted me because they had difficulties controlling their son and setting boundaries for him. In fact, the term "boundaries" was not mentioned at all in our first consultation meeting. His mother did not understand the need to set boundaries – she told me that her son sleeps between one and three hours every night and then gets up and plays quietly in his room until morning. She said that "he doesn't disturb anyone and I don't have the energy to force him to bed while he yells". She confessed that when she was a little girl, she was forced to go to sleep and this method is not acceptable to her, because it made her hate her parents. The father's opinion was different – he was willing to do almost anything in order to put his child to sleep. He confessed: "I don't have any patience to cope with him. This child has to understand that if I'm telling him to go to bed, then he must do it immediately, without any objections".

Figure 3-16: Elementary scribbling as an indication of lack of boundaries at home

Figure 3-17: After a month in therapy: more advanced drawing level, indicating clear boundaries and structuring

As you can see, the parents' approaches regarding this issue are directly in conflict. The mother has difficulty setting boundaries due to anger and frustration feelings toward her own parents. She wants to become a "perfect mom", who doesn't make her son frustrated, but content. She fears that if her son is faced with boundaries, he will distance himself from her, as she had from her parents. As a result, she feels confused and uncertain, which prevents her from establishing a clear and consistent set of boundaries based on her values. Conversely, the father views the process of setting boundaries as a rigid and immediate one. He believes avoiding the establishment of boundaries is a sign of weakness and helplessness, as well as another opportunity to humiliate the parent. This approach makes him prefer setting rigid boundaries, which place the parent in a superior position relative to his child.

My conclusion from the child's drawings was that there was clear and significant regression in his development. This 4 year-old's drawings were equivalent to drawings of 1–1½ year-olds, who scribble spontaneously. Note that he didn't have any developmental issue, so that the regression was expressed only in his drawing level. His amorphous drawing style, which had no continuity or clear structure, characterizes children with no more than 3 months' experience in drawing. During this stage, drawing style is unintentional and lacks any repetitions. Usually, after three months of drawing children develop a unique mark in their scribbles. However, he didn't develop such a unique mark even after experiencing drawing for three years. As he had no cognitive or motor issues, it was possible to conclude that these drawing characteristics were the result of lack in boundaries at home.

The sharp conflict between his parents' approaches made this child feel confused, as represented in his age-inappropriate amorphous drawing style. My guidance facilitated gradual change in the relationship between him and his parents, which resulted in a change in his drawing style that became more structured and developed.

Discipline

Parental discipline has great influence on the self-discipline a child develops in life. Through discipline a child learns to delay gratification, be responsible for his actions (and willing to pay the price) and also to accept undesirable realities. Avoiding this learning prevents a child from revealing his inner strength and finding adequate solutions for everyday problems (Greene, 2010).

Discipline is learning by way of modeling and sharing. Modeling means that a parent sets a role model for his child by not allowing himself something he denies his child. Sharing is when a parent stands by his child in a time of difficulty, which is a result of something his child did. The child then sees his parent as sensitive, and will not resist his parent when confronted with a boundary. Instead, the child will share his parent's goal and try to achieve it together with him.

The democratic era made parenting a complex task: should we hold elections within the family and make majoritarian decisions? Are parents considered authorities whose decisions are binding? How can you cope democratically with an anarchist child who behaves without boundaries? These are only some of the questions preoccupying today's parents who want their lifestyle outside and inside the family to correspond.

Punishments are part of the autocratic educational approach, which is why so many parents report they do not work anymore. Punishments used to be effective because the relationship between parent and child was more distant. A sentence such as: "When daddy gets home, I will tell him what you did…" used to be a real deterrent. Parents were the information agents of their children, who used to look up to them. Nowadays, technology has made information extremely accessible, narrowing and even reversing the intergenerational knowledge gap.

Moreover, in the past most parents didn't used to go back home feeling guilty for "abandoning" their children, but firm in their belief in an educational approach that considered respect and discipline an integral part of the parent-child relationship.

Nowadays, parents want a close relationship with their children when they return home. There are some parents that will clearly say, "I want to be my child's friend". Some parents also encourage their children to use other information sources such as the Internet for studying. This reality requires a more sophisticated educational approach than a simple set of threats and consequences. In fact, punishments are becoming ineffective and even exacerbate the conflict by giving the child a new reason for pursuing his struggle. As many parents report, "Punishments simply don't work, so we need to increase their level every time…"

So, what are punishments if not an external short-term disciplinary measure? Is fear or submission the right motivator for children? The turning point in making change is thinking about the action rather than the consequence. In order to make the change you can use the "natural consequences" and "logical consequences" method (Dreikurs & Goldman, 1986). Logical consequences are those which are reasonably but indirectly related to a certain action. For example, if a child objects to brushing his teeth, it is reasonable that you will prevent him from eating sweets. Natural consequences are directly related to reality, without adult mediation. For example, if a child does not take an umbrella on a rainy day, it is only natural that he will get wet.

Unlike the natural and logical consequences approach, punishment emphasizes the adult's authority and his power to judge and act on his judgment. The purpose of punishment is to create deterrence, involving feelings of anger and frustration towards the adult who punishes. Moreover, punishment refers mainly to the negative outcome rather than to the child's efforts. Just like adults, many children will do their best to avoid punishment by concealing and lying.

How to discipline without punishing:

- Share the natural and logical consequences method with your child and help him to anticipate the results of his actions.

- Establish a system of parental rules, with three types of rules: basic rules, which concern matters of life and death; family rules, which are mainly related to mutual respect; and norms, which may change over time following constructive dialog, due to age, family status and various life events. An example for such a role or norm is the bedtime hour, which may vary on vacations or according to the siblings' age. Naturally, you should set an example for following these rules.

- Under crisis conditions or power struggles, a child needs only few rules that will make it clear to him how you expect him to behave. The natural and logical consequences method is less effective in such cases.

- If you find it difficult to set boundaries, check with yourself if you have fears of conflicts or disagreements. Allow yourself to experience such conditions, both at home and in other surroundings. Refine your dialog abilities under conflict, without using aggressive or humiliating language.

- Truly believe that boundaries and rules, which are reasonable for a child, keep him from trouble and help shape a strong sense that his environment is safe for him. Regression in drawing level often indicates an ill-adjusted dialog a child has with his environment with regards to rules and boundaries.

- Constantly remind your child of the house rules and the reason for them.

- Let your child decide how to act, but not whether to act or not. For example, if taking a shower on a daily basis is important for you, let your child choose its exact time, the color of his towel or type of soap, etc. In other words, focus on priorities.

- Legitimize his emotions, but object to any violent expression style. In other words, your child's anger is acceptable, but he may not act out and beat others. Use drawings as a therapeutic tool for ventilating aggression and frustration. Let the child be angry on his drawing or draw controversial subjects. Encourage him to tell you more about his feelings, using the drawing as a medium.

- Remember that setting boundaries at a young age will help you cope with your child's natural rebelliousness as an adolescent.

- Identify his temperament through his drawings and adjust your set of norms accordingly. For example, when a child's drawing style is stormy and restless, it is better to use a small set of clear boundaries, and involve the child in the process of setting them. When a child's drawing style is slow and structured, it is better to proceed in an orderly and consistent manner. Follow the trends in his drawings and look for changing trends, which require behavioral change on your part as well.

Large Families

Parents to more than four children report two main trends in their relationships with their children: dominance and delegation. Dominance occurs when parents are regarded as the sources of authority at home and their children view them as the makers of rules.

Delegation is when parents hand over some of their authority to their older children, who are responsible for raising their younger siblings. In this case, the younger siblings may be considered "multiple parent children", while their older siblings will be forced to shift between their role as the "responsible grownup" and their need to remain children. Some of the children will have difficulty switching between these roles and may behave in an age inappropriate manner. For example, they may choose to remain "adults" with their siblings viewing them as 'little mother or father". Such decision may help the parents in the short-term, but it could harm the child in the long run, denying him some of his childhood experiences.

The purpose in analyzing large family drawings is to identify the viewpoints adopted by children and enable parents to allow their children a wide variety of attitudes and ways of action. For example, many young "responsible grownups" tend to make precise and structured drawings.

Figure 3-18: **Excessively structured drawing typical of a precocious older brother in a large family**

These children view adults as responsible, serious and infallible (although reality may be different). In these cases, the precise drawings symbolize the responsibility which the child feels. When such precision eventually creates a more advanced and age inappropriate drawing, you should see how the child may be allowed to draw freely, just for fun, including making mistakes. Drawing with mistakes will gradually enable the precocious child cope with his real-life mistakes.

A child in a large family cannot always get all the attention he needs. Therefore, when analyzing such children's drawings, you should first observe how a child stresses his figure compared to the other figures. For example, does a child use a template or colors that are different from his siblings? Does he tend to omit some of his siblings, while drawing only the ones closer to him? In what style are the parent figures drawn? The drawing style of a parent may provide us with valuable information about the relationship between him and his child.

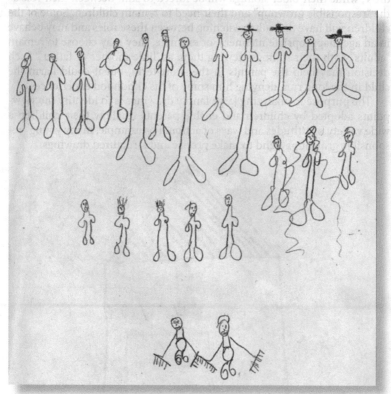

Figure 3-19: Enlarging the older brothers' figures as an indication of the quality of the relations with them

The ten year-old who made the next drawing grew up in an ultra-ortho-dox Jewish family. He chose to draw his family members in a same pat-tern, while relatively inflating the figures of his older brothers. There is no doubting his older brothers' function as his authorities. Such information is vital for understanding this family dynamic.

Hence, I concluded from his drawings that in order to transform his relationship with his parents, a preliminary dialog with his older brothers must take place.

The 9½ year-old girl who made the drawing in figure 3-20 was also raised in an ultra-orthodox family. As in the previous drawing I present-ed, she also uses a recurring pattern, but she adds another dimension to it, which is separation between boys and girls. Her family lives in a small house, which is why it is important for her to keep her privacy.

Figure 3-20: Graphic separation of the boys and girls indicating reli-gious-cultural separation

This separation is so meaningful for her that it becomes a part of her drawing; it is also important for understanding the dynamic between her and her parents. I concluded from her drawing that at least initially, her mother would be the best person to communicate with, mainly because of the cultural support for such gender segregation within this conservative society, of which the child seems keenly aware.

The same phenomenon, together with several other unique characteristics, is evident in religious Muslim families. The 7 year-old boy who made the following drawing grew up in a Bedouin family of 11 members. They are all drawn in the same pattern, but diversely colored. On the right side, you can see a group of children, including the boy, drawn in a similar way. This group includes siblings whose age is close to the child and with whom he has close relationship.

Figure 3-21: Similarity between the drawing style of older brothers and parents in a large family

The dominance of his older siblings is expressed in the similarity between them and their parents: both are drawn in the same pattern and stature. This uniform drawing style makes it hard to understand the parent-child relationship in this family. It is an example of confusion in the child's perception of the inner family coalitions.

According to this drawing everyone is equally important and there is no hierarchy, so it is hard to know who the head of the family is.

Figure 3-22: Multiple parent figures in a polygamous family

Another phenomenon which characterizes the Bedouin family is polygamy. In theory, every Muslim man is allowed to marry up to four women,
but polygamy is practiced only in very traditional communities, such as
the Bedouins'. In these cases, a child grows in a family with several mothers
and half siblings.

In drawings like the following by a 6 year-old, you see reference to this.
This drawing, made following my request to "draw your family", shows the

boy's father, drawn inside his house, and two of his wives.

Studies of children's drawings in polygamous families found a difference in trends between children of the father's first and last wives. The children of the first wife drew with more confidence than their half siblings, because they were more confident in their status.

Two other trends were enlarged mother figure and diminished father figure, as well as complete omission of the latter. These trends result from the distance those children feel from their father, who spends time with his other wives (Lev-Wiesel & Al-Krenawi 2000).

Additional trends found in polygamous family drawings are: differential reference to the mother and biological siblings (different size, color and shape); locating the biological family members on the upper or front part of the page; ignoring the half siblings while drawing only the biological family members; and drawing partitions between the biological and non-biological families, resulting from the child's confusion about his nuclear family boundaries.

The purpose of drawings in such cases will be to understand the way a child perceives his family dynamic and then help him cope with his complex reality in the best possible way for him and his family members.

Same-Sex Families

Many families are headed by lesbian or homosexual parents. Studies in this field are few and relatively new (Peterson 1995). Moreover, studies on children to male compared to female homosexual parents are particularly rare. Available findings show that growing up in a same-sex family doesn't necessarily affect a child's future sexual tendencies. These children develop normal self-image, and cognitive, social and sexual abilities. Only minor differences were found in gender functioning during childhood. In particular, children to same-sex parents allowed themselves greater freedom of choice when dressing, playing, etc. In fact, it appears that children of same-sex parents grow up with normal mental health and emotional development are more open to difference. In their adulthood, these children attend less to gender stereotypes when choosing their career or hobbies (Peterson 1995).

Peterson (ibid) found that parenting styles in same-sex families are distributed as in the rest of the population. The stigmas about short-term relationships between same-sex partners are apparently irrelevant to couples who decide to start a family. These couples have strong and steady relationships with their children and they have the same parenting dilemmas as heterosexual parents. Moreover, many of the same-sex parents, just like heterosexual adopting parents, spend more time discussing parental issues than heterosexual parents: because giving birth has not been trivial for them, they consider their children as a very central thing in their lives.

As part of my clinic work, I conducted a study of 30 same-sex families, which included interviews, observations and drawing analysis. My findings suggest the following unique characteristics of such families:

1. *"The second mother"* – One of the common (and infuriating) questions that lesbian parents are asked is "Which one of you is the child's mother?" The answer in most cases is, "We are both his mothers, and I'm the biological one". Most mothers feel frustrated by this question and by the fact that they are considered "the second mom", obliged to fight for the legitimacy of her motherhood.

2. *The child's perception* – A child usually has different perceptions of his parents: the father and mother are clearly perceived as different human beings. This perception also exists in same-sex families. For example, the 4½ year-old girl who made the next drawing used the same color and template to draw herself and her biological mother, thus differentiating between her two mothers. Another interesting observation is that she drew a circle within the body of her biological mother's figure, which symbolizes a womb, although her non-biological has just recently given birth. This phenomenon is unique, because children usually do not tend to draw their mother's womb after their own birth.

Figure 3-23: Unique graphic reference to the biological mother in a same-sex family

3. *Working hours* – Same-sex and particularly lesbian parents often both have the possibility of working shorter hours and spending more time with their children. This equality, which exists also in

this case, characterizes the relationship between the child's mothers and is represented by drawing both mothers in same color. In other drawings she made, I also noticed equal height, although the gap between her mothers is significant.

4. *The mother's self-image* – When a woman announces her sexual preference, she usually doesn't conceal her relationship. However, there are still cases in which men or women choose to hide their sexual tendency from their family or colleagues. When a mother is humiliated after confessing her tendency, her children often tend to draw her figure in a weak and unconfident line and sometimes with a sad expression. When a child feels that his mother has been excluded from her family, he will often draw a separating line between her figure and the rest of the family. In such cases, when the child experiences insecure attachment patterns with his environment, drawing – as opposed to verbal expressions – offer readily available and effective tools for understanding his inner world (Kaiser 1996).

Figure 3-24: Dividing line as a graphic indicator of family crisis

5. *Divorce* – In the course of my work, I have come across several cases of children who refused to draw their family after their heterosexual mother had divorced, deciding to be a lesbian. In some cases, the refusal resulted from a complex and painful divorce, which is typical also of heterosexual families, where the divorce is unrelated to sexual tendencies. Children who also gave a reason to

their refusal made it clear that they objected to their mother's new lifestyle. These children feared, mainly during the early adjustment stages, that their classmates will harass them. However, note that studies show that children born to lesbian mothers are equally popular at school – they receive as many social invitations as their friends (Green 1986), and they are equally exposed to harassments and bullying. Nevertheless, they are more harassed by their peers with regard to their sexuality (Tasker 1997).

Even so, some of the children of lesbian couples are still angry at them, as seen in their tendency to continue drawing their father even though their mother became a lesbian, and to ignore her new partner. Drawings in such cases are made with heavy pressure and impulsive coloring, which distinguishes them from drawings of children to divorced parents who have a good relationship or whose children still want their parents to reunite.

To conclude, drawings of children to same-sex parents have some unique characteristics, but you should not conclude from them on future differences or sexual tendencies. Naturally, same-sex parenting evokes, for some parents, fears that perhaps their sexual tendency will affect or burden their children in the long-term. However, most studies (e.g. Muir, 1992) show that parent's sexual tendency is not a factor that affects their children directly. The factors that affect them are the parents' perception of themselves and the way they explain their sexual tendency to their children. In this context, children's drawings may shed light on how a child perceives his parents' sexual tendency and their self-image.

Single-Parent Families

A single parent family is sometimes the result of divorce and in other cases of a wish to go at it alone. In the latter case, the father is sometimes known to his child and sometimes not. In general, the structure of a single parent family often promotes strong cohesion and emotional bonding between the parent and child. Such cohesion has been reported by some children as a significant source of emotional support, but for others it has become a burden (Mackay, 2005). It was found that the absence of the second parent often caused children difficulty developing emotional separation from their parents. When children have a parental alternative, it is easier for them to distance themselves from the parent they are angry at. However, such distance is more complex in a single parent family, because it will result in loneliness, so the rebellion of a child against his parent becomes more difficult than in dual parent families. The purpose of analyzing children's drawings in these families is to observe the family structure while helping the parent create such distance without the help of another parent. Another purpose in diagnosing the drawings is to adjust the psychological need for separation to cultural norms. In other words, our purpose is to ensure parent-child separation even in intensive daily family interactions.

The 6 year-old girl who made the next drawing grew up in a single par-ent family. In her drawing she draws her mother and herself in the same stature and pattern (Dunn et al, 2002). This drawing style emphasizes their relationship, which is based on equality. In this case, as in many others, the parent and child behave as a kind of couple.

Figure 3-25:   Mother and daughter identical in size indicating their equal relationship in a single-parent family

Indeed, the relationship between her mother and herself was good and open, to the extent that they both considered themselves friends more than a mother and daughter. Line quality and coloring are some of the indica-tors to this positive relationship.

Nevertheless, their relationship should be observed over the years, mainly in relation to conflict resolution and setting boundaries, because equal status between parent and child may sometimes become confusing.

On the other hand, some children to single parents draw themselves taller than their parent. This drawing style characterizes children who take advantage of the equality mentioned earlier. In many cases, this behavior is caused by the loneliness a parent feels and his need for partnership, as well as the child's dependency on his parent. Such a child demands to be partner to every decision and objects when his parent decides anything without consulting him. He sees in this behavior a betrayal of their partnership, and consequently fears that it might affect his status to the point that he will be "replaced" by another partner. This phenomenon can also be seen in families with two parents.

Figure 3-26: Enlarged mother figure indicating her centrality in the single-parent family

The drawing made by this child (aged 3 years and 9 months) represents another typical characteristic which is enlarging the mother's figure while placing her at the center of the page. Unlike dual parent families, this child and his sister have only one dominant authority figure. This dominancy is represented in the figure's location and size.

Since it is culturally acceptable to consider a mother figure as a source of attachment, old studies concluded that a father's presence is essential to set as a role model for gendered behavior. The number of untraditional family arrangements and their healthy children show that this conclusion is not necessarily true. However, the purpose in analyzing children's drawings is to assess the quality of relationship between a child and his only parent, and should the child require other figures to identify with, help his parent make this possible in a way that will benefit both.

How to Interpret Family Drawings

The objective of interpreting family drawings is to examine how the child experiences the relations with his family. Before we begin, it is important to remember that the way the child draws her family does not necessarily reflect her actual lived reality. Like adults, children also beautify reality or draw what the situation in which they want to be.

- Look for a **common denominator** between the figures. Drawing the images in an identical color, using an identical technique or with identical items (such as clothing or hairstyle) attests to the emotional connection the child experiences between the two or more similar figures.

- Notice the **size of the figures**. When a certain figure is more emotionally involved in the child's life, it will be drawn as bigger and more "positive" than the other figures.

- Check the **relations and distances between the figures**. Are the figures distant from one another? Are they close? Do they touch or hold hands? The relation in the drawing expresses the criticism or trust between the figures, as perceived by the child.

- Note **differences between the "parent unit" and "child unit"**. Who is drawn closer to whom? Who is relegated to the corner? Who is bigger than the others and occupies more space on the page? Who is smaller and shrunk compares to the rest? These differences indicate how the child perceives the emotional place of each family member.

- Check the **color and line quality** in which each figure is drawn. If the child has trouble in emotional communication with one of the family member, that figure will be drawn in a weak or disjointed line.

- **Has any figure been omitted?** Sometimes, children omit certain figures and draw only those closest to them. In this case, check why the figure has been omitted – whether due to lack of interest in it or an active desire for it to "disappear" (such as a new sibling in the family).

- **Try to sense the overall tone:** Is the drawing detailed? Is it joyful? Is it creative and imaginative, or is it lacking in detail, withdrawn, sad and makes the observer uneasy?

4 SIBLING RELATIONSHIPS

Analysis focused on understanding the dynamics between the child who made the drawing and his siblings provides answers to many issues that preoccupy parents on a daily basis. Children's drawings shed light on their character and enable us to understand how they prefer to cope with conflicts and define their self. In order to understand the dynamic between a child and his siblings you should first pay attention to the child's perception of his family members. One of the significant factors that affect his perception is order of birth.

When discussing sibling relationships, my starting point is that disagreements are a natural and integral part of any relationship, regardless of age. Children, like adults, argue about shared resources, territory, leadership, and even about whose turn it is to talk. Through their disputes with their peer group, which usually includes the siblings, children develop conflict resolution skills. In the future, these skills will help them cope with other disputes outside their home, with unfamiliar children.

These fights lead children to work through their definition of separation. In other words, through the conflict the child learns what "alone" and "together" mean, and most importantly, how can one be alone, but still be part of a group – to maintain autonomy in a relationship. Through his conflicts, the child learns to present his opinion despite other, sometimes conflicting opinions in the group. He also learns how to negotiate over limited resources and maintain an open relationship after the dispute and resulting anger subside.

In nature the influence of birth order is clear and significant: heron birds, for example, lay their eggs and then incubate the first two and only then tend to the rest. Because of this parental decision, the chicks that hatch out first have a competitive advantage and better chances of surviving. Fish also tend to prefer the older siblings, as they would rather risk themselves to protect the older rather than the younger ones. Wolves, which are considered social animals, show a clear tendency to protect their older siblings by letting them grow up in their own territory. This way, the older siblings avoid the need to fight for their own territory, but still they have to help their parents raise the younger siblings.

This natural preference is also evident in the plant kingdom. Orange trees, for example, bloom with some 100,000 flowers that can each develop into fruit. However, only 500 will eventually ripen, because the upper, more "mature" flowers overshadow the latecomers, preventing them from growing (Kluger 2007).

One of the best known psychological approaches to birth order is Adler's (Adler, 1964). Adler argued that birth order may significantly affect an individual's social behavior. According to his theory, firstborns are pulled away from the center of parental attention following the birth of the second child, resulting in long-term effects. Conversely, younger and only children may be described as spoiled.

Adler also referred to three factors as key to every person's personality: the number of children in his family, the parents' financial status and the age difference between siblings.

However, Adler's theory on birth order has become controversial over the years. During my clinic experience over the last few years I found that children's characteristics were not always related to birth order. Sometimes, I met older siblings with middle-child traits and in other cases it was the youngest kids who had personality traits that are considered typical of firstborns. For example, a firstborn with ADHD will not function, as predicted by the Adlerian approach, like an additional parent, and will not help with the daily chores, as he already finds it too difficult to manage on his own. Accordingly, treating all older siblings as children with similar personality traits might be an inaccurate generalization. The very purpose of observing and treating each child as an individual is to find out what his unique characteristics are in the context of his own being. And it's precisely in this respect that drawing analysis proves to be a powerful diagnostic and therapeutic tool.

Older Children: Characteristics and Drawings

The oldest child is the one who turned the two people who brought him into the world into parents for the first time in their lives. So why don't we automatically refer to the firstborn as the oldest when discussing personality traits? The answer is that parenthood is not only quantitative but also qualitative. Some parents refer to their first parenting with emotional detachment, as a rather technical matter, and admit to discovering their real parental feelings only with their second child.

The discussion of the private moment which caused the parent to feel like one has been and still is one of the greatest taboos of parenthood. Many parents are familiar with this feeling and are able to talk about it in therapy, which allows them to work it through and learn to live and grow with their parental approach. The parent's subjective approach determines the true atmosphere into which the child is born. The firstborn is sometimes born into a family that has expected him, turning him into the center of attention. In other cases, however, the family is not prepared for the challenges involved in raising a child, so he becomes a burden.

A child who has the oldest sibling's characteristics is the one who has managed to create and maintain a unique and private communication channel with his parents. His parent will admit that: "I can discuss things with him just like with adults", making the impression that they both speak the same language. Such a child will tend to identify and communicate with adults just as easily as with peers. Adults will usually enjoy his company and his ability to adjust his fields of interest to theirs. Note that such an approach enables us to identify multiple children as having "oldest sibling" characteristics in one family.

Usually, the oldest children (or siblings with their attributes) consume the largest portion of their family's time and energy: their behavior is watched carefully and quite often they become the subject of debates among other family members: "What can we do about him? What's the best way to help him?"

Sometimes it's actually the firstborn who make their parents feel inexperienced and hesitate about the right education approach. But in other cases it's the second or third child who forces his parents to face new dilemmas, without any preparation.

Figure 4-1:   Family hierarchy as perceived by a 4½ year-old

In the following drawing by a girl aged four years and four months, the youngest in a family of two children, it is possible to see how she places herself (the green figure) on top of everybody. Her parents are located beneath her and her brother is not part of the "tower coalition". In doing so, she emphasizes a clear separation between her and her brother and defines herself as the "eldest" child, who occupies her parents' attention, while her brother is sidelined.

Children who have "eldest child" characteristics are those who experience a sense of uniqueness or receive most of attention their parents' attention. However, such a feeling may be the result of a unique family situation. Such, for example, is the case of sick children (whether firstborn or not) who receive most of their parents' attention because of their illness. Although it wasn't their decision to fall ill, their siblings could develop characteristics which represent a direct reaction to his illness-related "eldest sibling" status.

Figure 4-2:   **Structured and dense drawing indicating crisis-induced precociousness**

The next drawing was made by a 4½ year-old middle child. His drawings changed significantly after his older brother had been diagnosed with cancer. Before the diagnosis, his drawing level matched the pre-schematic phase and he drew recurring graphic elements. It was possible to see in his drawing spaces between the various elements and the overall impression was well-spaced and relaxed.

As the disease progressed and the parents' attention resources focused on the brother's medical condition, to the detriment of his siblings, this child's drawings became more "elderly". Almost without any graphical progress, his drawings became very schematic and structured. At the same time, the drawings became much denser, to the point of being overcrowded, and lost some of their previous airiness. These drawing trends, which characterize many of the child's drawings, also characterize many other children who grow up in the shadow of a family crisis.

Such children are forced to "give up" some of their childhood, so to speak, and "skip" to a more mature developmental phase in order to be able to cope with the crisis. This precociousness, this premature disillusionment, is represented in their drawings by the change in drawing trends.

The child with the "eldest" characteristics has a richer relationship with the adult content world and with authority figures. These characteristics enable him to conduct a more effective dialog with adults, sometimes better than his peer group.

These "eldest" children also act as emotional mediators within the sibling group (Hodgetts & Hegar 2007). They talk to their siblings, understand their needs and calm them down. They are, in a sense, the family's glue. Just like with their siblings, they also have an emotional dialog with their parents, who expect from them to understand their needs and share issues that are usually discussed between themselves, more so than their other children.

This sharing might lead to a situation known as "parental vacuum" (Carter & McGoldrick 1981). The "eldest" child enters into the parental dyad and plays the emotional role of the other parent, for the other. In such cases, the child will adopt a mature tone of speech and comfort his parent in a time of crisis, supporting him as if he was his partner rather than his child. This coalition might naturally tip the balance in the family and lead to reactions by the other siblings.

In this case, it is also possible for the firstborn to be already grown up and living outside the family home, while his younger sibling enters the "parental vacuum".

Figure 4-3:   A father-older daughter coalition

The next drawing by a 5 year-old girl is an example of such case. The girl was told to "draw your family". According to her, the two figures in the drawing are herself and her father.

The scribbles around the figures represent her family members, whom she started drawing and then stopped. This drawing style, although extreme, represents the coalition between the father and his daughter. Her status as "daddy's girl" thus affects the family equilibrium and might cause long-term family conflicts.

Middle Children: Characteristics and Drawings

A child with "middle" characteristics is the one who defines and stretches the inner family boundaries. Such a child will commonly be referred to as one who has trouble finding his place in the family, mostly because he doesn't have the advantages associated with being the oldest or youngest.

In this case also, I recommend referring to "middle" child characteristics, rather than attributing these characteristics automatically to all middle children. In other words, checking the inner family territory means checking where the child is placed compared to his family members. For example, you could say that after the birth of a second sibling, the eldest become a middle child, because he is now placed between his parents and younger sibling. This approach enables better understanding of the eldest child's behavior following the birth of his sibling.

A "middle" child is characterized by constantly insisting on his uniqueness compared to his peers. He is less occupied by what adults or other authority figures have to say about him and he negotiates less with them compared to his other siblings. He is highly motivated and often acts out of competitive motives, giving the impression that he never stays still, but is constantly preoccupied with proving his status.

As a result of his behavior and never-ending comparison with others, he develops characteristics like envy or a sense of deprivation. A "middle" child might therefore feel he is not good enough if he didn't manage to secure his own niche within the family structure.

Similarly to the "eldest" brother, the "middle" brother has also various personality elements in addition to the ones defined in the classic Adlerian model. For example, a "middle" child is not necessarily the most deprived child in his family. Some "middle" children define themselves as central to their family structure, thereby stressing the advantages of their birth order. Gender is also an important factor in family structure and dynamics. For example, a girl who is the middle child with elder and younger brothers may define her status and territory based on her gender. Such a definition counteracts feelings of deprivation and frustration, as well as uncertainty regarding her place in the family. Moreover, in some cases, parents who prefer raising girls may reinforce such emergent feelings.

Figure 4-4: An enlarged or overemphasized central object indicating perceived dominance

This drawing, made by a 6 year-old middle girl with two brothers, is an example of such case. The girl defines herself at the center of the family, which enables her to be younger (compared to her elder brother) and older (compared to her younger brother) at the same time. Her drawings usually include three objects, and in most cases the middle element is enlarged and more dominant than the others.

Younger Children: Characteristics and Drawings

The main characteristic of the "youngest" child is his feeling that his status within the family is not obvious. He usually has high social skills and knows how to interact with his peers. Observed with his siblings, he seems in his natural environment where he spends most of his time. He tends to be ambitious, curious and opinionated. The "youngest" child is also characterized by treating (at least) one of his older siblings as a secondary parent. Such a child has to cope with multiple parents and each child has his ways of maintaining or changing this situation (Salter 2006).

The parents of the youngest child affect his behavior in that he marks the end of their childbearing years. This milestone, whether brought about by menopause or the parents' decision not to have any more children is critical, but may also prove temporary, since some parents may bear children unexpectedly after a hiatus of 10 years or more. The parents' separation from the childbearing phase is complex and may be expressed in many different ways. Some will decide to spoil their lastborn by overprotecting and helping him unnecessarily and age-inappropriately, just because it makes them feel like a young couple taking care of their "baby".

Figure 4-5: **Regression in terms of human figure drawing quality and graphic indicators**

The boy who made the following drawing (aged 6 years and 7 months) is the youngest in his family. My talks with his parents indicated that for them he signifies the end of the childbearing years, and this insight was both complex and painful for them. Since he was born they considered him their "little boy". This caused them to continue help him get dressed every morning. At dinner time, he would sit at the table waiting to be served, without helping at all. His behavior is evident in his drawings, which are relatively regressive in their overall quality, figures' details and inaccurate graphics.

All of these trends are typical of children with motor difficulties, but that's not the case with this child – hence, the reason for his regression is mainly emotional.

Some "youngest" children are mainly characterized by particular lack of parental attention. For example, in many families, parents will have several children and demanding jobs, preventing them from giving enough attention to each child. As a result of this situation, the "youngest" child will develop in his drawing a unique mark, unlike his siblings who will tend to copy drawing elements from each other.

Finally, many young children are affected by their parent's inability to make free time for them. Often, these children are born many years after the oldest sibling. Although they may not necessarily be the youngest chronologically, it is their parents' relative unavailability which determines their "youngest" status.

In this context, the parents' worldview is critical. Many parents, having brought their firstborn into the world at a relatively late age, have clearly defined worldviews, as well as free time to raise their lastborn. They know what parents they would like to be and their family atmosphere is therefore calm and confident. Note that some parents report on such feelings of confidence and calmness upon the birth of their first child, so, as usual, birth order should be disregarded.

To conclude, observing children's behavior without attaching undue importance to their birth order may share light on their personality characteristics. In addition, such an approach enables a more dynamic perception of the family structure, as it allows children to shift their status and position in their family. This shift is significant to the development of every child, as well as to the entire family unit.

Birth of a New Sibling: From Crisis to Coping

"Mommy, I don't want a brother! I will throw him into the garbage!" Elder children experience the birth of a new sibling in many ways, from indifference to anger and obvious frustration. As my starting point was that "eldest" children may be any of the family's children rather than just the firstborn, the crisis following the birth of a new sibling may be experienced by any of them. Likewise, the parents' reaction to the birth of a new sibling in their family may vary. For some parents, the transition from being a couple to couple +1 is significant, while other parents report that having two or three kids is particularly difficult and complex. The reasons for these gaps may include objective events in the parents' lives which affect their emotional preparedness and availability as parents as well as the child's own innate temperament (Palkovitz & Sussman 1989).

Similarly to the parents' subjective experience, many second-born children undergo a crisis following the birth of a third sibling, even though you could expect them to adapt more easily, having been born into a reality of a family with another child and not just parents. In most cases, the birth of the second child is considered significant for all family members and there are some who mark it as the transition to a "real family". For the firstborn, who used to be an only child until the birth of his sibling, the new family member is met with is a mixture of feelings: on the one hand, he has a chance to be a big brother and an authority figure, but on the other, he feels like a king who had to give up his thrown: he's not the only one anymore and from now on he will have to fight for his parents' attention, which was taken for granted until that point (Rathus 2007).

For some children, the birth of a new sibling precipitates regressive behaviors such as bedwetting, childish tone of speech, use of bottle and pacifier, attachment to transition objects like a doll or a piece of clothing, detachment and withdrawal. Such behavior makes many parents feel frustrated and helpless. From the child's perspective, you may often observe feelings of loneliness and betrayal. He is anxious that the birth of his sibling is just the beginning of an inevitable deterioration in the wonderful relationship he used to have with his parents. He is unable to see how things can change in the future and tends to blame his younger sibling for his condition.

The way children cope with the birth of their sibling changes according to their age, emotional characteristics and family relationships. Note that between ages 2 to 4, children tend to become aggressive towards their mother and attached to a beloved object and act regressively (e.g. wet their bed, crawl or revert to the bottle). At age 4 onwards, you may still observe infantile behavior and confrontations with the mother, but also aggressive behavior towards toys and dolls. Interestingly, children younger than 2 also demonstrate behavioral change, but because a childish behavior is typical at this age parents do not attach importance to it (Gottlieb-Regev 1998).

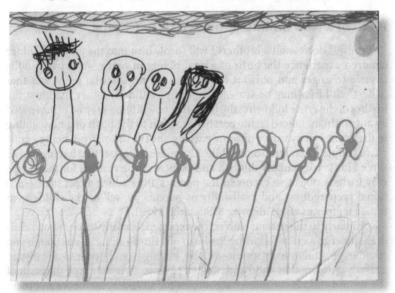

Figure 4-6:   Regression to an earlier developmental stage

In these cases, when a new sibling is born, it is possible to use the elder brother's drawings to better understand his needs at every stage. The following drawing by a 6 year-old girl illustrates the regression in the child's behavior after her sibling's birth. Before his birth, she used to draw figures with volume, whereas after his birth, she reverted to tadpole figures, with one limb only. My advice to her parents, based on her regressive drawings, was to treat her as a baby. Such a parental approach satisfied her regressive needs and she managed to overcome them after a while. Notably, there was a match between the improvement in her behavior and her figure drawing level.

Figure 4-7:   Graphic representation of restlessness and aggression

The drawings of the 7 year-old who made the next drawing also changed following the birth of his sibling, becoming more graphically "restless" and "aggressive". My recommendation in this case was to enable him to vent his aggression in other ways. Also, his parents were instructed to legitimize his feelings towards his sibling, including negative feelings such as anger or even sheer hatred. This legitimacy facilitated a significant change in the entire family atmosphere.

Figure 4-8:   Rigid and precise drawing indicating a behavioral transformation

The drawings of the 6 year-old girl who made the following drawing became rigid and exaggeratedly accurate since her little sister was born. Following this change in her drawing style, I recommended her parents to let her be herself, while emphasizing that she is not the baby's mother, but her older sister. Children like her who experience the birth of a new sibling for the first time, mistakenly think that they have two options: be either parents or little children. Since it is clear who the youngest member in the family is, she concluded that from now on she would have to become a secondary mother. This perception changed both her behavior and drawings style. In this case, like many others, analyzing children's drawings helped the parents understand the emotional situation of their child and tailor the most appropriate educational approach.

Figure 4-9:   Age-appropriate drawing, refuting behavioral regression

The following case is particularly interesting because the parents of this 6 year-old contacted me saying that she was immature and wouldn't help them take care of the new baby.

Analysis of her drawings, like the one presented here, indicated a different trend – her drawings were age-appropriate, as seen by their accuracy, coloring and overall drawing level. Hence, the idea that her behavior is regressive was rejected.

Observation at her home supported this conclusion, because her general behavior and emotional reactions were age-appropriate, considering the birth of the new sibling. In light of my observations, the conclusion was that her parents' attention should focus on their demands and communication patterns.

Following the birth of a new sibling, many parents tend to consider their eldest child as more mature than he really is, expecting him to behave independently and help raising the newborn. But how can the child help if he has never been asked to before? The eldest child experiences lack of control after the birth of his sibling. Without previous notice, his parents focus all their attention and efforts on the newborn, leaving him without a partner, giving him the feeling that he has no control over their quality time. This new situation might lead him to think that in order to get his parents' attention he must behave and act out like his younger sibling, so he develops a wide range of regressive behaviors.

His parents, already exhausted by taking care of the little child, now have to cope with his regression, so they become angry, tired and disappointed.

Figure 4-10: Omission of the little brother, indicating denial and re-pression

To cope with the new situation children use several defense mechanisms, which are reflected in their drawings. When this girl drew her family at age 4 and two months, she completely ignored her baby brother. This artistic choice is typical of defense mechanisms like repression and denial. Only later, after her friend turned her attention to this omission, did she add him to her drawing as the orange object, located at the upper part and some-what detached. Immediately after she added his figure to the drawing, she rose from the table, leaving her drawing on it, as if it no longer belonged to her...

Children use multiple defense mechanisms following the birth of a new sibling (Freud, 1971). The following list includes the major ones as reflect-ed in children's drawings:

1. *Reaction formation* – The child emphasizes the reverse impulse and rejects the undesirable urge. In drawings, this mechanism is represented by over-enlarging the baby's figure in an effort to hide the hostile feelings towards him.

2. *Projection* – The child projects the undesirable urge onto a differ-ent figure. For example, drawing the baby as a threatening figure that might harm the eldest sibling.

3. *Auto-aggression* – The child turns his aggressive emotions towards himself. This behavior might be represented by various anxiety in-dicators, refusal to draw or make any artwork.

4. *Regression* – The child regresses to an early developmental stage. We may see his regression in his behavior, as well as his drawings, which are made at a lower drawing level.

5. *Isolation* – The child separates his thoughts from their emotional content. For example, the child may behave tenderly and lovingly to his sibling, but communicate the exact opposite through his drawings. Sometimes this gap is created because the child represses his true feelings while helping his parents take care of the baby. These negative feelings, however, surface when he draws, and leave their mark on the page.

An example for this behavior may be seen in the following drawing, made by a girl aged 5 years and 10 months. Her younger brother, who is 6 months old, appears at the center of the drawing, in the middle of a storm at sea, surfing on a surfboard with evident pleasure. As a rule of the thumb, water in children's drawings represents emotions, among other things.

Figure 4-11: Acting out aggressions through drawings that reconstruct reality

This girl clearly communicates her hidden feelings towards her brother through her drawing, which is made in an impulsive drawing style. Her mother, however, reported that she takes good care of her young brother, treating him with dedication and love.

This example is one of many, representing the power of drawings: sometimes they are used to create a desired reality and in other cases, they are used as a platform for ventilating repressed aggressions. Sublimation – Together with the following defense mechanisms, sublimation represents more mature ways of coping. The sublimating child vents his aggression through a more socially acceptable channel. For example, a child may draw with high pressure instead of beating his younger brother.

1. *Identification* – The child redirects his aggression by positively identifying with its object. In children's drawings you may witness this phenomenon when a child draws himself as a parent caring for his baby.

2. *Emphasizing the father figure* – This mechanism, although not included among the classical defense mechanisms, is common in family drawings and is characterized by exaggerated attention to detail in the father figure and using a different color or line pressure compared to the other figures. This phenomenon is often due to the division of roles between the parents – the father may have more time to interact with his elder child, while the mother is busy breastfeeding. The father is perceived as a loyal figure, who didn't betray, as opposed to the mother's betrayal, which is obvious, because she carried her baby in her body for 9 months. Relatedly, the father's part in bringing a newborn into the world is repressed by the elder child (Goode 1971). Sometimes, enlargement of the father figure may be related to the Oedipus or Electra complex, which are manifested by identifying with one of the parents or by a desire to marry them.

3. *Other indicators in family drawings* – Many children who have experienced the birth of a new sibling omit arms from their own figures. This omission might be caused by their perception that they are liable to harm the baby with their arms. Another key finding in this regard is shifts in the child's position in family drawings, so that he draws himself near different family members each time. The last issue is a particularly significant trend in the case of children who used to draw themselves first in their family drawings prior to the birth of their sibling, and now do not.

Preparing Your Child for the Birth of a Little Brother or Sister

Here are some valuable tips that will help you prepare your child:

1. *Check his drawings* – Occasionally observe the child's drawings to observe his emotional state and which defense mechanisms he prefers to use.

2. *Avoid unnecessary discussions* – Try not to have discussions with your child about the relationship between him and the new sibling which is about to be born. In addition, try not to idealize the scene, describing a perfect reality after the sibling's birth.

3. *Comment on his drawings* – If you find that the child chooses to add his young brother to his drawings, use this opportunity to discuss the new family structure with him and to understand his perception of it.

4. *Plan your schedule* – It is very important to spend some quality, one-on-one, time with the elder child. This is a critical time for him, even if he doesn't show it, and he needs your support.

5. *Make slow changes* – It is recommended to avoid any drastic changes, such as entering into a new kindergarten or moving to a new home around the time the new sibling is born.

6. *Who makes decisions?* – A common issue among siblings is a quarrel about who is authorized to decide in the family. Sometimes, elder siblings try to force their opinion on their younger siblings. Avoid it by, for example, not letting the elder child decide on his sibling's room decoration.

7. *Mirror his difficulty* – When you encounter your child's negative reactions toward his younger sibling, talk to him about his difficulty, as well as your own. Remind him that you love both of them. However, don't gang up on the little one by turning your older child into your confidant and become his ally against the "crybaby" because this could make him think that crying is illegitimate.

8. *Be patient* – If your child chooses to omit his young sibling from his family drawings, you may disregard it for several months and keep track of it to see whether he eventually decides to draw him.

9. *Legitimize his feelings* – He is allowed not to love the newborn and it should be treated as a natural reaction. As a child, he might find it difficult to see the potential in his young sibling. Over time, he will discover his little sibling's personality and build a relationship with him.

The birth of a new sibling might trigger many exhausting disagreements or alternatively, promote personal and emotional development (Dreikurs 2000). Using children's drawings, it is possible to understand their emotional status and prepare them for the upcoming event. There are children who need detailed preparation and there are others who might recoil from that and even develop issues which did not exist before.

Twins: Raising an Individual within a Relationship

Being in a twin relationship is complex, partly because every argument between the two may be subjectively experienced as an effort by each one to define himself as a separate individual. For twins, this separation is more complex and should not be taken for granted, especially in case of identical twins (Joseph 2004).

Accordingly, twin drawings are a unique and fascinating phenomenon, as it helps us understand the similarities and differences between them. Through the drawings it is possible to receive answers to complex and important parenting issues such as: Will separating them into two kindergartens, classes or schools be beneficial for them? Is a twin's feeling that he's discriminated against really justified? What are each one's talents? And so on. Twins' drawings may have different trends than those made by singletons. In general, the same diagnostic tools will be used, but psychologically, a twin's reality is different than a singleton's. Hence, phenomena which must be addressed in drawings of singular child may be considered normative for twins.

The period between ages 6 months to 3 years is characterized by separation and individualization processes. During this period, a child internalizes the parents' role, as well as his emotional confidence in his own continuous existence. If a parent is absent from his life, it might give rise to separation anxiety and the difference between his parent and other figures in his life might cause stranger anxiety (Lansdown 2004).

Coping with separation is represented in drawings, among other things, in the child's ability to structure his elements on the entire page, his scribbling angle and the relative distances between the drawn figures. Twins, however, experience separation quite differently. First, they are not familiar with the feeling of being alone, because they constantly share their space with their twin sibling, from womb to baby carriage.

Secondly, their significant others often act as if they were an individual by referring to them as a single unit rather than two individuals, or dressing them in the same clothes. Some do it unintentionally, simply because it's easier.

The separation process requires the twin to search for consolation. Singletons often use transition objects such as a doll, toy, cloth or pacifier (Winnicott 1992). Some twins use their twin sibling as the transition object.

Figure 4-12: Twin sisters' symbiotic relationship

An example for that may be observed in the following drawing by a member of a triplet aged 6 years and three months. Her drawing communicates the strong relationship she has with her twin sisters, which is represented by the distances between the figures in the drawing. The three are drawn so close to one other that they all seem as one unit. Her parents were surprised by this expression in her drawing, but agreed that she has a close bond with her sisters. The bond is so strong that if one girl wishes to separate from it occasionally, she is unable to do so.

This example demonstrates the complexity of being a twin, because unlike a lifeless object, the twin sibling also has needs of his own, so he sometimes objects to the innate symbiosis. Another common difficulty is the environment's reaction to the twins' wish to separate. Significant others often view their bonding as graceful and magical, and encourage it.

Particularly in the case of identical twins, parents try to help their children develop their unique identity and prevent them from copying each other's behavior by sending them to different schools, classes or kindergartens.

The parents of the twin girls who made the next drawings at age 5 and seven months reported that the twins hardly ever quarrel. On the one hand, it seemed like an ideal situation, but on the other, they couldn't decide whether to send them to separate kindergartens.

Based on my analysis of their drawings I reached the following conclusions: the girl who made the left drawing is (perceived as) the dominant child – she fills the entire page with confidence and creativity, reflecting her high self-confidence and self-esteem, as well as and her ability to express her feelings around her friends and to develop relationships with them. Conversely, her sister is not as self-confident. Although she is also a clever girl, some indications in her drawings show that she has fears and anxieties following a medical intervention, including the shaky lines and hesitant movement which characterize her drawings.

Figures 4-13 & 4-14: A significant gap in drawing level between twin sisters

This significant gap between the drawing styles – creative and confident vs. shaky and poor – shows that the second sister is not yet ready to separate and that sending them to two kindergartens might be traumatic for her. In this case, it would be highly recommended for the second sister to be in therapy which will strengthen her and allow her to acknowledge her separateness and value herself without constantly comparing herself to her twin sister.

These drawings do well to illustrate the importance of analyzing each case separately rather than rushing to conclude that separating twins necessarily promotes individual identity-building or that avoiding it will necessarily make them feel safe because they are together.

Having said that, separating twins to different kindergartens or classes may often encourage them to build an inner individual identity that will support the outer, physical separation. In the case of the second sister, because of the lack of confidence evident in her drawings, the separation might be perceived as painful and arbitrary. She clings to her sister as if she were a transition object, borrowing energies from her for her own development. Thus, separation in this case can be very costly to her.

My recommendation to the parents, in addition to seeking therapy, was to start separating them as gently as possible by spending time with each child alone, dividing their room into two semi-autonomous spaces, enrolling each in a different extracurricular afternoon activity and continuing monitoring their drawings' development. My assumption was that these steps will encourage the second sister to develop her uniqueness in preparation for a more natural, smooth and confident separation.

When analyzing twins' drawings it is important to also take into account physical aspects which are typical of twins. Studies (e.g. Hurlock 1977) show that pregnancy complications, low birth weight, etc., affect physiological, cognitive, emotional and social development. Therefore, when a twin's drawing is age-inappropriate, it may be considered normative rather than an automatic indication of difficulty or distress.

Twins' Power Struggles

Twins cope with the need to separate and develop independent self-concepts also through power struggles and mutual hostility, designed to emphasize the psychological distance between them (Klein 2003).

Figure 4-15: Shadowing a figure's face as an indication of anger and aggression toward it

The following drawing by boy aged 5 years and seven months is a rare representation of this phenomenon's in children's artwork. This child drew his family, placing his parents between him and his sister, thus creating a large distance between them. In addition, he shadowed his sister's face, coloring it with high and angular pressure. This drawing style is characteristic of children who feel anger and aggression towards the drawn figure, particularly when this figure is drawn differently than others in the same drawing.

Shared resources, parallel development stages and other twin-related issues are a fertile ground for many disputes and struggles, which are sometimes difficult to resolve. These disagreements are often more intense than those between singletons.

Therefore, when analyzing twins' drawings, a fresh approach to disputes should be considered based on indicators such as line pressure, color combination or subject, based on the assumption that a twin finds himself struggling differently and often more intensively with his same-aged sibling than a singleton struggling against similarly aged siblings.

This particular intensity is largely due to the fact that many twins fear that the competition between them will endanger the symbiotic unity they were born to. Accordingly, on the one hand, they forge alliances against their environment and on the other hand, they fight with each other (Avtgis & Rancer 2010). These disputes are especially difficult for the parents because they are liable to experience the Cain and Abel syndrome: fearing that every passionate and intense fight might end in disaster and preference of one of the siblings. Therefore, it is important to note that twins who do not fight at all increase their symbiosis and counteract the natural psychological separation process (Plotnik 2003).

Twins' drawings often clearly demonstrate the difference in their characteristics. The 34 month-old girls who made the drawings shown below started to draw about a year ago. Note how the girl who made the left-hand drawing did it in a structured and accurate manner, while her sister enjoyed the appearance of movement created by the drawing tool, bursting in different directions.

Figures 4-16 & 4-17:
Different drawing styles – different personalities (34 month-old twins)

These differences in personality and twin relationships persist over the years. The parents of the twins who made the next drawings (aged 5 years and 3 months) contacted me for advice following intense fights between their children, which also became physical. Analysis of their drawings showed that the child who made the right-hand drawing was impulsive, while his brother was more balanced and organized. This could mainly be seen in the line quality and movement.

The differences between the brothers and their arguments forced their parents to designate separate territories for each child, but the impulsive brother continued to trespass on his brother's territory, in a way also evidenced by the lack of boundaries in his drawing – e.g. land overlaps the house. In contrast, his brother keeps to his boundaries, both in reality and in his drawings, evidence of his cautious and rigid attitude. In this case, my advice to the family was to designate better marked territories for the children, which will allow them to develop according to their own unique temperaments.

Figures 4-18 & 4-19:
Different drawing styles – different personalities (5 year-old twins)

In kindergarten and school twins develop social skills differently. Some cling to their dyad and constantly play together, while others build relationships with other children. The next drawings by twins aged five years and seven months were mailed to me by their parents, who wanted to assess their social status. They told me that their daughter, who made the left-hand drawing, was socially active and that her friends often came to visit, while their son was mainly busy interfering with his sister's games.

Figures 4-20 & 4-21:
Understanding non-identical twins' relationships by comparing their drawings

Indeed, the girl's drawings painted a clear social picture: she found it important to be structured and well understood and her drawing level was high compared to her age. She paid attention to the overall impression of her drawings, trying to keep it calm and esthetic. In contrast, her brother's drawings were mainly wild and angular, although he demonstrated the ability to draw well-structured objects like the flowers, and they communicated the general impression of an aggressive child.

Undoubtedly, the brother's behavior has social costs in kindergarten, but we should also discuss the prices his sister has to pay for his actions. When they play together, it seems that the brother is dominant, while she is busy tidying up the mess he did. Such a relationship might become permanent, so it is important that their parents intervene when needed to change the dynamics between them.

Sometimes, following twins' personality differences and their impact on their behavior, you may see twins copy from each other. In these cases, the more mature child – whether socially or in other respects – is worried by his twin's development, so he hides his talents, not to create too wide a gap between them. The less developed child chooses to give up on developing his personality and copy from his twin (John et al. 2008).

Just like other children in kindergarten or school who copy from their peers, twins copy from one another. However, in the twins' particular case the source for copying is available for most of the day. Hence, the twin who copies might develop an inferiority complex when his twin's drawings receive more acclaim.

To conclude, disagreements between twins might be experienced by their parents as more powerful than in the case of singletons. Nevertheless, because of the complexity of twins' relationships, disputes are vital to establishing separate identities. Conversely, when twins barely fight, copycatting and joint activities often camouflage gaps in their skills. Such gaps, which are often related to motor skills, are not always perceived by parents, but are clearly evident in the twins' drawings.

Sibling Rivalry

Quarrels and disputes between siblings, whether twins or not, are an integral part of any family's daily life. In most cases, families whose members rarely fight usually do not have significant emotional relationship, because fights are a legitimate part of any relationship. Through disagreements, children develop their conflict resolution skills with their peers, as in most cases they fight legitimately over limited resources, such as toys or their parents' attention. These struggles are often accompanied by feelings of envy, under-privilege and criticism.

I suggest you observe the reasons for sibling rivalry through three different personality lenses:

1. *Temperament* – Naturally, different temperaments lead to quarrels, because the children's behavioral patterns conflict when they play together. An example may be seen in the following drawings: the left-hand drawing is characterized by impulsiveness and restlessness, while the other is more accurate and drawn more slowly. The

cause of many of the girls' fights is their different temperament. For example, when one behaves cautiously and slowly, the other gets annoyed by it, as she wants things to happen quickly. When their parents understood the gap and reflected it to their daughters, it became possible to create a family atmosphere and activities that allowed each child to express her temperament without the need to interfere with the other.

Figures 4-22 & 4-23: Different temperament as a source of sibling rivalry

2. *Territory* – Defending one's territory against trespassing by other family members is common among both twins and singletons. In the following drawing made by a 6 year-old boy, you can see a classic example for territorial issues. The drawing is made with age-inappropriate drawing style, in that it is based on multiple elements that overlap each other. Analyzing drawings is important in such cases, because it enables us to formulate a solution plan for the entire family. The recommendation is to create new situations which will enable a more distinct territorial separation between the children, making them feel safer and calmer.

Figure 4-24:   Drawing elements "invading" other elements' "territory"

3. *Hierarchy and status* – Fights over hierarchy and status are common mainly during transformation in the family structure, such as the birth of a new sibling. In such cases, disputes are often fuelled by the assumption that whoever wins gets to dictate the rules, so they fight over control and leadership. In many cases, fights among siblings lead to alliances with the parents designed to promote one sibling's in the family hierarchy. In this case, I recommend that parents break such coalitions apart and downplay status differences.

Figure 4-25: Family coalitions

The parents must keep acting as leaders, but avoid situations in which one child is stereotyped as "serious and responsible", while the other is "fun and naughty". Unraveling hierarchies helps create a better family atmosphere and cope with legitimate conflicts as they arise.

Summary

Coping with sibling rivalry: Do's and don'ts

1. *Legitimacy* – When children fight many parents feel that they are responsible for it and that it is their failure. Learn to separate between yourselves and your children's behavior and to accept sibling rivalry as a natural and legitimate part of their relationship.

2. *Setting the rules* – As parents, you should define the basic rules of behavior at home and this includes rules governing disagreements. Agree on which behaviors are acceptable and which are not. If you accept a behavior, you should tolerate it when it actually occurs. Check, for example, the difference, in your opinion, between teasing and cursing, raising a voice and yelling or pushing and beating. After you set the rules, present them to the children and explain that these are the family's rules.

3. *Observe your children's drawings* – Drawings often include indications to sibling rivalry. When a child is in distress and experiences difficulties at kindergarten or school, is it reasonable that his frustration will be expressed at home, but also in his drawings.

4. *Don't judge* – Avoid, as much as possible, being the judge in your children's disputes. Such position is not beneficial to the child who won in the particular case, because the feeling of artificial coalition with his parents might lead him to think that he needs their backing. It is also detrimental for the child who lost, because he might feel that his parent abandoned him at a crucial moment, leaving him without protection. This perception might provide further legitimacy to continue fighting with his "stronger" sibling, who is supported by the parents.

5. *Maintain presence* – Not interfering in your children's disputes doesn't mean that you leave them alone, uncared, as if you haven't seen or heard anything. Show them that you are present at home and when fights occur choose the moment and act as a mediator, hearing each side's story, understanding their needs and trying to show them the golden path to an agreement.

6. *Bear in mind that rivalry can be beneficial* – It should be clear to you that during fights, children learn several important things, such as how to negotiate, reach an agreement and compromise. They also learn to identify and cope with threats, ultimatums and bullying.

7. *Don't beg for a favor* – When you ask a child to behave in a certain way as a favor to you, your child might feel more dominant in front of you and his younger sibling, who sees his power. Avoid, for example, saying "Please give up this toy, for me, just this once. I want peace and quiet in this house".

8. *Timing* – Try to interfere in children's disagreements when you see that one side behaves passively or when the quarrel repeats itself and it looks like the dispute has reached a dead end. When you join the conversation, do so in a way that will enable them to continue communicating also after you've left the scene. If you see that they continue their discussion after you've left, let them do so without your guidance.

9. *Timeout* – If you think the children need some timeout alone to cool down, maintain a one-minute-per-year ratio and not more: give the children two minutes to calm down separately if they are two years old. It is advised to force separation only in extreme cases and usually keep the sides together even when they fight, so that they learn not to run away from conflicts.

10. *Expression of feelings* – Teach the child to express his feelings and legitimize them at times of anger and frustration, as long as they are not violent.

11. *Search the drawings for clues* – Use children's drawings to better understand the source of their disputes. Search for one or more of these factors: temperament (drawing style and graphic indicators), territory (trespassing and spaces) and hierarchy gaps (coalitions in family drawings). Build the right solutions according to the dominant factor.

12. *Seek consultation* – If you feel that the tool you use does not improve the family atmosphere, do not hesitate to seek professional advice, whether through parental guidance, children's drawings analysis or therapy.

One of the unspoken secrets of parenting is the secret of the preferred child. This child is the one who is better loved because of his looks, temperament and the dialog with him, or the fact that he reminds the parent of himself, etc. It is difficult to cope with such preference, but a large part of the solution is being aware of it. Every parent should learn to see the uniqueness in every child. The challenge is to create a loving and close relationship with children who have different behavioral styles or personalities. Remember: sometimes we can learn more about ourselves from those who are different from us.

5 ADHD

Attention Deficit and Hyperactivity Disorder, also known as ADHD, is divided into three subtypes: predominantly hyperactive-impulsive, predominantly inattentive and combined hyperactive-impulsive and inattentive. It is common to consider ADHD as a neurobehavioral developmental disorder with an organic basis. As the years pass, children with ADHD develop emotional and social reactions around this basis. Hence, you may expect to see manifestations of ADHD in children's drawings.

According to research, ADHD affects about 5% of children globally and is diagnosed in about 2% to 16% of school-age children. This makes it the most common psychiatric and neuropsychological disorder in that age (DSM-IV-TR, APA, 2000). ADHD has long-term consequences for children: it is a chronic disorder with about 50% of those individuals diagnosed in childhood continuing to have symptoms into adulthood (Van Cleave & Leslie 2008; Hechtman 2000). Given those far-reaching effects, a variety of diagnostic approaches have been developed to identify ADHD at early age and help children who have it. One of the most available approaches currently available to parents and practitioners is children's drawings analysis. By school age, it is customary to also analyze children's handwriting for this purpose.

When analyzing a drawing, you should focus on the child's emotional and social reactions, because they are the most dominant in his functioning. Another important point you should note when diagnosing ADHD through children's drawings is that drawings reveal the subjective aspect of the disorder. Meaning, attention disorders vary individually in their intensity or patterns, so that every child experiences the disorder differently. Hence, when suggesting solutions following your analysis, they should be adapted to the child's individual disorder characteristics. Observing indications of ADHD through children's drawings will enable you to identify the critical issue for each child and provide him with the best solution for his needs.

Diagnosis and Evaluation

No specific cause of ADHD has yet been identified. There are, however, a number of contributory factors. These include psychological factors, genetics, diet (Bell & Peiper 2006) and the social and physical environments.

The genetic factor appears to be the dominant cause of ADHD, because genetics are a factor in about 75% of ADHD cases (Epstrin 2000).

Since drawings are influenced directly by the brain's neurochemistry, medicines like methylphenidate ("Ritalin") – which uses increases dopamine and norepinephrine brain levels by facilitating their neurotransmission, directly affect drawing style. Usually, when taking the drug, a child's drawings may become more organized and less stormy.

Therefore, in such case you should compare the child's drawings before and after medication, or when taking and avoiding the medicine (Barness, 2006).

Figure 5-1:   Drawing without the effects of Ritalin

Figure 5-2:   Drawing under the effects of Ritalin

In any case, analysis of children's drawings focuses mainly on the psychological aspects of a child's difficulty rather than on its neurobiological aspects that are directly influenced by diet or genetics.

Diagnosis of ADHD is made via clinical assessment, exclusively by certified professionals, such as neurologists, clinic psychologists, educational psychologists or neuropsychologists. Even so, as noted earlier, drawings are a complementary tool that helps many parents prior to making the clinic assessment.

When clinical assessment of ADHD is made, it is not based on one test only, because there isn't a single test that can confirm or deny the presence of the disorder. In some cases the assessment may find that a child has learning disability, eyesight or hearing disorder or behavioral disorder based on emotional background rather than due to ADHD. The purpose of the assessment is to check the difficulty level in psychological organization and cognitive control, as well as emotional or behavioral difficulties such as depression, anxiety, low self-esteem and social difficulties (Weingartner 1999).

Emotional Background

The purpose of analyzing drawings by children with ADHD is to identify their temperament and emotional background, including all the behavioral implications, and not necessarily to identify and define whether the child has ADHD or not. Sometimes, ADHD is a reaction to events that have emotionally overwhelmed the child. When this emotional overload is relieved, usually it is possible to see an improvement in the child's attention disorder patterns.

Hence, early diagnosis of a child's emotional condition may help parents and education professionals who have daily interaction with the child, because it will give them tools to better cope with ADHD and understand what the child is going through. In other words, the parents will not only know that their child has ADHD, but will also understand his needs and feelings and be better able to reach out to him and provide him with the specific help he needs.

Figure 5-3: **Drawing with indicators of emotional and developmental difficulties**

For example, the 11 year-old child who made this drawing was suspected to have ADHD. The results of his assessment showed that he had emotional developmental difficulties. Looking at his drawings, it was obvious that he suffered emotional distress. His distress is evident in the regression in his drawings: there are poor in detail and do not match the level appropriate for this age, which usually combines a plot. In particular, the figure to the right is drawn in a regressive manner: its arms are one-dimensional and are not proportional to its body. This drawing style usually characterizes children with social difficulties, who feel helpless in social situations. Since my analysis revealed the child's emotional difficulty as the dominant feature in his inner world, I focused on the emotional aspect, rather than ADHD, as the root cause of his impatience and attention and concentration difficulty. Indeed, when his parents checked his kindergarten environment, they discovered that children tended to harass him when the kindergarten teacher was not around and that he found it difficult to cope with them, so his distress only exacerbated.

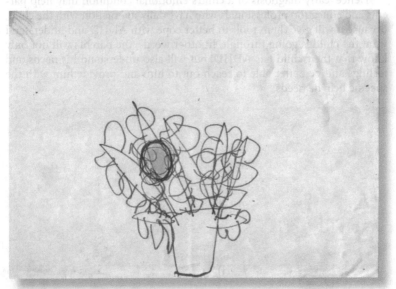

Figure 5-4: **Stressful learning environment as indicated in a drawing by an 8 year-old**

The following case of an 8 year-old is similar – the child began showing signs of attention disorder, but analysis of his drawings showed that his behavior was a result of a demanding and stressful academic environment. One of the indications for that was his treetop drawing style, which started off as an attempt to create an organized structure of the branches and leaves, but eventually the overall result included leaves overlapping each other and a stormy and confused scene. The combination of a large treetop and small trunk, together with other indicators in the drawing, symbolizes the cognitive overload this child experiences. Once his difficulty was made clear and treated by providing him with practical tools to cope with school requirements, his attention and concentration abilities improved significantly.

Figure 5-5:   Stress at home following divorce

The next case involves a 9 year-old child undergoing stress at home. As mentioned earlier, attention disorders are sometime a reaction to major life events and when these are resolved, the child's attention abilities are restored. This was the case with this boy: following deterioration in his parents' relationship and as a result of the rigid and alienated atmosphere at home this child began developing patterns of aggressive and willful behavior, as well as attention problems. His drawings changed dramatically: the pressure increased, indicating greater emotional stress; his drawing style became regressive; the houses in his drawings were drawn in an unstable way, bent sideways and in many cases with the door and windows omitted or drawn particularly small, symbolizing his emotional withdrawal. In this case, dialog with the family leading to a more complete understanding of each family member's feelings and needs proved key to improving his condition.

Is ADHD Really a Disorder?

Considering the incidence of ADHD – about 5% of children globally – many researchers argue that it is not a disorder but a natural trait that manifests itself in reaction to certain external stimuli experienced by the child (e.g., Timimi & Taylor 2004). Therefore, it is reasonable to assume that this trait offers evolutionary advantages, enabling it to persist from generation to generation (Hallowell & Ratey 1995). For example, a child's ability to see the wide space around him rather than focus on just a specific area or stimulus gives him a relative advantage in games that require wide perception such as football or soccer. In adulthood, this trait may be advantageous in professions such as teaching, management, marketing and computers.

This view is fundamental to children's drawing analysis. The focus in analysis is not to compare the child to his peers, checking whether he matches or deviates from the norm, but to truly understand why he behaves in a certain way and how this behavior benefits him. When the approach is not pathological, it is easier to assess ADHD at home and in school and to improve the child's behavioral outcomes. In other words, when the focus is not pathological, there is less stigma and stereotypes, hence less frustration and hostility from the child, facilitating a more positive environment that may contribute to the success of the therapeutic process. Note that although my focus is different, concentrating on how ADHD and its indicators are presented to a child and his family, I do recommend professional assessment.

ADHD in Children's Drawings and Handwritings

To diagnose ADHD, DSM-IV requires that six or more of the various signs of inattention or hyperactivity-impulsivity detailed in the manual have been present for at least 6 months to a point that is disruptive and age inappropriate. In order to determine whether a child has ADHD, he must be assessed by professionals. However, when in doubt, parents may use drawings as a preliminary tool to help them decide whether to undergo such an assessment. In addition, drawings provide in-depth analysis of a child's condition in various aspects. Naturally, it is recommended to corroborate the information from a child's drawings with behavioral events, gathered by objective observation and conversations with the child.

Inattention

First and foremost you must check the child's functioning level, when making a drawing, in comparison to his age. You should note the frequency of the child's inattention episodes. In this case, it is recommended to let the child draw freely, perhaps one of his favorite subjects, and make an observation: is he paying attention to details? Does he forget to draw important details? Compared to his peers, does he have difficulty drawing, so he quickly finishes his artwork? Does he understand the drawing instructions, as expected given his age? Does he prefer, out of difficulty, not to make complex drawings that require multiple levels (such as drawing houses or machines)? Does he have difficulty organizing in the drawing's setting?

Hyperactivity and Impulsivity

If you suspect that your child has an impulsivity element in addition to inattention, you should mainly focus on graphic indicators in his drawings, according to his age. Such indicators include rapid and overflowing drawing style, crossing lines and inconsistent organization of elements on the page.

In cases of hyperactivity which is not of the regular type but part of ADHD, you must observe the child's body language while he draws. Some children will be restless: they will swing their legs, move their behind on a chair or often rise and stand while drawing. Naturally, this observation must take the child's age into account. In drawings of hyperactive children, you may often notice disassembly of various elements, unfinished elements and irregular location of elements on a page.

Drawings are an integral part of diagnosing ADHD, mainly because most of the signs of ADHD appear before age 7. In the basis of ADHD lies a difficulty that children have in isolating a single stimulation out of many, in non-monotonous tasks. Therefore, drawing in this case is unique, because it is considered as a single stimulus and is not monotonous.

The Effects of ADHD on Cognitive Performance

Since children draw at home, in school or kindergarten, their drawings from all settings may be added to the teachers' behavior reports. Analyzing drawings helps focus on the various problems that children have because the symptoms are different in their intensity in each case. Furthermore, comparison of drawings made by a child throughout the years will also indicate changes in the disorder's trends and facilitate various solutions, according to these changes.

Figure 5-6:   Excessive details and a stormy and restless drawing style

The following drawing by a 6 year-old shows trends that characterize hyperactive children with ADHD. It is laden with details and motion in a way that indicates hyperactivity. The drawing style is overflowing and explosive, so that the lines sometimes exceed the page boundaries. Also, the child repeatedly applies strong pressure on the drawing tool, and his rhythm is stormy and restless and in some parts truncated. In the future, this child may also tend to avoid writing due to the static posture it requires (importantly, there are other reasons for avoiding drawing or writing, and not every case of avoidance necessarily indicates hyperactivity). When children are still at preschool, and are still not required to cope with task that require significant attention, such indicators are usually taken to indicate an impulsive temperament rather than bona fide ADHD. If in doubt, I recommend combining other diagnostic approaches.

Figure 5-7:   Formal overload and disorder typical of children with ADHD

Another point worthy of discussion in relation to drawings of children with ADHD is their ability to filter stimulations. The following drawing was made by a 7 year-old boy with ADHD. He tends to overburden his drawings with multiple small details, overwhelming the observer with forms, making it hard to comprehend the drawing. The unique aspect in this drawing is the general drawing style. The style can be either structured or chaotic. Some children have a high drawing level and draw with many details in a structured way, while children with ADHD will usually have an overloaded and chaotic drawing style.

Drawings of children with ADHD will often be overloaded and disordered, but the level of overload and disorder depends on the environment (therefore it is important to collect drawings from diverse settings). In some cases, when the surrounding is noisy, it will impair the child's ability to concentrate while drawing or studying in class. However, in other cases, external over-stimulation will increase his ability to concentrate. Analyzing a child's drawings will enable you to understand his personality and determine whether his concentration ability is increased or decreased in a noisy and over-stimulating environment, allowing you to come up with a better solution for him.

Figure 5-8:   Miniaturized head and poor detailing

This case is interesting also because it has to do with another aspect of children with ADHD. Often, parents of children with ADHD struggle with the question whether to keep their child for another year in kindergarten. The child who made this drawing spent another year in kindergarten, but this year was not beneficial for him. His lack of readiness was expressed mainly in his impulsive temperament and tendency to be distracted. When he subsequently entered first grade, his difficulties only exacerbated, because his temperament hasn't changed substantially and his learning abilities were still relatively low. Consequently, his drawings, just like the one shown here, included significant trends related to his low self-image: smaller drawings, figures with small heads and weak drawing style, as well as a generally poor drawing style, which did not characterize his drawings up to that point.

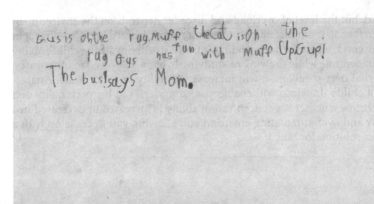

Figure 5-9:   **Disorganized handwriting with gaps**

During school, children with ADHD often hear the following sentence: "it is sad that you don't fulfill your potential". Nowadays, thanks to increasing awareness of ADHD and its signs, most teachers already know that this sentence is irrelevant, because these children tend to listen inconsistently to what is said in class, due to wide variety of noises and distractions. In their handwriting, you will often see evidence of the distractions they experience. The distractions will be manifested in irregular spaces between words.

Figure 5-10 illustrates these spaces, found on different places on the page, without any clear structure.

The learning process of the child who wrote this is similar to his handwriting – he writes half sentences, because he is able to hear only these parts and later he finds it difficult to organize these missing statements into complete and coherent learning.

In the early grades, the teacher tends to repeat her words several times to make sure all children understand what she says. However, in higher grades the child is responsible for completing the gaps that he did not manage to hear. Some children succeed in that, but others get tired of the cognitive effort and despair.

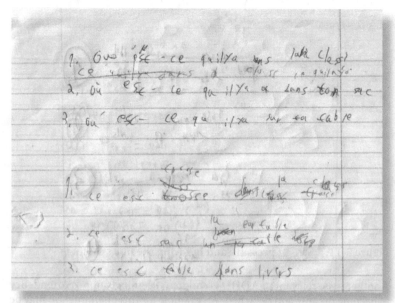

Figure 5-10:   An adolescent's handwriting filled with gaps

The hyperactive element in ADHD is often manifested in physical reactions (Barkley 2004). A hyperactive child tends to be involved in more fights and pranks. Sometimes, others join him and it is difficult for him to sit still in the classroom for a long period of time. Assuming that in each classroom there are between 20 and 35 students, it is almost impossible for one teacher to give effective attention to a child with hyperactive disorder and usually her frustration will only increase.

The handwriting you see in the next example, by a 9 year-old child, is illustrative in that regard. This child finds it difficult to sit still and hates going to school, where he suffers. He tends to be violent and fight with children from other classes. His impulsivity is evident in his drawing – he uses very heavy pressure on the page and chooses to ignore the structure of the page and its lines.

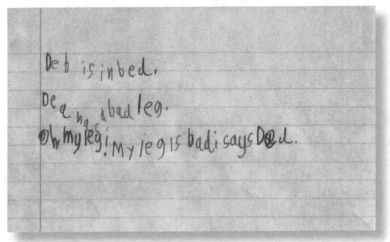

Figure 5-11:   Strong pressure and ignoring the line structure

Another issue relevant to ADHD is children's seemingly opposite tendency to become dreamy and detached. An example for this phenomenon may be seen in the following drawing by a seven year-old girl.

Her teacher reported that she does not interrupt during class and often seems invisible. Her drawings have similar characteristics, because she draws with light pressure and sometime her line almost vanishes from the page. She is a clever and full of potential, but her tendency to fade away – both socially and on the page – affects her self-esteem.

Figure 5-12: Weak and loose pressure, shaky and unconfident line (no motoric difficulties in this case)

In her case, motivation is not affected, because we see that she still has presence on the page and expresses her inner world. However, there is no doubt that treating her as invisible might eventually affect her motivation and self-image.

To conclude, the first obstacle that a child with ADHD has is related to learning – the attention level, concentration level and persistence and organization abilities are the first to affect his learning experience at kindergarten and school. Analyzing children's drawings at kindergarten age and observing their handwriting at the first stages of writing may prevent resistance to learning, as well as feelings of being unable to succeed in school. A child's belief that he is unable to succeed in school is very problematic and can lead to greater difficulty and decreased motivation. In such cases, a child may feel tired of failing and he will prefer to give up and try other fields he may be good at. The purpose of drawing analysis in these cases is to assess the degree of the child's difficulty and help him, as soon as possible, regain the belief that he is capable of learning.

The Effects of ADHD on Social Performance

Children's social functioning is influenced directly by their cognitive functioning level. When a child accumulates negative experiences due to failures at school, he may focus on his social life to compensate for his learning difficulty.

The parents of the 7 year-old girl who made the next drawing told me that she has no time or energy for studying, because she is completely occupied with various social activities.

In her drawings, you can see, on the one hand, trends that characterize her learning patterns – the sky is drawn in multiple patches made of various colors and drawn with different tools, there are scribbles made by pencil, a V sign was added at the center of the page, regardless of the subject or main theme of the drawing, the spaces are small and the drawing style is fast and stormy.

Figure 5-14: Overload and disorder combined with creative combinations of elements

All of these elements overburden the page and communicate her impulsive personality and difficulty managing tasks. Indeed, she usually fails to complete tasks, because her attention is distracted and this characteristic is evident in the irrelevant elements added to her drawings.

On the other hand, the overload and variety that characterize her drawings show that she has advanced social abilities. In the social arena, an impulsive temperament may be an advantage, because many social games require movement. Therefore, this child's personality affects her preferences and she finds pleasure in playing with others. It is easy for her to form social connections, just as she creates original connections between elements on the page. An example for such a connection or association is the lines stretched between the house and the swing's left pole. Her artistic decision to use laundry lines to connect these two elements and decorate them with shirts, a bra and pair of glasses is unique and impressive. Moreover, the multiple connections in her drawings also suggest that she can have social relationships with many friends at a time. Her impulsive and flexible temperament, represented by the variety in her drawings, enables her to adjust to a variety of children and show leadership skills while at the same time she finds a common language almost with everyone.

Nevertheless, some children find it difficult to use the social arena as compensation. In these cases, the difficulties they experience in their learning process compound their social difficulties (Wilde 1996). The boy who made the following drawing is 10 years old. His parents consulted me because they felt that his behavior was deteriorating. He was diagnosed with SPD (sensory processing disorder), which caused him to experience every light stimulus as much more intense. He was nervous during breaks at school, complained about noise and got into fights on a regular basis.

The combination of SPD with impulsivity, characteristic of ADHD, often creates the following worldview, as reported by this boy: "I was walking in the corridor and children were bumping into me like a bomb. I had to hit them back immediately for what they did to me. Later everyone blamed me for starting the fight and it's a lie! They don't understand, no one understands me, people always blame me and give me the worst punishments".

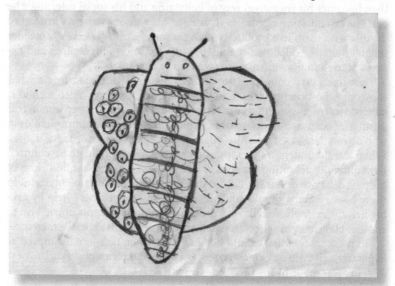

Figure 5-15: Constant heavy pressure on the entire page indicating imbalanced sensory regulation

His father reported that sometimes he taps gently on his son's shoulder, and his son then turns around to him in anger, asking: "Why are you pushing me?" These examples – at school and with his father – give us a glimpse into his sensory world. From his perspective, every touch is experienced as a blow which requires a violent reaction. Similarly, each whisper or light noise in class distracts his attention from his teacher. In addition, every invasion of his territory, such as his body or belongings is interpreted by him as a call for strong action.

Heavy pressure dominates his drawings and he often engraves on the page. It may be that his rigid and impulsive temperament is responsible for this pressure, but this could also be caused by his hypersensitivity. Just as every touch hurts him so does every line have to be rigid and engraved.

At this stage, analysis of his drawings helped his parents stop the social snowball from becoming an avalanche, and prevent the child from being officially stigmatized as "the violent and problematic child in class". In his case, the parents succeeded thanks to intervention in his social dynamics by way of frank discussion of events. His parents didn't punish him for every violent behavior, but helped him analyze the chains of events that caused him to lose his temper.

In other cases, violent behavior could offer a child an opportunity to belong. In these cases, a child is at a dead end, unable to stop his violent behavior – his behavior is violent because of his hypersensitivity, but then he achieves social benefits and feels a sense of belonging. The "violent child" then becomes his (negative) way of belonging and his social role. Since he gets the attention he needs, he maintains his sensory patterns instead of dealing with them in a productive way. In such cases, it is wise to consider mental therapy, which will enable the child to process his feelings and express himself in nonviolent ways (Nadeau & Dixon 1997).

Just like every coin has two sides, every social situation in class has someone who benefits from it and someone who suffers. When a child is labeled violent, usually there are other children who try to keep him in this position, because they draw some benefit from it. For example, children who do not dare to act violently, but encourage such behavior as spectators. When a child undergoes therapy and changes his behavior, these children have difficulty accepting the change and look for ways to "remind" him of his past behavior or harass him, so that he would become violent again. In these cases, parents should consider mobilizing the teacher's help by asking her, for example, to talk with the other children's parents, move him to another class or even school, to facilitate a more positive social experience.

In most cases, when a child has ADD, i.e. when he is not diagnosed as hyperactive, he will be characterized as a calm and pleasant child. The next drawing was made by a 9 year-old boy with ADD.

He draws slowly, with a pencil, and sometimes erases an element in order to correct a mistake and then continues with his work. Although the figure is located at the center of the page, it is very small, isolated and surrounded by emptiness. In addition, note the blackening of the figure's hands, which symbolizes deficient communication skills. The conclusion is that this child has low self-esteem and views himself as small and insignificant in real life as well as on the page.

Figure 5-16: Slow drawing rhythm; miniature and isolated figure

This child represents many children who deserve more attention from our society. On the one hand, their behavior does not interfere with society – they don't beat others, push or yell like their friends with the hyperactive element, but on the other hand, their silent and withdrawn behavior is not necessarily a sign of proper mental condition, but rather requires special attention.

Analysis of drawings made by children with ADHD in elementary school may enhance their performance in multiple areas because the disorder is still "new" and does not yet irreparably affect the way the child experiences himself. During these years, social experiences are the most intensive. Hence, the price a child pays for his social behavior is higher than at any other age and significantly affects his self-image.

During these years, parents also have greater influence on their children. Therefore, parents may allow themselves to be more involved in assisting their child directly while providing him with guidance.

ADHD Combined with Learning Difficulties

About 30% of children with ADHD are also diagnosed with learning disabilities (Gillis 1992). Contrary to common belief, there is no relation between learning disability and IQ. A child with learning disability is one who has significant difficulty in a certain field, compared to his age and his ability in other fields.

Drawings of children with ADHD and learning disabilities will include the following characteristics:

1. *Difficulty managing and filtering stimulations* – it would seem as though everything matters in a drawing, without separating the wheat from the chaff.

2. *Limited long-term concentration ability* – a child will have difficulty focusing on drawing or writing, compared to his age.

3. *Hyperactivity* – stormy line or movement and general restlessness in a drawing, multiplicity of elements and organization difficulties while drawing.

4. *Age-inappropriate difficulty regulating and delaying gratifications* – drawing many details, creating complex and unclear structures, and mixing up elements on the page.

The last indicator is material, because recent studies (e.g. Wilens 2004) clearly show that these children do not have difficulty gathering or processing information, but in controlling their movements and impulsive reactions to stimuli. In their drawings, it is easy to identify the level of their impulsivity, as well as the extent to which they are able to control it.

Analyzing drawings and handwriting is important, because in some cases there is a mistaken impression that a child does not complete his assignments because he is spoiled or lazy. When analyzing drawings made by these children, it is possible to see that this impression is indeed wrong – these children are full of vitality, but they find it difficult to organize it on a page. Thus, the result is a stormy, unstructured and non-methodical drawing.

The parents of the 7 year-old who made the drawing in figure 5-17 consulted me because they felt that doing homework has become an impossible task for their child. Analyzing this drawing, as well as others, revealed that he is constantly frustrated. He uses drawings as an excuse to externalize his aggressions and scribbles with heavy pressure. The pressure he applies is so strong that he almost tears the page. His drawings are loaded with lines and other add-ons, symbolizing his attention overload. He has a feeling that there are a lot of interesting stimulations around him, which are all equally important. The scribble he chose to add to the figure's forehead is uniquely and persuasively indicative of the white noise he experiences, as well as his concentration difficulties. Just like in this drawing, his head is packed with stimuli that make it difficult for him to listen to his teacher or complete his homework.

**Figure 5-17:   Self-portrait during a lesson in class; scribbling in the
forehead area indicating difficulty**

For his parents, just like many other parents of children with ADHD, getting him to do his homework or prepare for school in the morning are not
easy tasks. His parents report that the early morning hours are very tense
and full of angry outbursts and fights. They told me that when he finds
interest in a task, for example preparing for a ski vacation, he is able to
prepare for it quickly and efficiently. As a result, they assumed that he does
things on purpose, to annoy them, and this only made them even angrier
at him.

Learning disabilities also affect the way children with ADHD behave
during school breaks. This child's drawings are not overloaded like typical
drawings of children at this age. On the contrary, they are mostly empty,
except for few elements near the edges of the page. This drawing style characterizes children who feel extreme social isolation. In this case the combination of attention and hyperactivity disorders cause his social difficulties.
His classmates reject him because he insists to be at the center. (This insist-

ence was reflected in his drawings up to about a year ago: they were full of elements, spread all over the page, barely leaving uncolored areas). However, his violent behavior each time after not getting what he wanted severely affected his social status. His attention and concentration difficulties made it hard for him to improve his behavior and adjust himself to the prevailing social codes. This created a vicious circle of social deterioration.

His behavior had social implications and his recent drawings (including that shown here) clearly show the impact of his social environment on his feelings. He became more isolated, desperate, unmotivated and depressed. His difficulty making friends led to an ongoing sense of frustration, which caused him to avoid any social interaction with his peers.

A final word: as seen in this example, it is almost impossible to ignore the teacher's writing in red, commenting on the child's work. Using red or otherwise overemphasizing corrections could have a major effect on children's motivation. The relationship a child has with his teacher plays a key role in his academic achievements (Dendy 2000). Sometimes, adding a smiley, a heart or even a verbal comment near the final score may help the child feel accepted, heard, and trusted despite the difficulties.

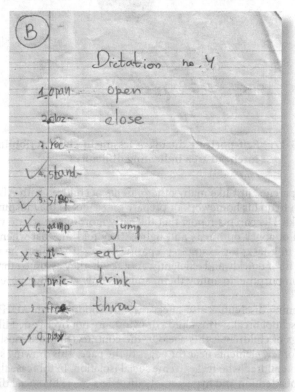

Figure 5-19:   Teacher's corrections and comments in red

Summary

Recommendations for Parents

1. Use drawings as a projective stimulus – sometimes it is easier to talk about the chaos in a child's drawing than to discuss the chaos in his schoolbag. Do not change his drawing or reject it as improper. Use his artwork as a tool to expand the dialog with him. Speak to him as if you were part of his drawings and encourage him to share his emotions, regardless of the chaos that he feels. Try to find ways to leave the drawing as it is, but organize other areas in his life.

2. Become proficient in the various methods used in corrective teaching. The tips and tricks learned in private lessons that help a child improve his learning habits are simple to perform and very helpful. Understanding these methods will enable your child to perform more effectively even in extracurricular settings.

3. Seek opportunities to give your child positive feedback, even for success in a minor task. This is your chance to observe his success from a different perspective and speak about it with your child according to his age. Your child's self-image is built gradually on success experiences. If you will succeed in pointing his attention to these experiences and show him that you notice them as well, he may avoid feelings of low self-esteem or incompetence that sometimes accompany ADHD. Encourage your child on a regular basis and believe in him and his abilities. As a result, he will also believe in himself and his success stories will be more frequent and effective.

4. Observe your child and try to understand his frustration – if he has temper tantrums each time he loses a game, speak to him about his difficulty and let him win. Be patient, because letting him win in few games will not necessarily prevent his aggression from being expressed in other places. Reflect his action by saying: "I can see that we should now play by your rules and not by the fair rules" and continue as if nothing happened. At the same time, try to jointly formulate a set of rules that will allow both of you to enjoy a pleasant and fair game.

5. When discussing events in your child's day, try to demonstrate to him the chain of actions and reactions that led to the final outcome. Children with ADHD or learning disabilities sometimes find it difficult to understand how things happened and thus feel that these events are out of their control. They will tell you that they suddenly began to be annoyed and beat other kids, or that they suddenly had

difficulty concentrating on the teacher's words. When you talk to your child, try to understand the situation together with him and check whether there were reasons for his anger or temporary concentration loss. It does not mean that the cause justifies the result, but it will enable your child to understand that he can control his behavior and consequently he will feel more confident in his ability to make a difference.

6. Following the analysis of your child's drawings and understanding ADHD, you may notice that other children in your family behave similarly. It is important that each child will be diagnosed separately, because some children acquire the ADHD behavioral pattern simply to get benefits such as attention from their parents. These children have false organization difficulties that are caused by their need to receive attention from their parents and not because they truly have ADHD.

7. Try to present your requests in stages: first ask to do the first part, then the second. Children with ADHD may find it difficult to perform multi-stage tasks, but at the same time may have abstract thinking and exceptional skills in many fields.

8. Check with your child whether hearing or speaking in a loud voice enables them to better understand what they are told. Many children with ADHD and learning disabilities report improvement in understanding when they hear a story while reading it. You may use audio versions of books for this purpose.

9. Children with ADHD or learning disabilities have difficulty with tasks that require order and organization. Therefore, check if you can reduce the amount of stimulations around your child and the number of tasks he is faced with, in addition to breaking these tasks into orderly stages. Children with ADHD might get lost in a room full of toys. Hence, reducing the number of toys and putting them in boxes may help them enjoy their games and make it easy for them to tidy up the room after they finish playing.

10. At home, create a set of predefined roles. When each child, even if he has ADHD, has a clearly defined role, he will perform it with greater enthusiasm.

11. Check your perceptions about your child and believe that you can make a change. Sometimes the road is long and hard and it includes moments of regression. If you say to your child in those moments: "you never listen to me... you never help me at home... anyway it's just a matter of time before you lose your temper again", referring

to his character instead of his actions, the behavioral change will be minor and the child might develop a stigma on himself. Therefore, say: "I disapprove of what you did" instead of "you are a bad boy!"

Recommendations for Practitioners

1. First and foremost, observing a child's drawings and handwriting may help you better understand his complex personality. Knowing his emotional status is important for improving his condition and the tools provided here may help you in that.

2. Notice whether you find yourselves writing some of the following comments to a child's parents: "Your son has to try and stay in focus and stop interrupting me..."; "Your daughter should start working seriously even in subjects she likes less..."; "Your child has to learn how to control himself and stop arriving late in class..."; "Your son constantly forgets his books and it looks like he is giving up on himself... If you work with him more intensively, everything can change". Such comments are very common among teachers of children not yet diagnosed with ADHD.

3. It is important to look at the class environment and check, perhaps even together with the child, where is the right place for him to sit. For example, seating a child with SPD or another attention disorder near a wall and not near a passage may help him, because his attention will be less distracted by children walking by or touching him. Nevertheless, it is important that his viewing angle in class will enable him to mainly see his teacher and not the other children in class.

4. In some schools around the world, a teacher may not touch a student. If the rules in your school are different, try to touch a child with ADHD when talking to him: put your hand on his shoulder or look into his eyes. Physical or eye contact helps increase his attention and facilitates better dialog.

5. Allow a child with ADHD short breaks during class. Physical exercise improves his attention and may help him return to class more focused.

6. Do not give up on real dialog with a child – sometimes it is easier to speak with a child's parents, because the child gives you the feeling that he doesn't listen, but you shouldn't give up on him. Write positive comments in his notebook, and add remarks on negative behavior when necessary. Just like with other children who don't have ADHD, good relationship with a teacher is based on positive feedbacks, true caring and human warmth.

7. Finally, ADHD, ADD or learning disabilities are no excuse for bad conduct. These disorders are a key which enables us to better understand the reasons for a child's misbehavior and how to resolve his difficulties.

Conclusion

ADHD is a widespread phenomenon among children and adolescents. Sometimes, this disorder has side effects, such as learning disabilities and social or emotional difficulties. The purpose of analyzing children's drawings is to gain profound understanding of a child's social and emotional status. This status would not necessarily change by taking a certain medicine and it often requires emotional therapy and parental guidance.

Analysis of children's drawings helps reveal children's compensation resources that can resolve the difficulties reported about them in school. Identifying and using these resources will enable children experience greater success. Drawings also help focus on children's perceptions of their surroundings and subjective feelings. Such focus promotes an effective solution, because it will help them cope with their weaknesses and perceive themselves as capable, just like their friends.

6 DIVORCE

Introduction

The moment when parents decide to separate is experienced by most children as shocking. From that moment on, reality is bound to change for them and in some cases they are forced to witness the bitter conflicts that often accompany the process. Even if divorce is the best solution, the child experiences the post-divorce period as traumatic. During this period difficult emotions arise, such as anger, fear, depression and guilt (Hetherington 1981). Given the fact that not all children have the verbal ability to express their feelings, drawings are often a significant tool for understanding their distress.

Still, not all children to divorced parents are doomed to suffer from mental trauma. When the parents succeed in isolating the intensity of the conflict and the anger and tensions around the divorce from the necessary coordination of their continued parental functions, this can ensure a productive and positive emotional atmosphere (Wesolowski 2008), evident also in the children's artwork.

Children tend to be highly sensitive to their social environment, but often the way they express their sensitivity is not fully registered or understood by adults. This sensitivity is sharpened in times of crisis, when the family cell encounters difficulties. Many divorced parents nowadays are highly aware of the need to educate their children on the impact of breaking up the marital bond. Many do the utmost to fully understand the long and short-term consequences and implications, for them and their children, in all aspects of life. In doing so, one of their primary concerns is to understand what the child is going through and the kind of support he needs.

In such cases, drawings may help understand the child's inner world. They provide us with the child's perspective on his emotional and social status when making the drawing. Hence, they provide insights to the child's adjustment process to his new family structure and the difficulties he may be experiencing. In this chapter, I will use real-life examples of children's drawings to shed light on the emotional and social status of children to divorced families, the difficulties they have had and the solutions they need.

Children's drawings enable us to evaluate, on the one hand, general emotional parameters that characterize different critical emotional responses that are not typical to divorce, such as development regression, low self-image, and stress. On the other hand, they also enable us to evaluate social issues that characterize divorce specifically, for example: What is the child's attitude to a noncustodial parent? How does the child grasp his new position in the family structure? Does he still wish for his parents to reunite?

Analysis of the children's drawings must include the entire family system. When checking the drawings you should also analyze drawings by the child's parents and siblings, because they provide insight into the child's unconscious perceptions of his family.

Children often perceive the breakup process as traumatic, a perception attended by behavioral changes. These may include introversion or extroversion, attention difficulties, domineering behavior, crying and angry outbursts. These behaviors are the result of conflictual emotions such as anger, fear, frustration, depression and guilt. These feelings and their behavioral expression reflect a normative response to non-normative situation the child is required to cope with. Note that despite the fact that the scope of divorce these days is wide to the extent it is considered normative, for a child it is almost never a normative situation.

My first example presents developmental regression and expression of anger. When children have emotional difficulty coping with an undesired reality, their drawings are often regressive. This regression is similar to children's behavioral regression patterns familiar to many parents in time of crisis, such as bedwetting and temper tantrums. In drawings, the regression is manifested by lower drawing quality.

This drawing was made by a 6 year-old who had already reached a high drawing level, but as a result of his parents' separation his drawing level deteriorated. This is evident in the drawing of tadpoles, which are typical of the scribbling stage (ages 2½–3). In addition, note that the brown figure (the upper middle tadpole) is actually erased – without separation of body parts so that its face and legs are erased using the same marker strokes. This drawing style is a typical expression of anger towards the figure.

Figure 6-1:   Regression following divorce

Before I continue, I would like to emphasize that when analyzing children's drawings, the focus should be on drawings made during the parental separation process. However, you must not forget the difficulties and challenges experienced by the parents. I believe that supporting parents is also important. Awareness of the parent's situation, as well as the child's as reflected in his drawings, together with variety of solutions, helps everyone cope with the new situation.

Phases in the Divorce Process

In general, the divorce process can be divided into 3 main phases. The first, pre-divorce phase is characterized by extreme tension at home, particularly between the parents. In some cases, you will witness incitement of the children to win their sympathy and to hurt the other partner. The child is subjected to great embarrassment in relation to his feelings toward his parents.

It is difficult for him to form a clearly defined relation toward each of his parents. The situation at home might interfere with his studies and the stress and pressure experienced at home might find its expression even in violence toward his close surroundings. If the dispute is long-term, the parents often cease to perform their parental role and may no longer be considered a model for correct and healthy attitudes towards members of the other gender.

The next example is a drawing by a 5½ year-old child made before his parents' divorce. Note the interesting parallel between the emotional storm brewing at home and the way the trees are drawn. Importantly, the trees' drawing style was not characteristic of his drawings a year earlier. The child is attempting to draw trees, and the general impression is of unrest and emotional burden. This impression is communicated by the wavy and non-homogenous lines, the treetops crossing into one another and the fragile looking trunks.

Figure 6-2:   The pre-divorce phase

Another indicative element evident in this drawing is the right's tree's foliage that touches the ground. We can attribute this element to the child's attempts to look for additional support for the tree and even for himself. Moreover, in all the trees you can see large treetops compared with fragile trunks drawn in thin and tortuous lines. This lack of proportion symbolizes the emotional burden on the child and his difficulty carrying it.

The aftermath or second phase is characterized by the family's transition and adaptation to the new situation. The ambience at home is relatively quiet and calm, in light of the fact that the overt conflicts and tensions have disappeared. At this stage, the parents and their children seek to start a new life: defining and updating schedules, work, dwellings, social contacts, etc.

The drawing presented in figure 6-3 was made by the same child six months after the previous one, after his parents had separated formally. Although this drawing is more structured, it is possible to see unusual elements. The house is not located on the ground and the windows are illustrated as crosses instead of squares that may be opened.

The drawing style of the windows symbolizes remoteness, withdrawal, and tendency not to expose the inner world. Evidently, the child still suffers difficulties, although in general it should be pointed out that the drawing is well-proportioned and age appropriate. Likewise, the quality of the line and rhythm of the drawing are once more similar to the trends typical of his drawings prior to the divorce.

Figure 6-3:   The aftermath of divorce

Stabilization: In this last phase, the remaining family members adopt a new routine without the parent who has left the house. Ideally, every family member knows his place and understands and accepts the new order. During this stage, it is usually also possible to witness stabilization in drawing trends. For example, during or after the divorce, a child's anger will be expressed by drawing with high pressure, but during the stabilization period the pressure on the drawing tool will be weaker. It should be noted that the stabilization period may take months or even years.

Psychological effects – coping stages

The child's reactions to divorce depend on his age, developmental status, visitation rules, adjustment level and relations with his parents. However, many reactions are typical to almost all children to divorced parents. Working through the loss of divorce is quite similar to mourning. In both processes of coping with loss, the child usually undergoes the following stages (Maureen 2000):

Denial – Many children try to reject or suspend the bitter reality. At this stage, children tend to believe the divorce is unreal and is nothing but a passing quarrel. At times, the child tries to deny he is affected by the divorce, emotionally or in any other way. In such children's drawings you can still see a family structure reminiscent of past drawings, just like in this example: the father and mother still hold hands and all family members smile and look happy together (and are also close together), despite the completely different reality.

Figure 6-4:   Denial

Guilt – During this stage the child might develop guilt feelings resulting from the omnipotent cognitions characteristic of younger children. He will tend to accuse himself and attribute his parents' quarrels and separation to his own behavior. On the one hand, at this stage you can see in the drawings omnipotent, dominant and powerful self-images: the child is at the center of the drawing, drawn in an emphasized and strong style compared to the other figures. But on the other hand, in a more advanced stage of guilt, it is possible to witness children drawing themselves as small and insignificant figures. We will then have an impression from the children's drawing that the child sees himself as primarily responsible for the divorce, causing feelings of guilt resulting in drawing a small and less dominant figure.

Anger – At this stage, the child tends to attach to the fact of separation emotional meanings of abandonment and neglect. As unwilling partners to the divorce, children experience emotionally distressed parents that are emotionally preoccupied and cannot give them the attention they have become accustomed to receive. Consequently, they begin to fear emotional neglect. These fears are now projected onto the parents or other authority figures such as teachers. His drawings will now be made using stronger pressure and stormy movement of the drawing tool, and possibly his aggressions will be directed to certain figures in the drawing – using strong pressure, deletion and destruction, lack of stylistic attention and the like.

Despair – By this stage, the child has already worked through the divorce, and starts to grieve the loss of the relationship in a more formal way.

Now, different behaviors that require emotional treatment may appear, such as different physical difficulties, hysterical weeping, and loss of interest in studies and in other age-appropriate activities. Those reactions are typical of most children, regardless of age, developmental stage, personality, relations with the parents, and past experiences.

Figure 6-5: **Weak pressure on the drawing tool indicating general reluctance**

Studies conducted among children to divorced partners (e.g. Gardner 1977) have suggested another, fifth stage, characterized by acceptance of the new reality and adjustment to the situation. In the following drawing, for example, you can see how the girl has managed to draw all family members on the same plain of the drawing, as well as three separate houses above them.

Drawing family members on the same plain indicates, in this case, the realistic status of the relationship between her divorced parents, who still celebrate family occasions and holidays together.

Figure 6-6:   Acceptance – coming to terms with the new reality

Children's Reactions to Divorce

During the first year or so after the divorce most families are in the first stages of dealing with the change. Oppawsky (2000) identified several key negative reaction patterns which characterize this period:

• **Aggressive reactions** enable the child to vent feelings of anger and helplessness, and in many cases take physiological form as in vomiting, facial spasms, weight fluctuations, sleeping disorders, and depression. These actually represent emotional adjustment difficulties. They are designed, in most cases, to signal overwhelming stress and distress he is experiencing in the aftermath of divorce. In most cases they are also unconsciously designed to force the parents to cope with the child's health problems rather than focus on their own emotional conflicts.

The drawing in figure 6-6 was made by a 10 year-old whose parents had divorced. Immediately after the formal divorce procedure had begun, the child started to experience eating and sleeping disorders.

Figure 6-7:   Anger at the parents

The child drew the house on the right but then erased it. Likewise, it's possible to notice the dense confused painting of the house. These two elements: deletion and density, communicate the child's anger and aggression towards his parents.

- **Attempts to mediate between the parents.** This reaction is combined with the intention of returning the family to its previous state, and development of age-inappropriate dependence on one of them. The development of such dependence is contingent on the child's age and personality, but it finds its expression in emotional patterns (emotional regression and need for intimacy that is not age appropriate), negative social reactions such as withdrawal or materialistic compensation mechanisms (like excessive demand to buy toys and the like).

- Regressive dependency characterizes those children who suffer from low self-image: the literature suggests a clear relationship between low self-image and parental separation (Schick 2002).

- **Identification with one of the parents.** Children who identify with one of the parents do so to gain power and meaningfulness. In their drawings it is easy to discern identification in the way the child draws himself and the parent he identifies with in a similar style, identical colors or clothes. In general, absolute identification with one of the parents requires the child to detach himself from the other parent or to reduce the frequency and quality of contacts with him.

- **Escapism.** Physically running away from home is characteristic of adolescents. It enables some children to avoid direct coping with the implications of divorce, and consequently, to evaluate the events around him from a more distant and objective perspective. There are children whose temporary escape from home enables them to find a supportive environment where they can cope emotionally with the divorce. Another, more subtle form of escape is cramming the day with a great variety of activities, to reduce the time spent at home to a minimum.

- **Preoccupation with the imaginary** world is another, more cognitive form of escape. This form of escape enables the child to avoid the painful facts of his daily life. Thus, the imaginary world serves as a haven in times of distress.

The next drawing provides a good example for a well-balanced and age-appropriate integration of the child's imaginary world into a drawing. A fairy can be seen on the right side. This fairy, according to the child who made this drawing, has an important role of changing reality and bringing her parents back together. However, a reservation is in order here: imagination is an integral part of children's drawings and therefore you must examine the drawing in its entirety and look for various indicators to the child's condition. It is important to remember that for children of separated parents, entering the imaginary world is therapeutic and therefore must not be prevented. Therefore, you must carefully assess the proportion of imaginary elements in the drawing, and remember that they comfort the child by providing protection and a safe haven.

Drawing 6-8: The imaginary world invades a realistic drawing made during divorce

The next example by a 7½ year-old child invites us to a reality of escape to the imagination which is not progressive or positive, but keeps the child from coping with his difficulties and receiving support from his close surroundings. The flowers are not abloom, the sun is distant and seems not to provide any heat and there is no interaction among the various elements on the page, as typical of his age. Consequently, we may assume that the child perceives his world as cold and remote, lacking happiness and social life.

Drawing 6-9: Social withdrawal following divorce

Note that about a year after the divorce, you may identify successful emotional working through of the divorce among most children: the pain and the suffering weakened, and were replaced by acceptance of the new reality. However, while most children accepted the divorce as final, younger children in particular tended to continue clinging to their fantasies of family reunion.

Parental Reactions to Divorce

In order to successfully meet the challenges of parenthood, and, in particular with the emotional pain that accompanies divorce, parents need to monitor the way their children cope with the new reality on an ongoing basis. Sometimes one of the children adjusts differently and more effectively, and consequently another sibling adopts regressive patterns, with new difficulties arising daily.

There is no reason that after the divorce you will not be able to continue educating your child to the same values, just as you have been doing before. The separation may have exacted an emotional price from all family members – depending of course on the emotional atmosphere around it – but even after a painful and quarrelsome separation, it is possible, little by little, to restore order. The more profoundly you understand what every family member is undergoing and what his needs are, the more wisely you are able to act and respond more effectively. Nevertheless, there is bound to be a period in which the relationship is oversensitive, and you will find yourself unable to communicate. Some relationships are problematic and quarrelsome for years. Particularly in these cases it is important to examine the effect of divorce on the children and try as much as possible to arrive at the optimal solution.

Just like their children, parents who are undergoing divorce tend to adopt negative behavioral patterns such as overcompensating the child and "buying his love", inciting against the other parent, exposing the child to sensitive and non age-appropriate information, and using the child to deliver messages to the other parent or to spy on him/her.

The child who made the next drawing was 6½ years-old. His parents had divorced several months before he made this drawing. The separation process was quarrelsome and painful to both sides.

Moreover, even after it ended the boy's parents continued to fight and disparate one another in every conversation they had. The gap between their educational approaches deepened with time, and each one of them saw in the child as compensation for the painful relationship with the former spouse.

As a result, the child himself was forced to bear the burden of having to choose between his parents, to prefer one over the other. In his drawings it is possible to see the result of his choice: the mother is drawn in a different physical pattern, which represents the gap he senses between her position and that of his father, both drawn similarly. Clearly this perception of the family members involves an emotional price, mainly because it distorts the perception of the parental versus the sibling unit.

Figure 6-10: Divorce in a hostile atmosphere

In the following drawing, you can see an example of a change in the family unit. This drawing is by a 4½ year-old boy, whose father was absent from home for a year since the couple had decided to separate. You can see how the child heightens himself, so that he and his mother have the same hierarchical importance in the family. Still, the father's image is present in the drawing, and its great height communicates his importance for the child. Besides this, he draws his father and his mother in a similar style using identical colors, presenting them as one unit.

Figure 6-11:　The father's influence on the divorce process

All these signs indicate that he still views his father as part of the family and part of the parental unit in particular. When the father's image is benign, his enduring presence in the family drawing is important. The very fact that he remains part of the family enables the child to retain the integrity of the family cell even if it has undergone such a critical change, and to continue examining the implications of the divorce for him. Studies show that as long as there is dialogue about the divorce, the child's emotional, cognitive and social performance is significantly higher.

　　To conclude, when the divorce is conflictual, children might find themselves at the heart of the conflict, a situation which may be characterized by three main patterns. The first involves blocking the family unit against the noncustodial parent, such that his visitation rights are revoked or not granted, and children are even incited against him. Such children may choose to draw the entire family but will find it difficult to visualize the parent who left, who will turn into a ghostly figure.

　　In the second pattern the child becomes a mediator between his aggressive parents, so that all insults are conveyed through him. In this case, drawings are likely to reveal a regression to an earlier developmental stage and indicator's of the child's confusion and distress.

Finally, the third pattern manifests itself in the absence of educational stability. In the drawings, a buffering line may appear between the parents who will also be drawn in a different graphic style to connote their separation (colors, physique, clothing, etc.).

The Effects of Divorce on Preschoolers

A study which analyzed drawings by children aged 4–6 (Cohen and Ronen 1999) found that children in their mother's custody which had a stable post-divorce relationship with their father coped better with the crisis and eventually reached acceptance.

Having said that, we can still chart several reasons for possible difficulties that are unique to preschoolers coping with divorce:

The first is **inexperience**. The experience of divorce is of course painful at any age, but older children have certain advantages over preschoolers. First, warm memories of the years preceding the marital crisis empower children. Preschoolers simply did not have a chance to experience the family as united and may be too young to remember the pre-divorce years.

An example for that is clearly evident in the following drawing by a five year-old. This drawing was made after the divorce, and is significantly different from drawings made before. The fact that there is no solid family basis (no ground in the drawing) is experienced by the child as a piercing, painful reality. This is represented by the figure which swings on the tip of a sharp edge and can fall at any moment, because it does not lean on solid ground and is surrounded entirely by sharp, thorn-like elements. Note that some children will experience this lack of stability also when their parents are together. In these cases you will sometimes notice an improvement when the parents formally divorce.

Dependence on the parents. Beyond the fact that the father has left the house, the family structure has entirely changed. The children are now raised (almost) exclusively by a mother who is forced to deal with new reality with all its implications. At times it is possible to feel a sense of relief and at times – the opposite is true – economic hardship, emotional stress, the mother's sense of failure, and so on. All these naturally transform family life, creating new dependencies.

Figure 6-12:   Lack of a solid family basis at an early age

A study on children in their mother's custody two years after the divorce of their parents analyzed family drawings and found that in time, these children tended to omit the father figure and enlarge the mother figure (Issacs & Levin 1984). It was also found that they tended to add figures which were not part of their nuclear family to the drawings.

The next drawing was made by a 3½ year-old and provides a good example of such dependency. In the drawing you can see a significant enlargement of the mother's image and her positioning in the center of the page. In doing so, the child affirms that his mother is important to him to the point of complete dependence, despite of the existence of other authoritative figures in the family.

Figure 6-13: **Dependency on the mother in a single-parent family**

Vulnerability. A sense of overexposure and trauma is typical of many children experiencing divorce. The departure of a parent from the house is experienced as a breakdown of the familiar family unit, and obviously this has a direct effect on the child's emotional world as well as on his drawings.

One of the most common examples in drawings related to divorce is drawing a house without any indication of separation. This is particularly typical of preschoolers, at an age in which not all children are able to fully grasp the complex realities of divorce. Consequently, they are preoccupied with creating an "idyllic family" that has not experienced divorce, or perhaps one that is about to return to its previous structure. In such drawings, the post-divorce home will be similar to the pre-divorce home.

The following drawing was made by a 6 year-old boy, illustrating a different vulnerable reaction. The parents of this boy had divorced several months before he made this drawing and since then, the relationship between them became unbearable, and even more severe than during the immediate pre-divorce period. The child witnessed verbal and physical aggression between them. When drawing his home, he added vertical lines along the house, creating separate units within it. This physical separation is typical of children who experience significant and unresolved conflicts between their parents.

Figure 6-14:   Indications of family conflict

New partners. Naturally, many divorced parents find new partners, with significant implications for the family unit, including step-parents and step-siblings. Sometimes, like in the famous legends, the child's step-parent has different educational approach than the original parent, or experience situation where a step-parent moves in with children from previous marriage and an effort is required to create a new, stable family unit.

Still, when the new relationship is successful, the new relatives may play an important and positive role in the child's life. A step-parent can provide the child things that lacked in his biological parent, who may have not been a good parent. In general, studies found that younger children have an easier time attaching to new family members compared with older children who need more time to accept the new reality. Children's drawings can be used as an effective way to understand children's perception of their step-parent, their relationship with him and the general stepfamily situation (Berger 1995).

In the next drawing, you may see the new woman in the father's life (dressed in red). It's possible to see that the girl has a good relationship with the new partner and that she has accepted her lovingly. Their loving relationship is indicated both by the hearts and the general happy atmosphere and by the fact that the new partner is drawn next to the father, in a harmonious style. Indeed, the girl is torn between the mothers, having doubts about whom it is proper to draw when asked to draw a family.

Figure 6-15:   The new woman in the father's life

Therefore, she finally decides to add a small image on the bottom left, drawn with a pencil, without identifying her explicitly as her biological mother. Be that as it may, it certainly seems as though she profits from having not one but two mothers who bestow love and affection on her.

Recommended Parental Approaches to Coping with Divorce

Education according to age

At each stage of the divorce process it is important to tailor your solutions and explanations to the child's age. The better you tailor your explanations to the child's age and needs, as arising from his drawings, the greater the chances for better emotional adjustment and effective coping with the new situation.

Ages 3 to 6

Since conceptualization level at these ages is low, children might conclude from the divorce that the separation between their parents also means separation from them. At this stage, their egocentric mode of thinking inevitably leads them to assume that they themselves are the cause of the divorce, and consequently they might develop guilt feelings. The separation scene itself is usually grasped in a simplistic, black-and-white manner: parent versus parent and parent versus child.

In the following drawing, you can see a parallel between the free scribbling stage characterized by the lack of structured forms and the child's low conceptualization ability as he still struggles with concepts of present-future tense. In other words, he finds it difficult to differentiate between the act of leaving the house and the possibility of continued relationship with his parent.

Figure 6-16: **Regressive spontaneous scribbling suggesting low conceptualization ability**

Therefore, I recommend at this stage to repeat to the child that the breakup is not from him – he will always remain both parents' child – and explain in detail how the family will function from now on. In addition, I advise explaining to the child the current state of affairs without using concepts of time that project to the future; for example, it is better to just say: "Now father lives in another home while we stay here".

Ages 6 to 9

The egocentric thinking style continues also in this age range. As a result, the child might develop guilt feelings also at this stage and blame himself for his parents' divorce. However, at this stage there is a broader perception of the family unit. The child is able to listen to the different parental viewpoints, but in many cases will experience a conflict of loyalty and struggle to contain the contradictions.

The drawing presented here was made by a 6½ year-old child, two months after his parents' formal divorce. Unlike his previous work, it is possible to see here disorder in the drawing of the figures and the space between them.

At this stage, the act of drawing is preceded by planning the figures' positions. The child figure's (second from left) proximity to the other figures symbolizes, among other things, his emotional closeness to these figures.

Figure 6-17: Disorderly and inadequately spaced figures

Children at this age are characterized, more than in other ages, by a tendency to please. In light of the new situation and the emotional difficulty that accompanies it some children develop a strong willingness to please by not expressing their feelings beyond a certain level.

As in the following drawing by an 8 year-old girl, you will witness in their drawings a tendency for a structured and precise drawing style characterized by dense, clean and accurate work that communicates her need to please her environment. You should pay attention to this tendency in children's drawings, because in most cases it reflects the child's reluctance to reveal his inner emotions and fears of the upcoming separation. The child prefers to wear a mask and present a positive, unrealistic attitude to his immediate social environment.

Figure 6-18:   Well-structured and carefully rendered drawing characterized by density and precision

Ages 9 to 12

At this stage most children are able to understand the emotional significance of the divorce. They are able to appreciate the complexity of emotional conflicts but will still try to mediate between the parents in the hope that the relationship between them will return to its previous state.

Age 12 and up

The level of autonomy from the adult world has increased by now and as a result, the parental approach to explaining the divorce must also change. The social support system (peer group) is now a central part of the adolescents' life and represents a viable alternative to the family unit.

The following drawing is an exceptional example which does not characterize drawings by 16 year-olds or adolescents in general. The accurate and esthetic drawing style, as well as his checking during the act of drawing to make sure the result is satisfactory, communicates his need for social support.

This drawing is not typical of adolescence because at this age, separation from adults increases, and the content that appears in the drawings is usually defiant and rebellious. In this case, the youngster seeks to draw an accurate and perfect view of the world; he is very dependent on his parents and his family and barely goes out to meet friends. Just as he draws without erasures and errors, so also in the dialogue with him, he seeks to paint a perfect picture of reality and takes care not to expose his anger toward his parents and their decisions.

Figure 6-19: Precise and esthetic drawing communicating a need for social support

Guiding your child

Good conceptualization is one that maintains equilibrium between explaining the situation in general and providing a more personal explanation. Your child's drawings enable you to know whether he needs general or more personal guidance. This can be learned by the age-appropriateness of your child's drawing level. If the drawing is below the drawing level expected of him, i.e. regressive, you should tailor your explanation level accordingly.

When the drawing level is relatively advanced, it may be possible to use more cognitively oriented explanations at first, although that you have to examine whether the high drawing level actually compensates for fear of direct dialogue about the child's emotional state.

In any case, it is also worthwhile to pay attention to the drawings' content, as they can shed light on the issues that concerns him and what he needs to receive from the adults around him: If he is busy with drawing real-life figures, you have to check whether he tries to reorganize the "family puzzle" through the drawings. Alternatively, he may hint through his choices at benign figures that provide him support in real life. If he is preoccupied with fantastic drawings, then concrete talk that explains the reality of divorce may be unsuitable just yet because at this stage he still needs to escape reality.

When exhausting this stage, he will be better prepared to attend to the new situation and accept reality.

Summary

The time that passes from the moment the parents decide to break up until the actual divorce is experienced very differently by different families. Moreover, within the same family, different family members take a different time to accept the reality of divorce. Using children's drawings you may arrive at a more informed understanding of how the divorce process is managed and coped with by each family member. Given this understanding, you can move on to cope with the issue more effectively.

The coping stages are typical of most families and should not be viewed rigidly or judgmentally. Through the drawings of the children and even adults, it is possible to identify whether all family members are in the same stage of the coping process or whether some members are in a different stage and therefore need a different kind of support.

Drawings also provide an indication of trends like regression (drawing level lower than expected by age), acting out (in drawing style and coloring), omission of certain body parts which symbolize difficulties in expressing feelings and coping with the crisis, and finally, drawing elements in a idiosyncratic way which symbolizes the subjective way the child sees reality and the solutions that are suitable for him.

When drawings become more schematic, it is possible to use them to identify wishes such as having a united family. You have to treat these drawings with understanding and not feel compelled to change them to suit reality.

It is nevertheless recommended to check whether these wishes reflect any misunderstanding by the child with regard to the current state of affairs, rather than just natural wishful thinking. In these cases, it is important to continue explaining to the child that the separation decision is final, and that although he may wish his parents to reunite, they don't intend to do so. According to the child's age, the parent has to explain the new situation to his child and all its practical implications.

Although some studies have expressed doubts regarding the potential for successful coping with divorce, I definitely believe that high awareness and professional tools can help the divorcing parents understand their children's needs and how to best fulfill them.

Drawings enable children to share their emotions in everyday life, and particularly in times of crisis. They provide children with a unique expressive ability that is often more powerful and revealing than words. Moreover, the act of drawing is in itself therapeutic, as it enables the child to vent his difficulties.

Analyzing children's drawings during the entire process is likely to help you better understand how your child experiences divorce – how he grows and develops in conjunction with the process, when he needs support and when he can manage by himself, when he needs concrete explanations, when he would rather escape to an imaginary world and mainly, what may be the solutions and conceptualizations optimally suited for your child.

7 TRANSITIONS AND TRANSFORMATIONS

Separations, transitions and transformations are an integral part of life. They begin with the parting from the mother's womb at birth and continue in age-appropriate transitions – to a new kindergarten, to school, to college, and so on. Separations are an important form of transition to a new and different reality, whether due to loss, such as death (whether in ripe old age or in tragic circumstances), or due to frequent and normative circumstances such as parting with one's diapers, pacifier, familiar toys, and of course one's parents as they go to work every morning – a separation experienced as a real loss by many children.

Factors Affecting Children's Coping with Separation

The child's temperament

A key factor affecting children's ability to cope with separation is their temperament. Using drawings, you can clearly distinguish between a peaceful temperament, as indicated in the following drawing by calm movement on the page, well-ordered and organized elements, and a more stormy temperament, as seen in the drawing below it with its tempestuous movement, disorder and unregulated pressure on the drawing tool.

Figure 7-1: An organized and peaceful drawing with regulated pressure on the drawing tool

Figure 7-2: A disorganized drawing with tempestuous movement and unregulated pressure

Of course these are only some of the indicators involved in diagnosing a child's temperament through his drawings. A peaceful child will adjust to transformations in a slower, more balanced way, while a tempestuous child will adjust quickly, but sometimes in an imbalanced way, so that you will witness rapid, superficial adaptation followed by regression.

Quality of relationship with the parents

A second factor directly related to coping with separation is the quality of children's relationship with their parents. Family drawings can be used to assess the perceived family dynamics. They can be used to distinguish between a subjective sense of security – for example, when the parent figures are close to the child or drawn in similar patterns as in figure 7-3 – as opposed to the sense of insecurity indicated by the distant and dissimilar figures in the second drawing.

Figure 7-3:   **Family members drawn in a similar pattern and close to one another**

Figure 7-4:   Distant family members drawn differently

In both cases, drawings can tell us how the child who made them experiences his world. They do not necessarily indicate, for example, that his parents are really distant. It may be that something in the nonverbal dialog between the child and his parents made him experience lack of understanding and confusion.

The child's independence level

A third key factor in coping with separation is the child's personal attitude. Using children's drawings you can distinguish between an autonomous attitude, as in the original and uniquely designed drawing in figure 7-5, and a more dependent attitude, as in the uninspired and over-structured drawing that follows it.

Figure 7-5:   Original and unique design

Figure 7-6:   Uninspired and over-structured design

Obviously, other factors also have to be taken into account, such as the history of the child's reactions to previous separations, the extent of support and explanations provided by his significant others. These other factors are significant, but cannot be inferred directly from the child's own drawings, as they are more related to his social environment.

6 Types of Children who Experience Difficulty with Separation

1. *Children who fear unfamiliar situations and need certainty and control* require advance preparation, and seek to control events in any transition. In many cases, their temperament will be rigid and inflexible, and their drawings likewise rigid, over-structured and precise, as in Figure 7-6.

2. *Children who experience their family as insecure* are afraid to move away from their parents because they do not wish to give up their "guardian" role. This is evident after the birth of a new sibling or when the parents go through divorce, and reflected in their drawings, particularly family drawings.

Figure 7-7: **Aggressive erasure of family members indicating insecure family structure**

3. *Children who find it difficult to emotionally understand reality* experience separation as unexpected, sharp, startling and even threatening. Their drawings will be regressive, or alternatively unstructured.

Figure 7-8: **Unstructured drawing indicating difficulty with emotional understanding**

4. *Children who experience a period of distress and anxieties* naturally face more difficulties when separating. Their drawing level will be typical of earlier ages and include specific graphic indicators of distress.

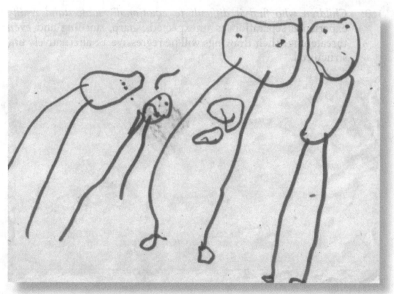

Figure 7-9: Regressive drawing level, organ omission and unstable line quality indicating anxieties

5. *Dependent children who fear to cope alone* will experience separation as threatening since it requires coping with the unknown. They may be truly unable to cope, perhaps even due to physiological difficulties. Having rejected such factors, their drawings may indicate weak coping ability.

Figure 7-10:   Regressive drawing (age 10) with unstable line quality, indicating dependency

6. *Children who experience the present social reality as benign and se-cure* will sometimes view any transition as an unnecessary move away from a familiar reality. In most cases, they will find the strength to cope, but often their longings will make their adjustment difficult and complex.

In one form or another, these characteristics will play a role in any separation, transition or transformation. Analyzing their drawings will be primarily designed to assess their readiness for transition, and if they are already experiencing it, find the best tools to help them cope.

Bedwetting

One of the first transitions children face involves diaper weaning. About half of the two-year olds still wet their pants or bedding occasionally, but by age five only 15% do, mainly at night. Most such cases involve primary bedwetting where the child has not yet completed toilet training. The remaining cases involve secondary bedwetting, that is, children who've completed their diaper weaning but revert to bedwetting under stress.

Bedwetting is considered a problem only after age five. At these ages, I recommend that you first eliminate all possible medical explanations before turning to drawing analysis to understand the emotional background.

Emotional maturity

The primary objective of drawing analysis in cases of diaper weaning is to determine whether the child is emotionally mature enough to complete the process. When the child's drawings are clearly below the age-appropriate level, as in the next example, this means he may be unprepared to part with the diapers and negotiate his independence. It is also possible that his regressive drawings indicate fear of growing up. Thus, his drawings remain "small" and through them, he too seeks to remain small rather than be weaned of the parental attention involved in using diapers.

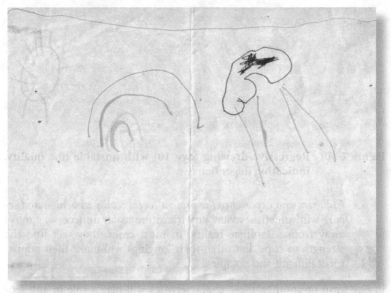

Figure 7-11:   A bedwetting 6 year-old drawing below his age level

On the other hand, drawings that are too "big" – over-precise and rigid – may also indicate difficulty with the weaning process. In the case of the child who made the next drawing, just as he is afraid to err in his drawing, he is also afraid to wet his bed again. Thus, despite the physical prepared-ness, fear of failure delays weaning.

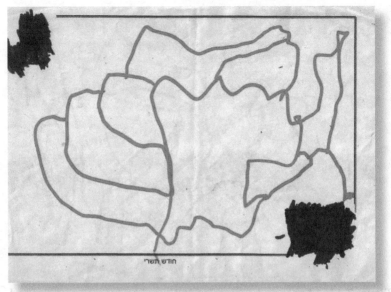

חודש ששי

Figure 7-12:   Over-precise and rigid drawing for a three year-old

Power struggles in the family

Another factor liable to delay weaning is related to power struggles. When the parent becomes used to sending the child to the toilet repeatedly, this could achieve the opposite result.

The child will start thinking that it is the parent who actually controls his evacuation and consequently seek to regain control by refusing to evacuate when asked to. In some of these cases, the children's drawings will communicate anger and aggression by intense pressure on the drawing tool and sharp, angular movements.

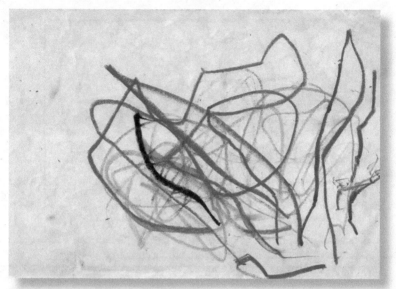

Figure 7-13:   Anger and aggression indicated by intense pressure and angular movements

The girl who made the following two drawings was raised until age 2½ at home without a nanny. At that age, her pregnant mother enrolled her in a private kindergarten. The girl started drawing around the age of 18 months, and by the time she was 2½, she started drawing relatively advanced figures as seen in figure 7-14.

Figure 7-14: Advanced drawing for a 2½, year-old

By the time when her little sister was born, a month after entering kinder-garten, this girl's drawings regressed significantly, as in the following exam-ple. Her infantile scribbles communicated considerable stress, as indicated by the angular lines, intense pressure and the multiple paint layers.

Figure 7-15:   Regression in drawing level due to difficulty upon entering kindergarten

This toddler's emotional overload following the major transitions in her life was also evident in her daily behavior: having stopped wetting her pants completely during the day, she reverted to a pattern of wetting several times a day.

After several months in which she found it difficult not to wet herself during the day, the girl's mother made the unusual decision of taking her out of the kindergarten and having her stay at home with her nanny. Personally, I would not necessarily recommend such a drastic step for all children. But I do believe that for any solution to be truly effective on the long run, it should take both the child's interests and the parent's educational approach into account. In this case, the mother was absolutely convinced that this was what she had to do.

The change in the girl's drawings was evident on the very same day she left kindergarten. As seen in figure 7-16, her drawings became figurative again, with an evident ability to organize space. Nevertheless, you can still notice some disquiet indicated mainly by the intense pressure on the drawing tool – to the point of tearing the page in certain places. Apparently, leaving kindergarten was not a magic solution and the girl continued to wet herself occasionally. Nevertheless, her overall functioning improved and she definitely wet herself less often during the day.

Figure 7-16: Improved drawing quality upon leaving kindergarten

Constipation

The parents of the five year-old who made the following two drawings sought to analyze his drawings to determine why their son used to ask them to diaper him so that he could defecate. When they would not respond, he would develop constipation and make matters even more difficult. Most children with constipation do not have any physiological problem. Indeed, in this boy's drawings you can see how the boundaries of the drawn figure are thin and fragile.

Figures 7-17a, b: Fragile figure boundaries typical of constipated children

Accordingly, my objective was to see how I could help this five year-old fortify his perceived body boundaries. I assumed that his insistence on being diapered was related to a wish for a kind of enveloping boundary for his body.

Next, I instructed his parents to allow him complete control over his body. The results were not long in coming: their son agreed to evacuate in the bathroom and his drawings also changed from poorly detailed and fragile to rich and complete.

Figure 7-18: Rich and complete drawing following parental guidance

We all wish for our children to grow up to be independent and confident adults. Therefore we must support them in certain stages in their lives and help them face unfamiliar realities. Denying the experience of transition is no solution, but it can help the child when he experiences too many transformations at the same time. The transition itself must be negotiated sooner or later, but only when the child is emotionally prepared for it.

Moving to a New Kindergarten

The move to a new kindergarten is part of every child's life. As in other transitions, it involves coping with the unknown. Children who find it difficult are often called upon to behave more maturely, but this requirement is not always in line with every child's emotional development.

Is the child ready for the move?

Drawing analysis can help parents assess their child's readiness for the move, how to cope with it and whether it is absolutely necessary.

The mother of five year-old twins considered placing them in two separate kindergartens. Until then, they used to be together most of the time, in the same room and in the same daycare facility. When she contacted me for counseling, the twins were about to move to kindergarten and it was recommended to her that they be separated. One of the twins expressed concern and asked whether there would be a joint fence or wall he would be able to cross in order to visit his sister. The mother therefore asked me to analyze their drawings in order to come up with ideas on how to smoothen the planned separation.

Some phenomena that would require special attention in the case of singletons may be considered normative amongst twins. Accordingly, analyzing the drawings of twins undergoing major transitions is somewhat more complex.

Figures 7-19, 20:
An independent girl (left) and her dependent twin brother (right)

As clearly seen above, at the time I analyzed these and other drawings by the twins, the girl drew in a much higher level. This artistic gap was directly related to issues of dependence vs. independence: the twin brother clearly required more adult attention and reinforcement than his sister. This was indicated by his poorly detailed drawings compared to his sister's, which were filled with colored shapes and other rich elements. Emotionally, while it was important to emphasize his separateness from his sister, it was also important to stress his continued relationship with her after the separation.

I therefore recommended to their parents to prepare two timetables at home, where the twins' parallel schedules could be clearly evident: the brother would be able to see that while he is busy with some activity in his kindergarten, his sister is not "gone", but rather busy doing something else. I also recommended that the twins discuss their experiences at kindergarten at the end of each day. Finally, I recommended that the twin brother keep a transition object that would remind him of his sister, such as a small souvenir or a drawing she had made especially for him.

The brother's drawings also indicated that any separation left a mark for a long time. I therefore recommended to the parents to check whether it would be easier for him when each parent took each twin to kindergarten separately, or when they went together, first to hers and then to his, so that he would know when he had "left his sister" last and not feel as though she had disappeared.

Separation was of course difficult for the sister as well. However, she could express it better in words or various emotional gestures. Her brother, on the other hand, tended to seek her closeness instead, and compare what each twin was doing at any given moment.

To conclude, moving to a new kindergarten is emotionally demanding, as it requires coping with a new reality. In the case of the twins discussed above, the transition was complicated by the fact that the brother was emotionally unprepared because he saw himself as inseparable from his sister.

Adoption

In cases of adoption, parents who contact me for drawing analysis are motivated by much more than the concerns typical of biological parents. Adopting parents are often moved by a sincere desire to get to know their child. The fact that the child was begotten by another often makes them dread the future: Who is my child? What should I beware of? What are his difficulties? What are his talents? Biological parents believe they have readymade answers to all those questions based on genetics. Adopting parents, on the other hand, feel in the dark, and want drawing analysis to provide them with a "manual" for coping with any difficulties their adopted child may have experienced earlier in life.

My approach to drawing analysis in this case is basically identical to the case of biological parents, although it does include particular reference to various distresses related to the adoption process and the transition crisis it involves. I believe adoptive parents who have been raising their children for several years discover every day how insignificant genetics actually is, and find real similarities between them and their adopted child. Thus, I want to help the parents connect to their adopted child not out of dread for the future, but rather view adoption as a transition that is part of his life.

The adopted child faces three integration tasks. My experience has taught me that these are usually expressed in drawings only when the adoption has occurred after the age of two or even three, that is, by the time the child has already realized who his parents are.

The "good" and "bad" mothers

The first task is *integrating the "good" and "bad" mothers.* The adopted child faces four psychological mother figures. He faces his biological mother who is good because she has given him life, but bad because she has abandoned him. He also faces an adoptive mother who is good because she has adopted him, but bad because she has not given him life and perhaps (in his fantasy) bought, stole or kidnapped him from the biological mother.

These splits are reflected in the child's self-image which is split between the image of the special child selected out of all other children and the image of the child rejected and abandoned in infancy. Such a child's drawings will be characterized by extreme trends and drastic alternations between them. For example, you will see large elements communicating confidence and presence right next to small and instable elements indicating abandonment.

Figure 7-21: **Extreme, contradictory trends in a drawing by an adopted child**

Second abandonment

On the one hand, the child seeks a golden path to contain both mothers within himself; on the other, he must abandon his biological mother and become convinced she would not come back for him one of those days. This second abandonment means that together with having been abandoned by his biological mother, the child also experiences abandonment of parts of his personality, as if he is required to distance himself from himself, from his very biology, from his body. We will see evidence of such inner struggles in family drawings, where the biological mother will sometime appear next to the adoptive family members. In other cases, as in the drawing shown here, the biological mother (the green figure) will be separated from the plane of the living where the child's figure is drawn. In other cases, the adopted child will adamantly refuse to draw her or, alternatively, attempt to draw her and himself as one.

Figure 7-22: An adopted child's biological mother as an abandoning
mother on a different plane

The artificial, forbidden and adopted self

The third task, or adopted self, is a product of the two previous tasks, following which the adopted child forms a different self. Before completing this task, the adopted child may have either an artificial self or a forbidden self.

The artificial self seeks to please others by being totally attuned to their expectations. He feels grateful that the adopting parents have agreed to adopt him despite his (perceived) defective biology, which caused his biological parents to abandon him. The drawing in figure 2-23 was made by such a child.

Figure 7-23: Drawing style characteristic of the artificial self

On the one hand, this drawing is precise and well-structured: the trees are flawless, and the coloring fills them perfectly. On the other hand, the dear price paid by the adopted child for her artificial self is also clearly evident: the trees are floating in the air, groundless. The child who made this drawing also feels this way. She is totally preoccupied with pleasing her social environment, obsessed by the fear that her biology (roots) might be "exposed" so that she would be abandoned again. As you can see in the drawing, this fear has actually materialized because the trees have been uprooted.

The forbidden or angry self is unwilling to deny his biological parents and views his adopting parents as an obstacle, preventing him from contacting his biological father and mother. The forbidden self becomes more evident when adopted children enter adolescence, and is reflected by direct and indirect anger. Indirect, or unspoken anger, is the inner reflection of the adoptive parents' anger at the biological parents for having abandoned such a child, or the biological parents' anger for having been forced to give him away. Direct anger is that of the adopted child himself, who is angry at his fate. Such children's drawings and handwriting samples will clearly indicate their anger and frustration. In many cases, the children will even refuse to draw at all – particularly family drawings.

The parents of the seven year-old who made the following drawing consulted me in order to better understand how he perceives his status in the family, having been adopted at age six. This relatively belated adoption involved various emotional issues which affected his overall functioning, and his parents sought additional tools to help him through the transition.

During the diagnostic process I analyzed over thirty drawings made by the recently adopted child over the previous several months and also examined his handwriting. House drawings are particularly revealing when it comes to adoption. As discussed in the online course, the way the house is drawn represents the way the child perceives himself and his nuclear family, his ambitions, realization of potential and need for territory and personal space.

Figure 2-24 conveys a highly insecure impression: the house is literally floating in the air, despite the fact that such a style is not age-appropriate; in addition, it leans on huge crutches make it seem highly unstable. Even when this child draws the ground, he does so in a style that communicates emotional disquiet and turbulence, in line with the angry or forbidden self as discussed above.

Figure 7-24: A floating house communicating instability and emotional turbulence

The house door symbolizes access to the individual's inner being and the choices he makes regarding emotional expression; the windows stand for the degree of exposure characteristic of his personality; while the outer walls serve as protection against external threats.

When looking at the drawing in figure 7-24, you get the feeling that this child's inner world is inaccessible. The door is locked and barred, and it is unclear what can be seen through the windows, if anything. I would like to refer in detail to the issue of barred windows and doors, because this has to do with one of the popular myths about children's drawings. In some cases, bars attest to the child's withdrawn and reclusive attitude. On the other hand, line quality, the amount of bars drawn and color selection all have a particularly significant role to play, because in many cases, locks and bars indicate the child's well-developed ability to observe his real-life environment in detail. In such cases, the child is actually rational and involved in his outer environment, spending considerable energy on documenting his actual reality, rather than drawing it based on his own perceptual world.

Finally, I would like to refer to the roof of the house, which is drawn in a shaky line compared to the rest of the drawing (particularly on the right side), lending further support to the conclusions based on the other parts of this house drawing.

This child's other drawings indicated further issues which reinforced the sense of uncertainty reported by his adoptive parents. They suggested significant separation anxiety, frequent use of lies and deceit, and a strong sense of confusion. Nevertheless, when comparing drawings made sooner after the adoption and drawings made a year later, I could see significant improvement. The more recent drawings showed the adoptive parents and it was clear that the adopted child was becoming more receptive to the intimacy and warmth they offered. My first recommendation to the parents was to acknowledge their child's sensitive condition at the specific point in time when his drawings had been analyzed. After about three months, when working on a family album, the child told them for the first time a significant detail about his past they had not known about, and through this revelation, so they told me, they felt they were getting closer to him.

Adoption is a complex and painful process for children. Their social environment often tries to ignore this, quick to create the alternative illusion that despite having been abandoned, they were adopted by a new family and have no need to think of the past ever again. In practice, the adopted child is ever torn between the two worlds and required to face various integration challenges. As loving and dedicated as his adoptive parents may be, he still struggles with difficult feelings of abandonment and fantasies about his future. The objective of drawing interpretation in such cases is to help the adopting parents face the challenges of adoption so as to be able to properly contain their child's emotions.

Moving to a New House

All over the world, children asked to draw a house draw a square with a triangular roof. This was first discovered by Rhoda Kellogg (1969), who studied more than a million drawings by children from thirty countries where people actually live in all kinds of houses. Although different children emphasize different parts of the house and draw them in different proportions, in most cases they follow the global pattern.

Home is a place of stability and confidence. Leaving home and moving to a new house is a significant transition for every child. This could be a planned move by the whole family, the establishment of two homes by divorced parents, or the sudden loss of home due to less normative circumstances such as violence or severe neglect. This section will focus on relocations under normative circumstances.

If the move is voluntary, it usually signifies a new beginning for the parents, a chance to improve their life. However, the child usually finds out about the move after the decision has been made. For him, the present situation is familiar and convenient, while the new situation may be perceived as strange and threatening. The child's present home represents familiar relationships with friends, neighbors and family members. It is where the child belongs, where he knows exactly how to get to wherever he wants.

Children who have difficulty moving will be those with a greater need for certainty and control, and their drawings will therefore be more precise and better structured compared to their peers'. Just as they require preparation and organization in reality, their drawings will also be well-organized and precise down to the smallest detail.

The drawing in figure 7-27 was made during a period of redecoration and moving. Since the child who made it was involved in the move and has been expecting it, you can see that it refers to several houses simultaneously.

Figure 7-27: Drawing several houses while moving to a new home

Examples for involuntary relocation the parents are opposed to include forced eviction for political reasons (such as evacuation of settlements following peace treaties), for national economic reasons (such as relocation of Chinese peasants due to massive public works projects), due to rent arrears or following a natural disaster. In these cases, the children often witness and identify with their parents' resistance to leaving the house. This resistance may be seen in their drawings in several ways, as detailed below.

Emphasized land line

In the example shown below, a 6½ year-old boy emphasizes the ground line. He spends considerable energy on coloring the ground and the edges of the house are planted within it, so that it seems as though the earth "overflows" and latches onto the house. The roof of the house is also "grounded" in the sky, contributing to the overall impression as though moving the house would be impossible – the elements would simply not allow it.

Figure 7-28:   Emphasized land line symbolizing the desire to avoid re-location

Reinforcing the house from outside

Another way of reinforcing the house is exemplified in the following drawing by a six year-old, who adds ladder-like supports to the house walls so as to thicken them.

Figure 7-29:   Reinforcing the house from outside

Omitting doors and windows

The seven year-old who made the next drawing found another way to protect his home. He avoids drawing any windows and doors, thereby barring entrance completely. In addition, the house is further protected by a fence, drawn in a strong and confident line, totally denying access.

Figure 7-30: Omitting doors and windows and adding a fence as protective measures

Drawing a double door

In the following drawing by a 5½ year-old, animals are drawn next to the house, and in the house itself (whose external walls have been drawn by the kindergarten teacher), two doors are drawn in different colors, with a large lock and fence-like horizontal lines.

Figure 7-31: A double door protecting the house

Disoriented house drawing

The seven year-old whose drawing is shown next also used the large fence motif and painstakingly drew symmetric squares within it. Interestingly, she also avoided drawing the house walls and drew the house as though it were a collection of separate items (window, roof, and door) without any connecting lines.

Figure 7-32:   Parts of the house drawn as separate elements

Decorating and emphasizing the door

In this drawing by a 6½ year-old, the same fence appears, but it does not block the access to the house. On the other hand, the door – which symbolizes entry into her individual and family life – has been painstakingly decorated. This child seems to be preoccupied with the issue of leaving home, and therefore has been focusing considerable energy on this part of the house.

Figure 7-33:   Decorating and emphasizing the door, indicating the desire to avoid relocation

Floating house

Another element which recurred in several of the drawings I collected is exemplified in the next drawing by a 5½ year-old girl. Although it does include a land line, the house is not positioned directly on it, but rather floats in the air, symbolizing her sense of being uprooted. The disjointed line, uncharacteristic of other drawings by the same child, communicates her intense anxiety.

Figure 7-34:   A floating house symbolizing a sense of groundlessness

Unsuccessful transition

In some cases, children's fears about the upcoming moving appear to have been realized and they consider their new home as an unsafe and unpleasant place. The following drawing made by a 7 year-old girl was made prior to moving. Note how rich and detailed this drawing is, and how the house is surrounded with blooming plants.

Figure 7-35: Prior to the move: a richly detailed and optimistic drawing

Five years after the move, I revisited this girl and she made another talented house drawing for me. It appeared that she did not work through this significant transition in a way that benefited her emotionally: the second drawing was characterized by various regressions in drawing level and omissions of key elements.

Figure 7-36:   Five years after the move: few details and an isolated atmosphere

This seven year-old's artistic choice tells us something about her sense of isolation. Just as the house stands alone in the middle of a huge desert, without any inviting doors or windows, the artist also experiences isolation and alienation which prevent her from truly expressing her emotions, her frustration.

Moving Overseas

Many countries have been blessed with immigrants arriving from all corners of the globe. Immigrating with the children requires more preparation for the move and usually involves coping with complex emotional issues following the transition.

Immigration is characterized by several stages of adjustment. The first is characterized by a sense of euphoria, accompanied by feelings of freedom and independence. This stage typically lasts several days or weeks.

In the second stage, the immigrant begins to acknowledge difficulties and frustrations. He may begin to feel dissatisfied, depressed, or alienated. Consequently, he is liable to withdraw to his country of origin for "emotional refueling", reminiscing on his beloved home(land), keeping close touch with family members left behind, and mainly idealizing the country of origin at the expense of the new country. This stage may continue several months and even years. In children's drawings made during this stage, you will notice trends such as clinging to a certain recurring style or theme, familiar landscapes from the country of origin, withdrawal and refusal do draw.

The third stage is re-involvement. Gradually, the immigrant begins to think positively about his new country, and adjusts to its physical and social environment. He comes to terms with having left his country of origin, and at the same time begins to form social contacts and to feel proud of his successful adjustment.

The drawing in figure 7-37, by a 6 year-old, exemplifies that stage. The girl has drawn her family and communicated an overall positive atmosphere: all figures are smiling and reaching out their hands. Interestingly however, she is the only one drawn with palms. In children's drawings, palms symbolize the ability to communicate with the social environment. Indeed, when I asked her parents whether she has adjusted to her environment better than they had, they confirmed my suspicions.

When this girl drew her family, she was well aware of those differences and even drew considerable strengths from them. She was aware of her skills as a translator for her parents, and therefore felt she was adjusting well. Accordingly, her drawing indicates that she is a strong, sociable girl, who has managed to take advantage of her talents to better adjust to living in the new country.

Figure 7-37:   The immigrant's social adjustment stage

Difficulties during the transition

Moving to a different country is always complex. For immigrants, the move follows a once-in-a-lifetime decision to start a new life elsewhere. In other cases, however, families move only temporarily. The children relocate together with their parents as part of their professional career, and are aware of the temporary nature of this relocation. The temporary nature of this transition does not always mean children adjust to it easily. Adjustment difficulties may be particularly severe among children whose parents move every few years – such as diplomats.

Relocating to a different country is more complex than relocating in the same country, since it involves enormous physical distance from friends and family, and often also the need to learn a new language. Withdrawn children who need certainty and control, younger children and children with learning disabilities will all have a particularly hard time in the new country.

The drawing in figure 7-38 was made by a 5½ year-old in the first days after moving to a different country. His parents reported a difficult and emotionally complex transition, and it does appear that this child uses angular coloring with intense pressure on the page. The resulting image is harsh and dense, symbolizing this boy's anger at his parents for having relocated.

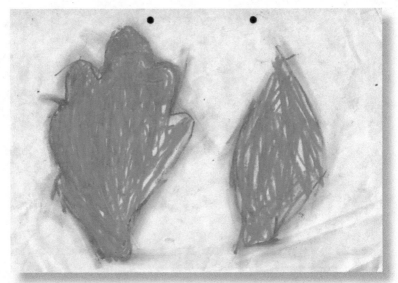

Figure 7-38:   Drawing style indicating difficulty and anger

Several months later, the same child drew the drawing seen in figure 7-39. His rebelliousness seemed to have subsided somewhat, but the trees still seem uprooted, crooked and unstable, giving the impression of instability and alienation. Nevertheless, the tree trunks have sprouted new branches, perhaps symbolic of an emerging sense of belonging to the new environment.

Figure 7-39:   Trees without a specified environment

Half a year into the transition, the drawings have changed. As seen in figure 7-40, the trees are now planted in the ground and have been joined by animals and visitors. The drawing is still rigid and angular, indicating emotional stress and disquiet, but we do see a group of trees connected by the various creatures – making the picture seem lively: no longer an isolated, groundless tree, but a tree which is an integral part of its environment.

Later on, as seen in the drawing to the right, the child drew more balanced graphic trends and better developed environmental elements. Like his drawings, this child slowly adjusted to his environment, acquired the new language and made new friends.

Figures 7-40: Trees as an integral part of the environment
Figures 7-41: Balanced graphic trends

Transitions in Adolescence

Like other transitions, the process of maturation and the passage of time involve coping with transformations. Although adolescence is a natural and normative transition, the fact that it is forced upon us and the inability to doubt its necessity (as when relocating, for example), often triggers a bona fide mental crisis.

Since adolescence usually involves puberty, you often witness significant changes in drawings and handwritings from year to year, and sometimes even from month to month. The objective of interpreting drawings in this case is to better understand how the adolescent experiences the multiple transformations involved in this period, and of course how to best help him in a time of crisis.

Before viewing some examples, it is important to realize the magnitude of the tasks facing the adolescent. The adolescent asks himself who he is and what he wants to be. This self-search is unsettling and disconcerting. Adolescents are busy looking for answers and at the same time processing huge amounts of information provided by their peer group. In the process, they formulate a worldview that provides a frame of reference to judge events and at the same time face the age-appropriate challenges of sexual development.

In what follows I use tree drawings made by an adolescent at ages 15–18. In the context of adolescence, tree drawings offer a unique model for assessing coping with transitions because of the charged emotional meaning of uprooting them. Indeed, in the first drawing, the tree is clearly out of balance, leaning to one direction to the point that some of its roots stick out of the ground.

Figure 7-42: **Imbalance in a tree reflecting an adolescent's emotional state**

This imbalance may be seen as representative of the unsettling nature of the complex self-search involved in adolescence. Just like the tree, the 15 year-old also feels shaken and out of balance.

Moreover, the tree is exfoliated and it branches seem like a thicket of thorns. This style is also characteristic of many adolescents' tendency to withdraw into themselves, making the adults around them feel as though they are hidden in an impenetrable thicket.

A year later, the tree became more balanced. It still communicates social withdrawal with the branches seeming to enclose the leaves within them. However, the 16 year-old who drew it was perhaps more self-forgiving, as he allowed his tree to grow leaves, despite his enduring need for an enclosed, private space.

Figure 7-43: A more balanced tree which still communicates withdrawal

In the third drawing, at age 17, the tree turns its thorny leaves outwards. Although it no longer has a frame, it is still difficult to approach this tree. Its bark is thick and multilayered, standing for the adolescent's need to avoid exposure by covering the tender trunk in an armor of sorts.

Figure 7-44:   A thick bark representing the desire to avoid exposure

The fourth drawing reverts to the initial trend of elaborate, leafless branches. This time, however, the branches seem more flexible and for the first
time you see a human figure next to the tree. The person resting on the
trunk communicates emotional attachment, suggesting that the tree is now
approachable, and that it has something to offer – on the whole, a significantly positive addition to the drawing.

Figure 7-45: Human figure added to the tree drawing, indicating openness

As you can see, the transformations typically experienced by adolescents are many and varied. The trends apparent in their drawings change very quickly with time. Tree drawings, in particular, offer an interesting opportunity to observe the transitions they undergo, mainly because trees may be rooted or uprooted, as well as bear fruits (objectives) and grow leaves (contact with one's social environment).

Five Keys for Making Changes and Transitions Easier for Kids

The objective of interpreting drawings is to identify the difficulty the child may be experiencing and the abilities and talents at his disposal that can help her cope. The drawings make it possible to identify the precise difficulty in the transition: language, need for control, contradictory messages from the environment, etc. Pinpointing the difficulty will enable you to formulate a better-focused and more effective action plan:

1. **Draw the transition with the child:** See how the two of you can be the transition "commanders".

2. **Minimize unnecessary transitions:** If the child is experiencing additional emotional transition such as the birth of a sibling or a divorce, this may not be the right time for any further changes.

3. **Look for signs** related to anxiety and emotional distress. If you identify such signs in the child's drawings, she may not be ready for change, but rather in need of emotional support for her anxiety.

4. **Talk about your character and the kid's:** The child's temperament and our own has a tremendous effect on how we cope with transitions. If we know that the child needs advance preparation and a slow transition, we can talk to him about it and thus "make friends" with his needs.

5. **Draw past, present and future:** Drawings can be therapeutic when the past and future are drawn side by side. At a more advanced stage, you can also draw a path or a bridge between the two periods, and talk to the child about the connection between them.

8 SOCIAL FUNCTIONING

The issue of children's social functioning preoccupies many parents. Social abilities and skills are some of the most common subjects assessed through drawings. Perhaps one of the reasons for that is because drawings enable parents to understand what their child is actually experiencing behind the kindergarten or school gate, just after they go to work and for hours thereafter. Assessing social skills is critical because most early childhood experiences – including learning experiences – are social experiences based on peer group contacts. In those contacts, the child learns about himself and his environment more than in any social contact with adults or books.

Cultural differences aside, it is obvious that parents throughout the world are busy asking themselves the same questions (albeit with varying intensity): Who are my boy's friends? Why is my daughter unpopular? Why does my boy hang out with the class bully? And above all – What is the relationship between social status, academic success and self-image?

The objective of interpreting children's drawings in this context is to complete the puzzle of the child's inner world, starting from the assumption that social conduct is intimately related to the child's overall subjective experience. According to Adler (Dreikurs 2000), for example, social conduct is the starting point of our entire personality structure. According to Adler, human beings are social creatures seeking to belong – when we experience a sense of belonging to society, we structure our entire personality and belief system around it. Thus, diagnosing children's drawings can help us understand how they experience their social environment and thereby understand how it affects his beliefs, perceptions and personality.

Popularity

Many people approach me for consulting after finding out that their child is not as socially popular as they thought. They may find their child charming, cute and smart, but kindergarten reality is slightly different. The child's peers have failed to be impressed with his qualities. One day, this wonderful, talented child comes home with a sad face and a voice choking on tears, saying: "They told me I'm stupid... and that they don't wanna play with me… they keep bullying me, and-and… I have no friends!" The parent stares at him, trying to take in the bad news, feeling the pain of rejection together with his child. Often this pain is familiar to the parent from his own childhood, and he now re-experiences it. So he thinks along the lines of: "I have to teach him how to manage… I won't have them tell him things like that! Who are they anyway? How can I turn him into the most popular kid in the 'hood?"

Social popularity and belonging are significant in every child's life. Children naturally want to belong to society, contribute to it and express themselves uniquely. There are many ways of doing so, and every child tries several paths, some more successful than others. The social contacts the child forms with his peers, as well as his family members, contribute considerably to his personal development, and in the future shape his conduct as an adult member of society (Shapiro 1998).

Naturally, it is important for parents to help their child make his first steps outside the family greenhouse. How can this be accomplished? For some parents, popularity means the ability to stand out. They will encourage their child to demonstrate their skills at any opportunity. Such children's drawings will often reflect this parental tendency, such that they will continue emphasizing their skills, as though these constitute their entire personality rather than just one aspect of it, even at the cost of detracting from their spontaneous and free expression. For example, a girl to whom belonging means occupying center stage and being admired by everyone around her may often choose to draw herself as a dancer, actor, etc. Talent will become her "calling card" – her gate to belonging. Accordingly, she will never draw herself in plain clothes that are not directly associated with her unique talent.

Obviously, standing out is not always the best way to achieve social popularity – all too often, it makes the child different and separate from the others. This does not mean that children have to be mediocre and talentless to become popular, but that children who always seek to stand out and require children around them to be their cheering audience will often find it hard to win their heartfelt sympathy. Moreover, parents who stress the child's uniqueness in order to resolve various social issues, and tend to interpret the rejection experienced by their child as envy (because he's so much smarter or richer than the others) may end up perpetuating the child's experience of being different, and thus rejected and unlovable.

Conversely, many parents think social popularity means getting along with all children without any fights. When disagreements arise, they immediately teach their child to give up and to empathize with the other, saying things like: "He didn't mean it, you must share…" Upon hearing that, many children tend to react by experiencing social encounters as unpleasant and develop resistance to them. On the other hand, some parents encourage their children never to give up, never be "losers", while reporting their own success using various "wartime tactics" that used to work for them as children. Be that as it may, the question arises – Should the child follow in his parents' footsteps to become popular, or should he find his own way?

In order to assist in their child's social adjustment, the parents are required to intervene in a highly focused way. Psychological studies based on observations of parents to more and less popular children found that the former tend to encourage their children to join in social games, while mirroring the others' perspective for them, but stop intervening once the child joins in (Duke 1996). On the other hand, parents of less popular children tended to intervene more intensively, by stopping the game, announcing their child's agreement to join in, and acting as referees.

Aged 8 years and four months, the girl who made the following drawing likes to spend time with her classmates. Her drawing style is unique, attesting to her independent ability to function socially and understand the social map. In her drawings, she makes a point not to copy subjects and techniques from her friend, but to focus on her own work and develop independent techniques as she goes along. In other words, while drawing she remains very attentive to all that is going on around her, but never at the expense of maintaining a unique approach to her drawing.

Figure 8-1:   Independent and unique drawing style

In order to effectively integrate in her peer group, she manages to adjust herself to the social situation (by taking part in social games, for example). In her drawings, this is evident in the flexible and soft – but not too soft – lines. This line style demonstrates that she can stand up for herself and get what she wants, so that integrating in the group does not come at the expense of her own desires.

For a child to develop from a popular child to a popular leader, he needs to be skilled in keeping several children together, in other words, the ability to achieve interpersonal integration. The drawing above is also characterized by diverse and original relationships among the various figures shown, indicating ability to forge fruitful contacts.

On the other hand, it is important to see how the child connects the various figures and objects in his drawings. Are those relationships productive and original? Or are they banal, without adding any meaning to the drawing?

Figure 8-2:   Banal relationship that adds no meaning to the drawing

In most cases, children who form multiple but rather banal relationships between the various objects and figures in their drawings will also tend not to take the initiative in social situations, but tag along. This means they may require safer playing environments, so that they would prefer inviting their friends over, where everything is safe and familiar. Later on, after their social skill develops further, some children will change this pattern and come to enjoy diverse playing environment, and this will be seen in their drawings, which will also become diverse in terms of subjects and general use of line, color and movement.

To return to the first drawing (Figure 8-1), you can also see an effort to make the drawing more intelligible, in that she adds a title to it, as well as explanatory signs to prevent misunderstandings. These add-ons, apart from being age-appropriate, are directly related to the drawing child's need to be understood by others, and of course to her social experience.

Another example is the drawing in figure 8-3. The 7½ year-old who made it loves initiating social encounters, and this is evident in the combination of the multiple subjects into a dynamic and fascinating plot. Each part of her drawing includes several elements that are originally and uniquely interrelated. For example, the laundry line which connects the house with the swing poles, also used for hanging a pair of glasses. She takes the page boundaries into due consideration and seems to draw enormous pleasure from the process itself, rather than just the outcome.

Figure 8-3:   Combining multiple elements

Another way of achieving popularity is pleasing an authority figure such as a kindergarten or school teacher. This helps the child socially, particularly in kindergarten and the lower classes. Later, this approach is liable to become irrelevant and even detrimental. Children who seek to please in kindergarten make efforts to become the teacher's favorite, thereby attaining a powerful position through positive reinforcements from the most significant authority figure around. To do so, they adjust to her demands, sometimes at the expense of true self-expression. They cater to her every whim, paying particular attention to how they do things, and need her to appreciate the outcome of everything they do. Their drawings will be characterized by the absence of a unique personal style, and a tendency to follow orders to the letter (in extreme cases, such children will also ask for help in choosing colors). The outcome will be a rigid drawing, with the artist demanding to know what everyone around him thinks of it.

Figure 8-4:   Rigid and banal drawing by a dependent child

The definition of social popularity varies with culture, as indicated by the interactions children from different cultures create among the various figures in their drawings. In cultures which attach great importance to social contacts, children tend to draw the figures closer to one another, while in cultures in which children stress good manners and social distance, the drawn figures will be physically more distant from one another (Cox et al. 2001).

Social Rejection

Many children seem not to want to be popular and not take any part in social play. Psychologically, this is often perceived as an indication to their fear of making contact, which prevents them from daring and taking positive steps to promote their social integration.

Such children are known to be shy from an early age, and to be relatively fearful of strangers. They would rather not experience anything new, including in artwork and drawings in particular. Their drawings will sometimes be characterized by thin lines and weak pressure on the drawing tool, but only when they are shy and find it difficult to express themselves beyond the narrow social circle of their kindergarten or class.

When a child feels socially rejected or finds it difficult to adjust to and communicate with his peers, this may be for many reasons, including learning difficulties and various physical disabilities, as well as personal issues such as low self-esteem, difficulty expressing himself confidently, family issues, etc. Physical appearance can also affect the ability to adjust, as well as various behaviors acquired in the family system (such as overindulgence) which can make it difficult for the child to manage in peer society, and may even be rebuked in kindergarten.

Such children's drawings will include various indications of their distress due to their difficulty dealing with social realities. Their drawings will also bear marks of complex emotional coping, particularly in terms of color combinations and line qualities (shaky, disjointed or varying line). Social rejection is also liable to undermine self-confidence, and consequently the desire to draw and create in general. In such cases, children feel that what they do does not promote them and therefore lose interest in doing, and in more extreme cases, lose confidence in their abilities.

In my work I have often analyzed children's drawings of social groups or families. I have noticed that when children feel popular, they tend to emphasize the similarities between them and the other figures in such drawings. Conversely, when they feel rejected, they tend to emphasize their uniqueness compared to the others.

The following drawing by a 7½ year-old illustrates the feeling of being socially rejected. Together with other drawings by the same boy, it sheds light on a painful personal world. Here, the flowers do not blossom, the sun is tiny and distant, not giving warmth, and there is no relationship among the various objects. Collectively, the drawings shown to me seemed to indicate significant trauma experienced by this boy at a tender age, which had made him lose trust in all adults around him. I therefore referred him to art therapy and thanks to the emotional process he underwent, he also found himself able to express his feelings through drawing.

Figure 8-5: A sense of distance and alienation indicative of early trauma

Social Anxiety Disorder

Social anxiety disorder (SAD) is common among adults, teenagers and children (mostly girls). Children with SAD experience disquiet and discomfort in a wide variety of situations related to interaction with others. The main difficulty often has to do with the fear of occupying the center of attention, including sometimes the difficulty of even asking for help, staying in another child's house, talk in class, etc. Such children may have a rich inner world, they may know the answer to the teacher's questions, but do not dare speak up. For these children, any social occasion, any birthday or class party, is a stressful and threatening event.

Some make the mistake of treating these children as introverted and shy, but for the children themselves this is not a desirable condition that corresponds to their general mood, but more in the way of "still waters run deep". In other words, to them, what is perceived as shyness is forced withdrawal and they experience it as failure rather than a constructive solution – failure coping with their social anxiety. When they do have to face this anxiety they respond with a variety of somatic symptoms such as excessive perspiration, blushing, hyperventilation and tachycardia, dizziness, stomach ache and paralysis, as well as temper tantrums. About half the children diagnosed with SAD will suffer from generalized social anxiety disorder, while the rest will react adversely mainly to a specific stimulus such as having to read aloud in front of an audience (non-generalized SAD).

The parents of the six year-old who made the following drawings asked me to diagnose her drawings because they felt she had social difficulties. After analyzing the drawings, I held guidance meetings with the parents, later followed by regular emotional treatment for the child. Initially, the drawings clearly indicated her social difficulties. As seen in the representative example below, she drew an almost totally deserted playground: the slide and seesaw at the center are unused, while the human figure to the right is drawn with a large mouth, giving the impression of a sealed mouth more of a mouth that can speak. As I have already explained, one indication of social popularity is human interactions within the drawing itself. As you can see, in this drawing each element is completely isolated and unrelated to the others.

Figure 8-6: **Limited interactions between elements indicating unpopularity**

The next drawing also represents her style upon arriving for treatment: the human figures are colored in a stormy and disquiet line, body boundaries are often exceeded, the legs are drawn in a thin and shaky line, and some facial organs have been omitted from the figures to the extreme right and left. This drawing style, combined with the social trends indicated by the previous drawing, suggested a key diagnostic conclusion: this girl is experiencing major social difficulty, and consequently lashes out at others and experiences bona fide anxiety when interacting with her peers.

Figure 8-7:　Thin and shaky line and exceeding body boundaries indicating social difficulty

My conversation with the parents after the diagnosis supported my conclusions: over the past two years, when their daughter was at kindergarten, she would not come out to play. In the afternoons, when her parents took her to the playground, she would not approach other children from her kindergarten, but stand frozen next to them. At home, her parents had to cope with extreme temper tantrums which included throwing objects. After several talks, the parents and I decided to start weekly emotional therapy with their daughter. In those sessions, this girl brought contents from her inner world to the therapy room and together we worked through the difficulties she presented. The drawing in figure 8-8 is from the midst of the therapeutic process, and is typical of drawings in such stages. The line quality is calmer, and she allows herself to add creative decorative elements. In other drawings made during therapy, she also allowed herself to invent and create, and thus be occupied with her subjective uniqueness more than with what her social environment expects of her.

Figure 8-8: **During therapy: rigid drawing, albeit with slight signs of improvement**

This drawing was made at the end of the therapy process. By this point, the girl's kindergarten teacher reported that she agreed to go outside and play together with the other children.

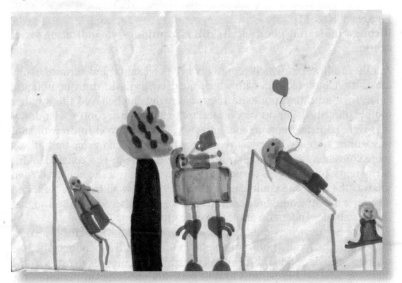

Figure 8-9: **At the end of therapy: improved social integration**

The parents also reported that her temper tantrums subsided and that when they did occur, they were not as prolonged and intense as before.

Note how compared to her first drawing (Figure 8-6), the playground became filled with children, each drawn differently with his or her unique look (hair color, clothing and handheld object). Also, the human figures are drawn in a more clearly specified environment and no expressive organs such as eyes or mouth are omitted. Accordingly, at the end of therapy, the girl reported that she made new friends and that she enjoyed spending time with them.

The following case is more subtle, although also representative of many children. The 5½ year-old girl who made the next drawing refused to go to her friends' houses, but was willing to host them. Her parents wanted me to use her drawings to find out the source of this difficulty, and how she could be helped. Interestingly, I could see in her drawings many indications of well-developed social skills – primarily their high quality and rich detailing, as seen in the house drawing in figure 8-11.

Figures 8-10 & 11:
Richness indicating good social skills vs. cautious style indicating social caution

Another indication, which represents her persistence and seriousness, is the caution and precision with which she drew, as in the drawing in figure 8-11. This indication points to the reason why she behaved the way her mother described – it was very important to her to be in control. Her drawings were painstakingly precise, and she wanted to excel in drawing and was willing to make the effort required. Due to this character trait, it was more convenient for her to play host. Perhaps this was less convenient for her parents, but for her it ensured the degree of control she needed. When she was the host, she could call the shots, she knew all the toys well, and whenever a fight would break out she knew her mother was around so that she was not dependent on another parent's judgment.

Since her drawings did indicate well-developed social skills, I recommended to the family not to intervene too much in her conduct. She had no extraordinary social difficulties requiring guidance or therapy, and I therefore advised her parents to wait patiently until she rid herself of the habit.

Having said that I did ask them to look into some issues, in order to see whether the source of their daughter's habit lay in her personality, or in the environment, such as in some parental pattern. First, I asked them to check how they intervened during fights between their daughter and her guests. Perhaps her need to host was due to her dependency on the parent's style – for example, the fact that her mother would immediately come over and take care of everything. When she was at another girl's house, perhaps the parents there would respond differently, making her feel less protected. In this regard, I recommended that they help her acquire some social skills. Most likely, she had the requisite skills, as evidenced in her drawings, but perhaps the parental pattern at home did not allow her natural skills to be fully expressed.

Second, I asked the parents to see what girls she hosted. Were these girls that she felt more "appropriate" to host in a familiar environment? Perhaps these girls acted domineeringly towards her, and therefore had to be hosted on the home turf, where she had the upper hand. This is a critical point relevant to many cases of social difficulties in childhood, particularly because in kindergarten the territory belongs to everyone and there is one teacher, while at home the boundaries are usually less clearly drawn.

Last but not least, I implored the parents to support, encourage and mirror. I instructed them to talk to their daughter about her need to host rather than be hosted, to show her that they were aware of that need, and that they could listen to her. In time, a child with social skills as developed as hers will surely manage to attenuate her need for control so as to better deal with uncertain situations.

One of the most interesting things about children's drawings is that the change is often indicated on the page before it appears in real life. It seems that children find it is more appropriate to for them to express the transformation they are undergoing in a nonverbal manner, and only later express it in words and conduct. This was also true in the case of this 5½ year-old. When the change occurred, it was first noticeable in her drawings, primarily through two main indicators: her drawing line became more flexible, and the coloring, although still very precise, could slip now and then as she allowed herself to express herself more freely, less cautiously. At the same time, her parents began noticing that she agreed to be hosted by some of her friends, so that her social conduct became more balanced.

Figure 8-12: Social transformation prefigured by flexible line with occasional glitches

Aggression and Violence

Children's aggression is one of the most complex behaviors a parent is required to face. First of all, it makes many parents feel as though they have failed as educators. They stand abashed in front of the kindergarten or school teacher and other parents, and find it hard to understand how their child could have stooped so low.

Other parents find themselves responding aggressively to their children's aggression, using either verbal or physical violence themselves.

Still other parents find themselves at an educational dead end: they communicate contradictory and confusing messages about how the child should behave in confrontations with other children, such as: "You must not be violent, but if others hit you – hit them back!" This makes many children feel very confused. In response to such contradictory messages, some of them begin to "tell on" others consistently, which makes their peers see them as squealers, which often exacerbates their social situation.

There may be several possible reasons for overt aggression by children:

1. **Age-appropriate aggression.** Many children aged 1–3 will beat, bite, or push others. At these ages, children are in the midst of the egocentric stage, and are very possessive about their toys. As far as they are concerned, there is no reason for any toy to be taken away from them, and the end justifies the means. At this point in their psychological development, their drawings are largely characterized by scribbles, and as these scribbles progress, so do their social cognition and experience, causing their aggression to subside in favor of new negotiation tactics.

Figure 8-13:   Scribble indicating age-appropriate aggression

2. **Aggression as a socialization strategy.** In this case, the child realizes that using aggression he can improve his social status. Accordingly, as in the next example, such a child's drawings will be characterized by aggressive and even violent trends, such as intense

pressure on the drawing tool and stormy, disquiet movement on the page. When analyzing such drawings it is important to check whether this child used to draw this way prior to becoming part of a peer society or started doing so as a result of his new (false) insight.

Figure 8-14:   Intense pressure and stormy movement

3. **Aggression due to frustration and low self-image.** As the saying goes, "there are no bad boys, only boys yet unreached". Aggression in these cases is better seen as a sign of distress. In these children's drawings, beyond classic indications of aggression, you also see motifs related to low self-image and feelings of frustration and helplessness. This is illustrated by the next drawing, where the figures are drawn in a weak and fluttering line and they are relatively thin, somewhat fragile and marginal compared to the rest of the elements in the drawing, which are made with a high pressure, rigid line and dominant presence on the page.

Figure 8-15:   Figures drawn with weak pressure

4. **Aggression due to family stress.** In this case, aggression is specific
    to a certain time and place, and follows upon negative life events
    such as death, disease, divorce or alternatively, momentous events
    such as the birth of a new sibling that may be perceived as negative
    in the short term. In such cases, family drawings in particular may
    shed light on the cause of aggression. The drawing shown here,
    for example, was made in the midst of a prolonged and difficult
    divorce process. The father is drawn to the right and the mother
    to the left, separated by a large Star of David. The father is drawn
    with arms, while the mother is armless. Interpreting this drawing
    helped me pinpoint their son's aggression as directly related to the
    overt and covert conflicts between them, and the way he experi-
    ences both of them.

Figure 8-16: Aggression in a family drawing

5. **Aggression due to learning disability.** Due to their cognitive processing difficulties, children with learning disabilities often misinterpret social reactions to them and social overtures made by peers. Their drawings will be typically characterized by trends related to children with learning disabilities such as adding elements not related to the main theme, etc.

6. **Aggression as conduct problem** occurs mainly when the entire environment communicates contradictory messages to the child. In these cases, the child conducts himself in an inconsistent environment in terms of its reactions to his behavior, with right and wrong being unclear. If he cries or expresses any difficulty, sometimes others (teachers, parents) give up on demands from him, sometimes the mother takes a different stand than the father, and in other times the parents have a completely different opinion than the teachers, etc. In such cases, the child's drawings will lack any clear trends, as in the following example.

Figure 8-17: Blurred boundaries as a source of aggression

7. **Aggression as a form of release.** Many children act out aggressively to vent multiple stressors such as competition with the peer group or parental demands for high achievements. In this case, the most common indication of stress in their drawings will be rigidity, as seen below, in the dense coloring.

Figure 8-18: External pressure as a source of aggression

8. **Parental modeling** is often a source of aggression, particularly in cases of child abuse. In such cases, the child's aggression is a direct response to the harsh educational methods, to put it euphemistically, he experiences at home. Accordingly, the child's drawings will show clear indications of ill-treatment.

The parents of the girl who made the following drawings contacted me for consultation due to her violent behavior. They reported their daughter, aged 2 and 9 months, throws temper tantrums in which she is able to bash another child's head against the floor. Naturally, her parents were afraid of her violence and sought to determine its cause.

Figure 8-19:   Intense pressure and rigid movement indicating stress

This girl is full of presence and confidence, as evidenced mainly by her fluent and self-assured use of the entire page area. The rhythm with which she draws indicates that she has a quick grasp and able to express herself clearly in a way that enchants everyone around her. She likes the attention she manages to get and knows how to take advantage of it to influence her social environment. Nevertheless, the intense pressure she applies to the drawing tool, to the point of tearing the page in certain places, also indicates that she is a very obstinate and stubborn child.

However, her drawings indicate that her willfulness actually results from a deep sense of frustration. They also indicate that she tends to act out "violently" when things do not go her way – for example, she would vomit voluntarily when her parents left her or demanded that she behave in a way that was not acceptable to her.

Based on my analysis of this girl's older drawings, it seemed there was something in her present environment that significantly stressed her out. In her previous drawings, she applied less pressure to the drawing tool and her movement was looser in the entire drawing style.

Figure 8-20: Weak pressure and loose movement

I came to the realization that this girl's social difficulties and violent behavior in kindergarten resulted from a non-age-appropriate punitive system. A high achiever, she often found herself challenged by competition. The common punishment in her kindergarten – having children sit in the time-out corner to reflect upon their misbehavior – achieved the opposite result in her case. While sitting there, she found it very difficult to learn any real lessons but rather used the time to identify the "guilty" parties – a pattern repeated in her relationships with her parents. Therefore, my first recommendation to the family was to see how her need for attention and influence on her environment could be channeled to directions that will help her understand the costs involved in her behavior.

As already mentioned, she liked being at the center of things and was totally present on the drawing page. Consequently, the solution of keeping her away could only achieve partial results. I thought it better to look into the various roles she liked to play and through them find out how she can contribute to her family and peer society. I also recommended to her parents to clarify the relationship between responsible and considerate behavior and taking responsibility in other areas.

My bottom line is that no child is born violent. Regrettably, some children find out that their violent behavior patterns have powerful effects on their environment and can benefit them in many ways.

Social Functioning and Temperament

Studies (e.g. Heimberg 2004) found a relationship between generalized social anxiety and certain types of temperament, with specific type most related to social functioning disorders being inhibited temperament. This temperament is evident already in infancy and is characterized by a tendency to shy away and withdraw from new situations, to the point of complete avoidance.

Parents of inhibited children can tell that from very early on, their children avoided playing with new toys or approaching unfamiliar children. Often, the child's temperament is woven into the parenting pattern he experiences. For example, when his parents are overprotective, restraining and anxious of his independence, the child may develop an insecure attachment style. Since the primary attachment pattern is a model for future relationships, a vicious circle develops, making it difficult for the child to take advantage of new social situations.

Nevertheless, it is important to reiterate that no particular parenting pattern can be the source of this or that anxiety. It is always about the synergy between parent and child, between the innate temperament which responds to the environmental conditions in the parent-child relationship, and vice versa.

Educating children is no mean task. In bookstores you will find many books encouraging liberal and open educational approaches, together with others that preach a harsher, more disciplinary approach. However, I feel that many of the parents who read these books from cover to cover are uncertain of their approach and often wonder if they had done right with their children.

Whoever has some experience in raising children knows there is no "proven formula". Even within the same family, parents are often required to use different approaches with different children – this boy always asks for explanations and you have to discuss everything with him, while his sister feels such family discussions are confusing and useless, or can be used manipulatively. Some react to disciplinary measures the way the parents expect, while others only resist and regress even further behaviorally. At the end of the day, the proverb "educate the child according to his way" always proves to be powerfully true – all parents have to understand their child's "way" and once they do, it will be easier for them to tailor the right approach to him.

Rigid and stormy temperament

The parents of the 4½ year-old who made the following drawing asked me to analyze her drawings because they felt that her hot-temperedness and capriciousness affect her social functioning.

Indeed, this girl's drawings showed that she was curious and spicy. The "hot-temperedness" her parents inquired about was indicated in her drawings mainly in her extensive movements on the page and the speed in which she manage to complete the coloring of broad areas.

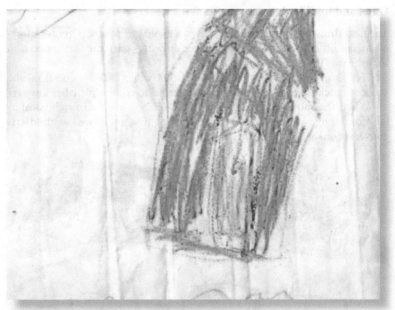

Figure 8-21: Rapid drawing style indicating impulsiveness

Generally, temperament is innate and cannot be controlled, nor is it recommended to try and control it. This is because in most cases, parents who try to fight this battle are bound to lose. In the long run, the child's temperament will not change due to this or that punishment.

Accordingly, in this girl's case, I did not recommend looking into ways of controlling her hot temper, but rather to see how the parents could communicate with her in accordance with her impulsive pace and style. In general, when she behaved impetuously and capriciously, the parents could mirror her intense excitement at the moment (but do it sincerely, rather than cynically or patronizingly), for example: "Yes, I understand you are very excited and must have this now, and very soon I will be able to attend to it". It was important to reinforce her for every minute she managed to hold back and at the same time see if anything could be done to make it easier for her, and not have her be forced to hold back for too long. In this girl's case, it was important to change the parents' attitude, because once they were locked into viewing her as "impulsive", this narrowed down the range of potential educational approaches, mainly due to the negative and antisocial connotations of this word.

When you can pinpoint the "fuse" that sparks in the parent's brain in response to a given behavior by his child, you can often isolate the source of that parent's anger and determine how much it derives from the child's own behavioral patterns as opposed to the parent's character and related, perhaps, to traumatic childhood memories.

Quiet and inhibited temperament

The next drawings were made by a five year-old girl whose parents reported social difficulties. My analysis of her drawings gave me the impression that she was intelligent.

Her slow pace of drawing indicated that when asked a question, she was not quick to respond, but rather preferred to contemplate her answer.

When she spoke, she was pleasant to listen to – she had a rich vocabulary for her age and she enjoyed participating in adult as well as children's conversations.

Figure 8-22:   Slow, careful and high-quality drawing style in keeping with the child's character

Nevertheless, this girl's very cautious drawing and coloring style indicated that she was quite demanding of herself – she sometimes behaved maturely for her age, but on other occasions she would surprisingly behave regressively. In addition, she tended to take assignments seriously, there was no need to rush her and she could set very high objectives for herself. This attitude made her pay a heavy price in her daily conduct, because she would often experience daily tasks as if there were truly "missions" she had to accomplish at any cost.

Next year, this five year-old will enter first grade. On the face of it, she seemed cognitively prepared. Moreover, her achievement-oriented attitude could be very helpful at school, where she would receive numerical or verbal feedback on her accomplishment and act accordingly.

Perfectionism and achievements

Based on my conclusions from the drawing analysis, my main recommendations for the parents was to look into their daughter's achievement mindset as a fundamental worldview. As explained above, children's inhibited temperament is intimately related to the parenting pattern they experience. In this case, the parents are overprotective of their daughter and at the same time expect her to perform and achieve at the highest level. This perfectionist approach, as reflected in her drawings, is typical of the family atmosphere, not just of her.

I want to stress that there is nothing wrong in pushing children to achieve. The thing is that in doing so, the children have to learn to cope with failure, so as not to arrive at extreme situations. In this girl's case, she would suddenly burst out in anger or seek intense intimacy and refuse to let go (for example, before going to sleep or to the kindergarten). On such occasions, her parents wonder how this mature and intelligent girl can act so regressively. Most adults know how to cope with losses and failures, but children usually need guidance from their parents in such moments, and it is important to provide this guidance even if the immediate results seem disappointing.

Figure 8-23: Attention to detail as an indication of a perfectionist family attitude

When using the term "perfectionist family attitude" the idea is not to diagnose the family or brand it, but simply to say that the dosage of attention to achievements in a given family may be higher than that devoted to other areas in the child's life. When you put this mirror in front of the parents and try to analyze its communication patterns, you will do well to include nonverbal messages as well: everyone knows that a B in fourth grade is not the end of the world, but does our face communicate the same message? When we find our child is not such a good math student, do we truly believe in his abilities to succeed in the future or do we envision the long hours we would have to spend on his homeroom and the money we would have to spend on private tutors? Remember, children can sense, "sniff out", what their parents truly expect of them.

The second area that deserves your attention is how you reinforce good achievements. There is no need to elaborate too much on this point – just remember to say a good word or two commending the effort and the final outcome. At the same time, you must be keenly aware of how you treat failures: do they mobilize the entire family to help the child overcome the difficulty? When the family is mobilized this way, the child gets the message that failure or loss means working together to win the next time, thus become more focused on achievements.

In some families, one of the siblings learns to stand out through his achievements – his report card is his strength and family role. As children enter first grade and advance in school, learning becomes more complex and difficult. For the achievement-oriented child this increasingly threatens his family role, making him feel that if he does not continue to excel, his very identity is endangered.

In view of the relationship found in the literature (e.g. McNeil and Hembree-Kigin 2001) between the parent's responses to the child's social functioning, another point parents will do well to look into has to do with the way they talk about their life in terms of success or failure. Like this inhibited five year-old's parents, many parents see their children as tools for self-realization, so that every accomplishment by their child proves they are good parents. Every time their child presents his achievements to them, they are filled with pride and tend to refer to this often in social occasions. I do not mean you must not be proud in your child's achievements, but only to be careful not to focus on the outcome rather than on the process that led to it. By the same token, when the child fails the focus is on the disappointing end result rather than on the daring and curiosity which made the child try something that proved too difficult for him.

When this girl draws, she is very precise. She thoughtfully analyzes the various elements on the page. When she writes, she does it slowly, being careful to keep it aligned and accurate. When she colors, she fills the entire area and usually does not leave a single uncolored point in the designated colored area. When interacting, she throws her arms out to her sides expressing her keen desire to make friends, but despite all that, occasionally, her drawing lines are shaky, attesting to the price she has to pay in order to continue being as good (and even excellent) as she expects of herself.

Nevertheless, you should be aware of the fact that perfectionist drawings can also be seen in families with a different atmosphere. For example, many children who grow in an overly liberal environment draw with painstaking accuracy, indicating their need for clear boundaries. Since such are not provided by their parents, the children themselves develop an entire array of behavioral rules and prohibitions that demand high standards of them.

When perfectionist children approach drawings, beyond the indicators mentioned above with reference to the 5 year-old about to enter first grade, they treat them as an "assignment". They try to glance at others' drawings, repeatedly ask the kindergarten or school teacher what they "should" draw, and try to avoid mistakes. When the drawing is complete, they will need to hear what others think of it, and will not take kindly to light-hearted or humoristic responses. Perfectionist children often use extreme terms such as "this is the most beautiful drawing in the world", or "I draw better than everyone else", or conversely, "I will never be able to draw". When they encounter failure, they often tear up the page, crumple it and throw it in the garbage. In such cases, it is important to respect their wishes, but at the same time show forgiveness and love for every product of their work. Perfectionist children would rather use pencils because they are erasable, and do not like gouache or finger paints that cannot be applied with accuracy.

In itself, perfectionism is neither a good nor a bad quality. In this girl's case, it affected her social functioning – she was rigid in dialogues with her peers, always insisted on playing by the rules and when anyone suggested changing the rules she would become upset and lash out in anger.

At the right doses, children can get very far when they are achievers, when they are thorough, responsible and disciplined. Just remember to let them understand that at least at home, with the family, and also with their closest friends, their failures, doubts and fears will always be accepted with love. Perfectionism is one of the behavioral aspects of innate temperament. Analyzing this girl's case through the prism of her temperament proved to be the beginning of resolving her social difficulties.

To conclude, since children use their drawings as a second language, their artwork communicates their inner world and experiences. This is particularly true of the social interactions which take up such a significant part of the child's day, and which can be analyzed through their drawings in order to better understand social dynamics which as parents, we are not always able to observe directly.

Nine Keys for Coping with Social Difficulties

1. **Reinterpretation.** Work with the child on negative interpretations for social situations. Ask the child to draw the social situation, "before" and "after". Together with the child, understand how she analyses the event and start talking about alternative interpretations that could lead to better coping.

2. **Staging.** Invite the child to give voice to the characters in the drawing. When the situation involves high anxiety for the child, it can be left "distant" on the page and watched like a play. This distancing through the drawing enables the child to "visit" the social world and still feel secure.

3. **My child and the child within me.** It is reasonable to assume that the parent and child share the sources of anxiety and social difficulties. In such cases, I invite both the parent and child to the clinic, and we create a "game" situation where both draw their greatest fear. In a calm and facilitative atmosphere, we talk about it and come up with solutions.

4. **Compensatory moves.** Many parents ask me, why does my child hang out with the class bully? For the child, this relation enables to compensate for his weaker sides by developing them vicariously. I usually recommend not interfering with those social choices. As the child reinterprets situations around him, his social choices will change as well.

5. **Dos and don'ts.** Decide on a consistent educational response to aggressive (and other) behaviors by the child and stick to it. Use words to explain what the child may and may not do, and provide a role model by responding accordingly.

6. **Where can I possibly run here?** Look for alternative legitimate contexts for channeling aggression. Today, children spent most of their time sitting down, which is completely unsuitable for their temperament and motor development needs. Give them a place where they can move around, do some sports, let off some steam.

7. **Off-screen.** Check whether your child's aggressive behavior occur soon after watching TV or playing a computer game. Although academic studies have yet to find a significant relation between the two, many parents have found their children to be ill affected by staring at a screen for long hours.

8. **Provide positive reinforcement** of behaviors such as delaying gratification or using words to resolve conflicts.

9. **Let the drawings talk.** Observe your child's drawings closely to understand trends and reasons related to aggression.

9 THE HUMAN BODY

Human Figure Drawings

Children find human figure drawings fascinating. Developmentally, they will start at around age three, with tadpole figures, shaped like round heads to which lines are attached to represent the limbs and these will gradually develop into more humanlike two-dimensional figures. At first, you will see two-dimensional limbs replace the lines, and then, gradually, around age five, children will draw the torso and neck, with the main emphasis being on the organ's bodily function. During the school years (but for some children even earlier), you will see the shoulders and smaller organs detailed, down to the level of drawing eyelashes and pupils. From then on, human figures will develop and seem more realistic, with each figure having its unique characteristics.

When a child draws a human figure, he does not necessarily look at people around him for reference, but often negotiates with himself and his own bodily organs. Therefore, children's human figure drawings can tell us a lot about how they perceive themselves and their families, in terms of body image and self-image in general (Koppitz 1990).

In the first half of the 20th century, children's intelligence was often measured according to the number of items they referenced in human figure drawings, according to age (Goodenough 1926). Today this approach is largely unaccepted (Eno 1981), mainly because no significant relationship has been found between the number of items and intelligence level, particularly among children with various learning disorders and motor difficulties. Moreover, recent studies (Moschini 2004) suggest that certain omissions in such drawings are characteristic of specific age ranges and are due to purely developmental issues that have little bearing on children's IQ; these include, for example, the tendency to omit arms around ages 5–7.

Moreover, recent approaches to IQ (e.g. Terman 2009) emphasize a multi-systemic approach, conceiving of several types of intelligences that children may apply in varying degrees. Therefore, unlike Goodenough's approach (ibid.), quantitative scales are insufficient when it comes to drawing a broad picture of children's intelligences mosaic.

Drawings centered on human figures are highly common and highly diverse. In some cases, children treat the body as purely physical, while in others they treat it as the receptacle of personality. In the first case, children document reality. On the other hand, when they treat the body as the receptacle of personality, they use the drawing to express various emotional meanings associated with bodily organs.

Such references – whether physical or emotional – appear in children's drawings both in reference to normative, daily physical conditions, such as lice or asthma, and in reference to more unusual circumstances such as crises involving serious illness. In all such cases, the children refer in their drawings to their own body or to that of a close friend or relative undergoing a serious crisis. I will first discuss the first group of ordinary physical experiences, followed by the second group of serious illnesses.

Human Figure Drawings and Their Emotional Meaning

This drawing was made by an 8½ year-old who had contracted lice in school, and drew it soon after returning home. In this case, the experience of contracting lice made her preoccupied with her body, so that this human figure drawing is also indicative of her overall subjective bodily experience. The way she drew her own figure (to the right) is different compared to earlier drawings, and the two figures seen here are clearly qualitatively different.

Figure 9-1: **Applying intense pressure to highlight certain organs**

One of the first things you should assess when interpreting human figure drawings is the figure's size compared to other elements in the drawing (naturally, this can only be done after the child has started making proportional drawings, that is, not before the schematic stage). For example, children with social anxiety, low self-esteem, a sense of inferiority and extreme self-criticism will draw themselves as significantly smaller in comparison (Di Leo 1973).

Clearly, contracting lice has social implications, possibly making the child feel outcast. Many adults remember how nervous they used to feel whenever the school nurse would come in to examine children's heads for lice, and how those found "guilty" were seated far away from their classmates.

In this girl's drawing, the head is enlarged, representing her preoccupation with the lice. This overcompensation is a common trend in children's drawing. In this case, the enlarge head not only symbolizes her preoccupation, but communicates a sense of otherness, which is even more evident in comparison with the other figure with its much smaller head.

As in other types of drawings, line quality is significant in human figure drawings. For example, when children draw one of the figures using intense pressure on the drawing tool and an angular line, this could mean that this specific figure makes him feel stressful and is perceived to be rigid and inflexible (Klepsch 1988). When another figure is drawn using a broken and shaky line and with weak pressure, I recommend looking into why the child perceives this figure as unconfident, hesitant and even anxious.

In general, it is important to compare the various figures drawn by the child in order to detect any gaps between them. When all figures are drawn the same way, this is often indicative of the child's tendency to project his qualities on those around him.

In this example, you can see a clear difference between the pressure she applies to the figure's torso, head and limbs and the pressure applied to the hair, to the point of making the penciled hair look almost black. When representing the area that preoccupies her, and particularly the scratching palms, she applies particularly intense pressure. Some researchers (e.g. Craft & Denehy 1990), believe that such blackening should be interpreted as suggesting anxieties and emotional conflicts. But in this case as in others, duration is the key: indeed, this girl's drawing style changed after she got rid of her lice.

Another important qualification concerning blackening is the difference between it and shading. Some children use high-quality shadowing because they are talented, and in such cases, the emotional conclusion is usually more positive, particularly in cases of subtly graded shades. Blackening, on the other hand, is drastic, and tends to appear in a certain area of the drawing, usually with a uniform shade. Unlike shading, blackening significantly detracts from the drawing's quality or creates an impression of concealing and even destroying the original figure. In such cases, blackening – combined, as usual, with other suggestive elements in the drawing

– indicates fears, anxieties and aggressions.

An additional key indicator in human figure drawings has to do with drawing figures in profile or with their back to the viewer. This is suggestive of social anxiety and attempts to withdraw and slip away. Note that in this case, however, the human figure is frontal and clearly visible. In my experience, I found many children and teenagers take up drawing figures in profile as a graphic challenge. Also note that many drawing classes in school focus on techniques of drawing figures in profile, so that children taking such lessons make such attempts on a regular basis. Thus, when interpreting profile drawings you must follow the golden rule of integrating other aspects of the drawing in your analysis – including line quality, color combinations, the drawing's subject, etc. – prior to arriving at any conclusions regarding social withdrawal. In some cases, drawing a figure in profile at an early age may suggest a high IQ, given the level of spatial perception it requires.

Body parts: Detailed review

After forming a general impression about the figure's character, you can examine the various body parts in greater details. First, the eyes represent the child's attachment style. Interestingly, this 8½ year-old drew the profiled, smaller figure's eye with a pupil, while omitting the pupils from her own frontal figure. Such an omission in children's drawings is suggestive of social detachment and withdrawal. Moreover, girls her age usually add eyebrows, lashes and even makeup to figures' eyes, expressing their desire to please society.

Another hypothesis related to facial organs is that oversized and over-emphasized ears are typical of hearing-impaired children, or children suffering from chronic ear pain/infection. This hypothesis was not supported, however, in a study of deaf and hearing impaired children (Di Leo 1983). Again, in order to truly extract significant emotional meaning out of a drawing, attention to graphic parameters such as line quality is critical. When the line is high-quality, enlarged ears may indicate enhanced sensitivity and musical talent. As a rule, enlarged sensory organs suggests heightened attunement and sensitivity to the environment, such that according to line quality and pressure this may suggest an either negative attitude, such as suspiciousness or hyper-vigilance, or a positive attitude such as social awareness, expressive skills, etc. (Frick et al. 2009).

My next example involves another sensory organ – the mouth. The mouth is rich in significance, beginning in infancy (sucking on the mother's breast or pacifier) through emotional issues related to nurturing, to expressive abilities in later ages (talking, crying, raising one's voice). Due to its centrality, its location in children's drawings and the way it is rendered are highly significant. For example, ignoring mouth drawings is typical of asthma patients (Gabriels et al. 2000), perhaps due to the difficulty of breathing through it during an attack. In this example, the mouth is omitted by a child drawing his autistic brother. When no physiological issue is involved, omitting the mouth may indicate unsatisfied oral needs in the past or difficulties communicating with others in the present.

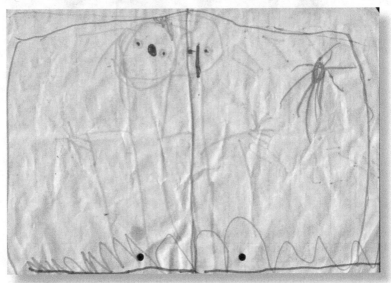

Figure 9-2:   Mouth omitted by a child drawing his autistic brother

Nevertheless, as with other organs, the way the mouth is drawn is related to developmental motifs appearing in certain ages, without necessarily bearing any emotional significance. For example, the smiling mouth is very typical of drawings by 5–6 year-olds, and is normative for that age range. If the constantly smiling mouth continues to dominate human figure drawings at later ages, this may indicate childishness or alternatively, the child's feeling as though he must maintain a certain façade and always seem agreeable and talented.

Figure 9-3:   Typical smiling figure at age 5

One of the common myths associated with mouth drawings has to do with teeth. Teeth are often regarded as indicating aggression, but this is not always the case. I have often seen teeth drawn by children who became keenly aware of them following dental treatments. Relatedly, it was found that children tend to draw breasts soon after the birth of a breastfed baby, or sexual organs around the time they were scheduled to undergo hernia operations (Di Leo 1973).

Figure 9-4: **Teeth added to a human figure following dental treatment**

Indeed, sexual organs immediately draw the viewer's attention. First, it is important to stress the developmental aspect: in ages 3–6, drawing sexual organs may suggest normative awareness of one's body, as seen in the following example by a 4 year-old.

Figure 9-5: **Age-appropriate drawing of sexual organs**

Nevertheless, it is important for me to stress that when analyzing children's drawings at this age range in particular – 3–6 – attention to sexual organs is critical, as this is the typical age of onset of sexual abuse. Thus, the conclusion whether drawing sexual organs is age-appropriate or indicates sexual abuse requires analyzing multiple examples, as well as applying additional diagnostic approaches.

Arms make their first appearance already in tadpole figures. Children use their hands to interact with their environment, whether by touching or by attacking it. They use them to get what they want. Thus, arms drawn right next to the body indicate self-restraint in social interactions (as in the next drawing), while looser arms indicate the opposite. If you return to my first example, you can see that at first glance, the larger figure's arms seem like enlarged ears. The arms are grotesquely linear, while the other, smaller figure has a two-dimensional arm (in profile).

Figure 9-6: **Arms held close to the body, indicating self-restraint**

This distinction is yet another indication of this girl's acute sense of differentness in terms of her common use of her hands during that period – to scratch her lice-infested head. This grotesques impression is enhanced when she draws her palms like comb teeth. Her linear and rigid fingers convey considerable aggression and anger. Conversely, the other figure's palms are drawn with a softer line.

Legs symbolize children's everyday sense of security and stability. Accordingly, you can see legless figures or figures with legs clenched together, drawn in a thin and shaky line, among dependent children who are anxious of changes. In the first drawing in this chapter, the child's figure is drawn with asymmetric feet, indicating instability, particularly given the fact that in her previous drawings, her figures had had similarly sized feet.

Unlike the first example, which is rich in indications related to specific bodily organs, the next drawing has to do with overall body and self-image. The girl who made it, aged six and 7 months, was overweight and described by her parents as having a low self-image. Among other things, her mother complained about her rebelliousness. The way this girl drew her body was age-inappropriate, particularly given the clearly evident blurred body boundaries, typical of overweight children (Nathan 1973). In this drawing, the legs seem to extend in all direction, and the line movement is very impulsive. Based on this drawing and others, it appeared that this girl was undergoing a daily struggle for survival. She had to speak out, and raise her voice, or else she would be ignored. Often, she would be willful and rebellious to spite her family members and attract their attention.

Figure 9-7:   Blurred body boundaries indicating low body image

When I examined her siblings' drawings I found that this attitude was typical of the entire family, creating a snowball effect, with each family member entrenching in his or her position, poisoning the entire atmosphere. An analysis of her previous drawings enabled me to pinpoint the onset of her spiteful behavior, as well as the causes that made it snowball. Based on these findings, I could provide her parents with tools to cope with it, tailored to her character as well as to theirs.

This example points to the thin line between the body's purely physical aspect and the body as an emotional receptacle representing the mind, or more particularly, self-image. Self-image appears in children's drawing in a variety of ways. When a child hates the way he looks, he may refuse to draw himself, and if he does, he is liable to draw his body in a twisted (often amorphous) way, using a weak, shaky and soft line indicating indifference on his part. We will also find inconsistency between a generally high drawing level and low-quality self-portraits that seem to have been made offhandedly.

To conclude, remember that emotional conclusions may not be reached based on the way a single body organ is drawn. You must cross-reference with other indications in the same drawing and others made during the same period and before. It is important to refer to the overall impression of the human figure on the page, and see where the child has invested most of his energy while drawing. For example, a child having difficulty with gross motor skills who finds physical education lessons challenging may emphasize the leg area one way or another. This is because in most cases, the body parts drawn with greater energy investment are also the most emotionally significant in the child's subjective self-experience.

Drawings by Sick Children

Human figure drawings and curable diseases

When children fall seriously ill, this often comes as an unpleasant surprise, followed by a long trail of anxieties, fears and difficult and complex daily coping by the child and his family. Health conditions vary widely in type and intensity: some are only temporary (a case of the flu, or a broken limb), and evident in drawing over a limited time period, while others are chronic, with diverse articulations over a prolonged period of time.

Children's human figure drawings often refer to various bodily conditions. This does not mean that they can be used as a tool to diagnose certain diseases and health-related issues, but that they may provide important clues to the implications of children's health on their emotional world. In other words, what the child draws on the page mirrors his subjective health situation, enabling us to form an impression of his illness that goes beyond strictly medical and biological parameters (Lowenfeld 1987).

Thus, for example, while in some cases respiratory organs may be omitted in drawings by asthmatic children, and ears by deaf children, my own experience shows that such phenomena are not necessarily related to actual disabilities experienced by the child. To reiterate, it is the internal reality, the way the health condition is experienced and how it affects the child's self-image that will be represented on the page.

The following drawing by a 5½ year-old shows how his asthma "chokes" him, preventing him from breathing and expressing himself properly. This boy stresses a certain body part to indicate the source of the disease, a technique commonly used among sick children (Mathers 2001), who tend to feel that the stressed body part is something they do not know enough about, or that is out of their control.

Figure 9-8:   Drawing by an asthmatic boy

This drawing was made on a specific day when his asthma was a focus of discussion in the kindergarten. On that day, it probably became indistinguishable from his self-image. It is expressed in the drawing not necessarily in the choice of black – which has been found to be insignificantly related to emotional stress (Malchiodi 1998) – but more in the evident gaps between the areas where intense pressure has been applied (the neck) and other areas drawn with less pressure.

Such a direct relationship between health conditions and children's awareness of them has been found in a large number of studies conducted over the past decades (e.g. Shapiro 2010). According to recent findings on the nature of cognition and its physical underpinnings, which form the basis of a new theory embodied cognition, thought processes are intimately related to sensory and motor experience. It thus seems that children's drawings, affected as they are by the physical experience of producing the drawing, are a reflection of children's cognitions regarding their physiological experiences.

During my work I often encountered remarkable cases that demonstrated the directness of the relationship between children's health and drawings. When the child is mature and aware of his illness, you may expect him to refer to it (one way or another) in his human figure drawings. Interestingly, however, children often indicate awareness of their disease at a very young age, sometimes even before its first symptoms appear.

For example, the next drawing was made by a child aged three and 3 months, several days before severe pneumonia symptoms first made their appearance, following which he had to be hospitalized. The drawing clearly shows the shape of the lungs. Moreover, it was distinctly unlike this boy's earlier scribbles, and he did not draw that way afterwards.

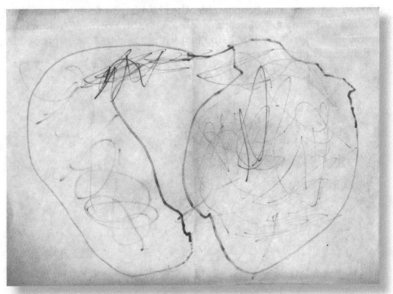

Figure 9-9: **Drawing made before the appearance of pneumonia symptoms**

As early as the 1940s researchers noticed that children with various disabilities draw figures with exaggerated or omitted organs, expressing how they feel about their defective or sick body part (Lowenfeld 1947). More recent studies (e.g. Krampen 1991) found that children use drawings to indicate their physical condition, and more importantly, their concerns and fears regarding their prognosis and the treatments they would have to undergo.

Another study focused on the healing stage found that green is often used to symbolize growth and renewal (Back 1990). Another study (Gilad & Florian 1987) showed how the child's body image can be seen to improve when not suffering from an incurable disease: the drawings convey the impression of an overall improvement evidenced by positive reference to all body parts. Schwartz and Shafir (1980) found that sick or disabled children tend to stress certain body parts by taking them apart and coloring each part differently, suggesting a problematic body image and low self-image. Finally, Malchiodi (1993) describes an interesting way of identifying the source of pain and fear experienced by the sick child. The child is given a page with human contour lines and asked to use any of several colors to paint areas of concern, anger, fear, sadness or any other emotion. This helps practitioners understand where children suffer psychologically and helps children articulate their own feelings and emotions.

Human figure drawings and incurable diseases

When the disease may be incurable, the child has to face the possibility of living in the shadow of death. Coping with this possibility follows five typical stages (Or-Bach 1989). The first is the *stage of shock*, expressed by anxiety and withdrawal.

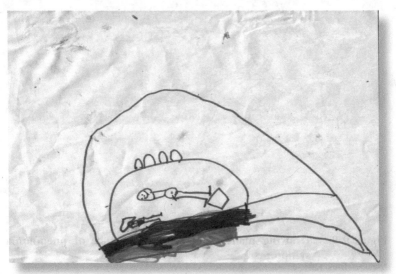

Figure 9-10:   Coping with a severe illness: the stage of shock

At this stage, human figures in the child's drawings will be small and even tiny, shaded, and with facial expressions of fear and helplessness. The child's withdrawal could be further indicated by framing the human figures, or formal drawings without reference to reality (Abraham 1989).

The second stage is *denial*. At this stage, drawings are replete with erasures and often focus on subjects related to sanctuaries.

In the third stage, the disease is *referenced directly*, typically through overcompensation, such that the diseased body part is overemphasized (Pinchover 2002). In the next drawing for example, you can see the child on a surgery bed with his abdominal area stressed by a black contour line.

Figure 9-11: Coping with a severe illness: the direct reference stage

Next, in the fourth stage the child begins to cope with the disease on a more *realistic* level, and will start referring to it in the drawings by adding cartoon talk balloons with references to his health condition.

Finally, in the fifth stage the child *comes to terms with death*. He begins to prepare himself for it by drawing graves, funerals, or angels and other heavenly references (Kubler-Ross 1969). Importantly, I have noticed similar phenomena among completely healthy children who have experienced the sudden death of a loved one, whether due to an accident or natural causes.

Figure 9-12: Coping with a severe illness: the acceptance stage

Several years ago, I was contacted by a mother whose 6½ year-old child made the drawing shown above. Overcome with emotion, she told me she had placed this drawing at the center of her child's bedroom throughout the morning over her death due to a severe illness. She said the drawing was made several days before her daughter's death, but was discovered only afterwards. When she first saw it, she burst out crying. I asked her how she interpreted the drawing, and she gave me an immediate and simple explanation: the figure to the right, which seems to hover above ground, indicates that her daughter realized she was about to die, prepared for it, and drew it. This interpretation empowered the mother in that it helped her think of her tragic circumstances as though they were destined to be.

This case was particularly moving and exceptional. Nevertheless, I must qualify the description above by saying that hovering figures in children's drawings do not necessarily prophesy disaster. Sometimes they refer to completely imaginary worlds, or may be age appropriate, typical of the pre-schematic stage. In this case as well, the figure may have been drawn for reasons completely unrelated to the disease, with the mother's interpretation being conjectural, albeit psychologically beneficial.

Other subjects in drawings by sick children

Apart for human figure drawings, house and tree drawings can also be indirectly suggestive of children's health condition and its emotional consequences. For example, trees and houses supported by various objects may stand for the social environment's support of the child, or suggest that like the child, the tree (being also a living organism) has been uprooted before its time (Shafir 1991).

House drawings may be particularly significant for severely ill children, beyond their usual symbolism of the self and family relationship among all children. When drawing a house, these children convey their coping with the reality of living in a hospital, away from their familiar home environment.

Sick children also often draw clowns. Some attribute this choice to the child's inner sense of being a stranger in his own body. Sick children are required to wear a new mask, and in some cases also undergo treatments which affect their actual appearance (Pinchover 2002). Clown drawings may be related to the sick child's lived reality in another way as well. When friends come to visit him, he tries to seem happy and cheerful rather than talk about the difficult moments of coping with the illness and its associated treatments. Consequently, many children portray their sense of being detached from their physical condition by producing grotesque drawings of children and surreal figures such as robots and other imaginary beings. In many cases, this is accompanied by refusal to draw themselves, but only a generic human figure. These are all typical of the distancing defense mechanism, which helps coping with the disease and the various anxieties it arouses (Freud 1971).

To conclude this section, drawings can be used by sick children not only to represent their condition, but also to cope with it by creating a new reality. Children may use art therapeutically by drawing themselves after having convalesced, or as managing to overcome the disease using various creative solutions depicted on the white page.

Drawings by Children with Sick Parents

Diseases feature in children's drawings even if they do not experience in person. Often, such drawings can shed light on how the child experiences the family crisis that results when a parent is diagnosed with a severe illness.

The mother of the girl who made the next drawing (aged four and 7 months) has been in and out of hospitals for about a year. During that time, the girl's drawings have changed completely. Her concerned mother wanted to analyze them in order to see how she could help her daughter out in their joint struggle.

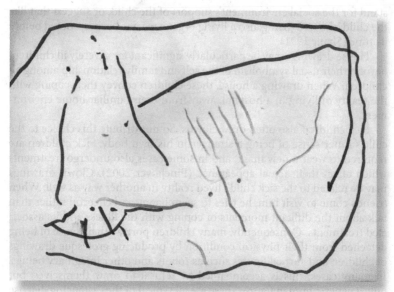

Figure 9-13: Regression following the mother's hospitalization

The most significant change in her drawings was abrupt regression to an earlier developmental stage. Such regression is typical of children undergoing crises, and is evident not only in their drawings, but also in their behavior (reverting to the pacifier, bedwetting, and latching on to transitional objects). Such regression is a defensive mechanism designed to protect the child by withdrawing to an older, more familiar reality.

In this drawing, regression is seen in two main aspects: first, the human figure drawing has not developed to an age-appropriate level, and second, the girl has chosen to omit the body's contour line, creating a figure without a clear boundary, liable to "spill" at any time or alternatively, be invaded by another (this is perhaps related to invasive medical treatments).

Nevertheless, it is interesting to see that when this girl made this drawing, she drew a line from the figure to the left around the other figure, and when doing so, she said that this was her arm embracing her mother. That is, the girl's subjective interpretation in this case was more empowering and positive, reminding us the analytic importance of listening closely to the child as he performs or describes his own drawing.

The next drawing was made by a boy four years and 2 months old, whose mother had a cervical tumor. It seems to convey subconscious awareness of the disease although, at the time this drawing was made, his parents did not share the traumatic information with him. The parents contacted me for counseling on how to talk to him about the complex reality of the difficult treatments his mother was expected to undergo. As he told me while depicting his mother in this family drawing, he defined her as the central figure. It was the first he drew, and he started by drawing her head in a shaky and unconfident line. He then turned to the other two figures and demonstrated himself to be perfectly able, in terms of motor skills, to draw a nice, rounded line to designate the head. In other words, in this drawing he made a graphic distinction between the various figures, regardless of his actual skill.

Figure 9-14: **A child who may be subconsciously aware of his mother's disease**

When children draw illness, the diseased organ is often depicted with weak, shattered and shaky lines, with multiple erasures and line that seem "welded together". Conversely, other children use strong, rigid lines, as well as emphases in the diseased area to express the anger they feel about the disease. Despite the formal contradiction between those two motifs, analytically they are one, as both represent reactions to physiologically-related stress situations, with the specific graphic response (rigidity vs. softness) related mainly to the child's personal character.

The next drawing is another example of unconscious awareness. The four year-old who made this drawing depicted her mother, as she said, at a time when, unbeknownst to her, her mother was diagnosed with cervical cancer and had to face chemotherapy and possibly even hysterectomy. Until the actual treatments began, this girl's family was very cautious and told her nothing about the disease, so that, as her mother told me at the time the drawing was made, there was "no chance" her daughter had any inkling about her condition.

Figure 9-15:   A child who may be subconsciously aware of her mother's disease

The mother contacted me for drawing analysis about a year after her disease had been diagnosed. She brought me dozens of drawing and wanted to know how her child was coping with the family crisis over that year. This drawing was there as well, its date revealing that it had been made before the disease was diagnosed. According to the girl, the bent-over figure in the drawing depicts the mother. Her body organs are depicted pretty ordinarily and age-appropriately. However, the area corresponding to the womb is blackened and depicted in an angular and dense line, indicating an area of stress and anxiety, raising the possibility that the child may have been (at least subconsciously) aware of her mother's condition.

When I asked the girl who made the following drawing to draw her family, she immediately asked for a ruler. A baby brother was born to this 4,5-year-old girl several months before the drawing. Since he suffered from a congenital heart defect, her parents kept taking him to the hospital. When she made this drawing, she ignored the parents and drew only herself and her two brothers. The parents' absence is keenly felt in the drawing, and naturally, in her recent lifestyle as well. This extreme transformation is further emphasized by her use of the ruler: she needs it to draw straight, well-structured lines, just as she would have liked her reality to be.

Figure 9-16: Using a ruler in times of crisis

The next drawing was made by a six year-old when his entire family was preoccupied with his father's severe illness. The threat of death kept hanging over everyone and the mother had to do everything she could to support her children and communicate the difficult reality to them. The drawing was the boy's response to the request that he draw a tree.

Figure 9-17: **A tree drawing indicating a child's fears during his father's illness**

This drawing speaks for itself: the tree, symbolizing growth, development and new beginning is relegated to the edge of the page, while the emptiness – typical of times of fear and anxiety – takes over the entire space. The trunk, symbolic of the ability to withstand environmental difficulties (storms, etc.) is thin and fragile, representing the mental fragility experienced by the child (and perhaps other family members as well (Jolley 2009).

Often, the power of drawings lies in their function as records. They often accompany families during times of crisis, and can be a source of strength after successful coping with a crisis, as they make the families' psychological achievements clearly evident. The next drawings illustrate regression followed by progression, consistent with a parent's developing condition.

Figure 9-18:   Regression in a drawing made before a parent's surgery

The mother of the ten year-old who made the drawing seen above had to undergo surgical removal of an inner organ. She was very fearful of this invasive procedure and it seems her son was keenly aware of her fears, sharing her concern in the period leading up to the operation. This drawing was made the day before the surgery.

Compared to previous drawings by this child, the overall drawing quality, and particularly the mother figure, has regressed. The mother's arms are one-dimensional, symbolizing her difficulty coping with her imminent surgery. Note that some of the other figures have two-dimensional arms, thereby distinguished graphically and demonstrating that the child who drew them attributes the inability to cope emotionally to a specific figure – his mother – in that he is perfectly capable of drawing otherwise. Moreover, the mother's legs are unstable, reflecting her emotional stability due to her health condition.

Only three days later, while his mother was convalescing at home, the same boy made the next drawing. Here, his drawing skill is back to its normal level, before the operation. The mother figure appears at the center and seems clear and secure. Her arms are two-dimensional, her legs are stable, the line in which she is drawn is stronger and of higher quality compared to the previous drawing, and finally, the entire figure is painted (including body color). All these new indicators suggest that this boy experiences renewed confidence in his mother now that she has survived her surgery.

Figure 9-19: Improved drawing quality after the mother's convalescence

The last series of drawings in this section represents a successful family process of coping with a parent's illness. The mother went through chemotherapy as a result of her breast cancer. She not only coped with her own difficult treatments, but made a considerable effort to find creative ways to help her daughters work through the family crisis on the emotional level.

The solutions this family came up with were diverse and moving, from the father's decision to shave his head to express solidarity with the mother's hair loss, through many conversations in which they had to field their daughters' difficult questions (Can any disease turn into lethal cancer? Why do these treatments make mommy bald? Can any medicine do it?"), to solutions tailored to the concrete cognitive style of children that age and designed to make the girls feel part of what is going on. To accomplish the latter objective, the mother made an intuitive choice to use drawings. She drew a diagram of a female breast, and used a rubber stamp to depict the "tumor". She then invited her daughters to talk to the drawing, express anger against it, and scribble all over it; and when she returned from chemo, she invited them to draw a huge "X" over it, as seen here.

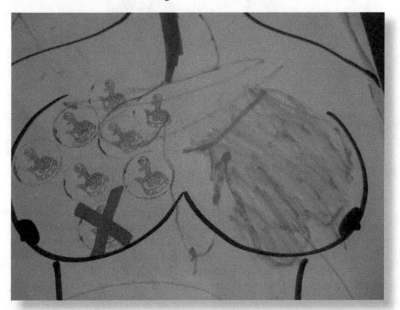

Figure 9-20: Drawing as a therapeutic tool focused on the diseased area

The first drawing was made when the younger daughter was four and 5 months-old. It clearly mirrors the disquiet and stress experienced by her entire family: unstable figures that seem to "spill" into the drawing, with broken, spindly legs, all drawn using one color. Although the mother's figure is still at the center, it seems that hers is no real presence. The mother, drawn between her two daughters, is drawn with particularly intense pressure on the hair, perhaps due to the daughter's preoccupation with her hair loss.

Figure 9-21: Family stress due to the mother's illness

The painter's figure, to the left, is drawn with weak pressure and a shaky line, perhaps indicating difficulty to express her feelings, as well as the fears and difficulties attendant on her mother's treatment process.

In a drawing made a year later, all family members are represented, including the father. Although he has always been there, now the focus is no longer exclusively on the mother, and the family can become more balanced. This drawing is richer and more colorful. The mother is still at the center, with her long hair seeming to shelter her daughter. The figures' mouths (symbolizing expressiveness), seem more proportional and smiling.

Figure 9-22: **Well-balanced and rich drawing about a year into cancer treatment**

Clearly, in this case, these and other drawings played a significant role in the family's coping and came to occupy a unique place in their photo album. They are highly moving and convincing representations of "before" and "after" – a record of this family's courage and sensitivity in the face of adversity.

How to Help Children Cope with Illness?

- Together with the child, **draw the sick body next to the healthy body.** Ask the child to draw a bridge between them and place all the words, colors and feelings that will help the body turn from sick to healthy on that bridge.

- Check the drawings to see whether **the child is aware of the illness** even if you haven't talked about it openly at home. Signs of emotional distress may appear in drawings before they do in real life.

- **Answer all questions matter-of-factly.** Young children think in concrete terms. They ask direct questions and these needs to be answered, without however providing excessive or frightening information.

- **Make it clear that the illness is not a punishment!** In terms of her emotional development, the child is in an egocentric stage, and is therefore liable to think that illness is punishment for her behavior.

- **An overly precise and rigid drawing style** can indicate that the child experiences guilt feelings about the illness and attempts to compensate by creating a perfect reality. It is important to talk to him about it and "relieve" him of his responsibility.

- When the child's drawing is far removed from the difficult reality, **forgive her for trying to create an idealized reality.** Tell her, "I hope all that you have drawn will come true", and keep the painting for her like a lucky charm, so that she understand it is highly valuable to you.

- **Share your beliefs about life after death.** Every family has its own beliefs about death, and you must prepare for the child's questions: If they go up to heaven after death, why are people buried in the ground? If death means going to sleep, what will happen to me when I go to sleep at night? If grandpa's illness won, can every illness also get the best of me? Ask the child what he things happens after death, and adopt the images and metaphors he uses.

- **Calm the child down** when she starts developing fears that all her relatives will die soon. Show her that not everyone in the family died young, and that many overcome illnesses, and share some of the solutions science has to offer. Stress to her that life is long and full of surprises, some complex and difficult and others good and pleasant.

- **Provide yourselves with emotional support** so that you can be strong for your children. Search the drawings for indications for the child's emotional condition, and support her accordingly.

10 FEARS

Identifying Children's Fears

The words "I'm scared!" are thrown into the air at various moments and circumstances during every child's life: before visiting a new place, when meeting strangers, or when unfamiliar sounds are heard on a stormy winter night. Children may be scared of certain animals, the doctor, the sight of blood, or syringes. Some are scared of clowns and masks, or need a little light in the room at night, fear to flush the toilet, and so on.

As parents and practitioners, we observe children every day and follow their progress and choices. They often invite us to take part in these processes, but we are also often requested or forced not to intervene in their world. Consequently, many questions remain unanswered. What do we really know about the child's fears? Have we correctly understood his hints? Will he turn to us when he's really afraid? Would we be able to identify more profound difficulties on time, or would it be too late?

In drawings, children are allowed to express themselves freely, with less emphasis on rules of expression. As opposed to when a child learns to write, the choices made when drawing are affected by the child's physical, cognitive and emotional situation, and less by the need to complete a task dictated from above. Even when it is important for the child to show the finished drawing to his friends and family, he is engrossed with the drawing while working on it, and as a rule draws according to his personal preferences rather than what he "should". Thus, drawings offer a particularly effective diagnostic and therapeutic tool, particularly when children are shy or reticent about emotions such as fear.

Fear and its various manifestations are an integral part of every child's development. Around age three, for example, we observe an age-appropriate intensification of fears. As part of the growing process, the child learns how to trust his abilities in dealing with events around him. Naturally, this raises certain doubts and fears: Am I able to sleep alone? Can I cope with this scary monster on my own, or do I still need my parents' protection? Fear is not only age-appropriate; it is also a key survival mechanism. A totally fearless child can find himself in dangerous situations without being aware of the danger. Fear, in such cases, protects children and helps them develop awareness of their bodies and understand the limits of their powers in the world.

Coping with a child's fears

Parents often feel as though their child uses fear as a manipulation against them. Whether this is true or not, in most cases the child still experiences the fear as very real and terrible. Although he manages to use fear to control the parent's behavior, it is worthwhile checking why he chooses this negative course of action, and what he stands to gain from it (Dreikurs 1973). In addition, you should provide your child with tools to enable him to cope with fears on his own, and give him the sense that he is not alone in the fight. On the other hand you must not embark on nocturnal voyages and "ambushes" of monsters and demons…

Among the various tools suggested for coping with fears, it is known that the artistic medium is particularly helpful for children (Malchiodi 2002). When the child draws, he is not required to talk about his fears and conceptualize his scary emotions. Children find it natural and easy to express themselves nonverbally, and in most cases their visual expressive skills are richer than their emerging verbal abilities.

There are several methods of coping with fears through drawings. One of them breaks the process into three stages. First, the child is asked to draw the fear, with the idea being to "project" the scary emotions on a page of limited size and boundaries, facilitating an initial sense of control. Second, the child draws a situation where he doesn't experience fear, or where the fear still exists but does not affect him; at this point, the drawing focuses the child on his own strengths. Third, the child redraws the fear, adding to his figure somebody or something that can help him overcome it. This stage challenges the child to use resources that are available to him and render the possibility of overcoming the fear more realistic (Mills & Crowley 1986).

Representation of fears in drawings

The manifestations of various fears in drawings are particularly complex, since children express their fears in many ways. Many do so by withdrawing socially, while others act out aggressively or do so indirectly through nightmares. In any case, drawings are a natural language for children, and as such, may provide important diagnostic clues.

When using drawings to detect and analyze a child's fears, you must first see how the child approaches the task of drawing. Most children like to draw and are proud of their work. The older they become, the stronger their desire to make a nicer and more unique drawing. They invest in drawing details, and then strut around and show everyone how well they have drawn. But when a child does not like drawing, only in some cases would the reason for that be physiological (optical problem, low muscle tone, learning disability etc.). In many other cases, it could be emotional, related to the intervention the child experiences when drawing, or to his inner sense as though what he is doing is insignificant.

There are also cases of *sudden* refusal to draw. This refers to children who have enjoyed drawing up to a certain age, and suddenly stopped and began to refuse drawing under any circumstances. In such cases, it is important to check why the child shies away from an activity that used to be pleasurable? When total and absolute, sudden refusal to draw should be considered as a cause for concern.

Second, you should observe how the child refers to the drawing materials. Some children approach the crayons with hesitation and draw carelessly, while others seem to draw very rigidly, constantly concerned with how others around them may react. It is also important to notice how children cope with errors (such as applying too much paint or drawing inaccurately). Children who suffer from certain fears will often consider their errors a problem rather than an opportunity to change or improve their artwork.

When a child draws, he is engrossed in a personal creative act that is meaningful to him. Nevertheless, some children may become "upset" with their drawing: they start drawing impatiently, grit their teeth, shake their legs, and when they finish – tear up the page, crumple it and even throw it away. In such cases, it is clear that the task of drawing invokes feelings and emotions the child finds it difficult to express directly, and that he would rather articulate indirectly.

Some of the children who tear up the page and throw it away tend to make beautiful and highly accurate drawings – drawings often praised by adults. When the drawing is not a product of free expression, many children are too careful not to exceed boundaries when drawing frames, paint so hard they punch a hole through the page, and most importantly "lose it" when they fail. In such cases, you must check what makes them draw so rigidly.

The following drawing is an example of fears in drawings. The mother of the boy aged five and 7 months who made this drawing had suffered post-partum depression. When this drawing was made, she was already being treated with psychiatric medicine and her mental state was deteriorating: she stopped functioning and would lie in bed and cry all day. The father described a difficult reality at home, and commented that he had no doubt that his son was keenly aware of and concerned with it.

Figure 10-1: Regression, intensive pressure and arches indicating the child's fears

From the moment this boy's mother returned from hospital, his drawings regressed significantly. He reverted to the "tadpole" stage, typical of his drawings at age three and a half. Such regression is typical of children with fears, also in other behavioral areas such as bedwetting, and reverting back to the pacifier. To them, such regression is a particularly powerful defense mechanism, as it takes them back to an earlier, familiar and therefore less threatening stage in their lives.

The sad expression on the faces of figures drawn by this boy is also a concern, as it clearly reflects his inner feelings. It also documents the reality he saw around him. He also added tears to the figures, drawn with particularly intense pressure. The intense pressure applied to the drawing tool is an indication of his frustration.

The girl who made the following drawing was described by her mother as a "girl who's afraid of everything". She told me that her daughter (aged four and 3 months) would always cling to her at every opportunity, fear every animal (even the sweetest and cuddliest) and start crying and screaming whenever she was about to face one. One indication of her fears is the way she consistently frames her figure. Note that such framing, in the form of arches, can be seen around the head of the figure in the drawing in figure 10-1.

Figure 10-2: Framing one's figure as protection against fear

The five year-old who made the next drawing woke up one night after hearing noises at home. A burglar entered his home, and he was scared and ran away to his parents. The next day, he refused to go to kindergarten claiming he had to stay and watch over the house. His parents accepted this behavior and let him stay. After several days, he made the next drawing, which was very different from his usual drawings.

Figure 10-3:   Shrunk elements indicating fear

Beyond the regression in drawing level, he used black here, where he didn't use to before. In previous drawings, he used to paint the sky blue and the rainbow in the colors of the rainbow. Moreover, the black paint in the drawing was applied with intense pressure and a broken, shaky line, while in previous drawings his line quality used to be higher. Another significant indicator was the style in which the clouds were rendered. Compared to previous drawings, these elements are clearly narrowed. This shrinkage is akin to the biological phenomenon where inner organs become more constricted under stress. In drawings as well, this is a clear indicator of inner distress, assuming of course that the elements in question used to be drawn differently in the past.

After a time, as this boy's fear subsided, and the memory of the event became more blurred, the clouds grew thicker again and black was used just like any other color, and rendered in the same secure, high-quality line that used to characterize his drawings in the past.

There are many myths about fear in children's drawings, myths that can stigmatize children and lead to a misguided approach towards them. One such myth is related to the color black. The use of black, it appears, does not necessarily indicate distress. Gulbro-Leavitt and Schimmel (1991), for example, found that depressed children tend to use more colors than non-depressed children.

The seven year-old who made the next drawing was afraid of cock-

roaches. She would start screaming whenever she saw one and find it difficult to relax even hours later. Her protective behaviors included checking
out places before entering them and asking her parents to spray her room
every day. When asked to draw herself and her fear, she drew a gigantic and
terrible cockroach, with sharp teeth.

Figure 10-4: The feared object (cockroach) is exaggerated in size

The feared object does not only occupy most of the page area, it is also
richly colored. Usually, coloring a single element in a drawing more than
others represents the child's attempt to focus our attention on this element,
which indicates a certain issue or need. In other words, rich colors do not
necessarily represent a positive emotional state. To the contrary, the time
the child invests in each element in the drawing is a rough indicator of the
inner time he dedicates to the issue in question in his emotional world.

After drawing the cockroach, I asked her to draw herself in relation to
the object of her fear. She added her figure next to the cockroach, drawn
in a particularly regressive style. Her figure stands on a pair of shaky legs,
her arms one-dimensional and thin. She is mouth-less and her eyes are intensely blackened. All together, these signs indicate her helplessness when
faced with her fear. She experiences herself as unstable and as having difficulty expressing herself in her social environment. She draws herself as tiny
and defenseless against the gigantic, aggressive object of her fear.

At later stages, thanks to her emotional therapy, this girl's drawings also
became transformed and this absolute dichotomy of good-vs.-evil, weak-

vs.-strong, victimizer-vs.-victim, balanced out gradually as her behavior improved.

The eight year-old who made the next drawing had a phobia of doctors and syringes. As in the previous case, it is important to stress that many children (and adults as well), have similar fears. In most cases, these particular children are referred to treatment because their parents or the child himself feel that he is overwhelmed by fear to the point that it obstructs his daily functioning. In such cases, you should start therapy and see what can be done to make your daily routine more manageable.

This boy's fear of syringes had appeared over the years before this drawing was made in varying degrees of intensity. By the time this and other drawings were brought to me for diagnosis, the fear reached its highest level. In fact, he could not even walk within a block from a clinic without screaming loudly.

Figure 10-5: Fear of doctors and syringes

Interpreting these drawings led to interesting findings. As seen in the drawing above, in this case also the object of fear is exaggeratedly large and points directly at the "victim's" head (note that children are very rarely "shot in the head" like this). This particular, unrealistic point of view, offered the clue to this child's trypanopobia, or fear of syringes. When I talked to his parents, it turned out that his uncle died as a result of a head surgery, and he misattributed the cause of death to the material contained in the syringe. In the guidance I provided to the parents, I suggested that they try to encourage their son to talk about "that" case without forcing the issue. The results were not long in coming. The boy showed great interest in these talks, and repeatedly requested to understand what exactly had happened. He shared his point of view and listened to his parents' version attentively. Gradually, his parents began reporting significant improvement in his preparedness to undergo any procedures that involved syringes.

Night Terrors

Psychologists have offered non-physiological explanations for night terror. Psychologically, night terrors can be an age-appropriate phenomenon that is part of the normative emotional development, mainly at age two to four. In these normative cases, the child uses the dreamlike vision to work through certain emotional or even sensory contents from the past day. Perhaps the psychological reason for the appearance of night terrors after age two is that at this age, the child begins to realize the limits of his abilities, and hence begins to experience all kinds of fears (Ronald 2008). The child realizes that help means being dependent on others, and that he is therefore vulnerable. This is also the cause for the famous "terrible two" power struggles – the attempt to understand the boundaries of power. The contents of most normative night terrors have to do with anger at the kindergarten teacher, competition with other children and anger at the parents.

The second type of night terrors, which should raise more concern, has to do with persisting stress and difficulties in the child's life. The parents of the 4½ year-old who made the next drawing reported that over a period of six months, she would wake up terrified every night, sometimes several times in one night. They consulted me because they could not manage to pacify her, and didn't know the cause for the stress she was evidently experiencing.

Indeed, inability to pacify a child is a frequent complaint by parents of children with night terrors. It appears as though the child is actually still asleep, and does not really register their presence or notice their soothing words and caresses. This is actually true – although his eyes may be open, the child is still asleep and all you can do is to wait for the terror to go away.

Analyzing drawings in such cases can help practitioners and parents discover the sources of the child's stress. Note that although night terrors are experienced by many children, they must not be treated lightly – not all children have them, and it may indicate certain issues in the child's life that are unresolved.

Figure 10-6: Regression in drawing level indicating stress that is also evident in night terrors

Interpreting this girl's drawings showed that her nocturnal stress was also typical of her general behavior during the day. In the drawings her parents had collected for over a year, I could see severe regression over the last six months, to the point of reverting to the primary scribbling stage. Her drawings were not only regressed, but also characterized by intense pressure and rigid, angular movements. After this eight year-old was hospitalized for tests due to a suspected rare disease, I could more easily help the family by relating her younger sister's terrors to the general uncertainty which was naturally a major stressor for the entire family.

Summary and Recommendations

1. Check for sources of stress at home – children can sense stress even if it remains underground and unspoken. Maintaining stress covertly, "under the radar", can intensify it and affect your child's emotional integrity. Therefore, when you identify stress-related elements in your child's drawings, invite him for an open talk, in a pleasant atmosphere, to try and see how this stress may be abated.

2. Try to maintain a regular and calm sleeping routine. Studies show that clear boundaries at home, compared to over-permissiveness, tend to reduce fears.

3. When your child wakes up from a nightmare or night terror, do not trifle with his fears and visions, but let him feel safe and secure when you are around.

4. Invite your child to draw his fear – let him express his anger at the drawing. The advantage of drawings as a therapeutic tool is that they can be used to uniquely express any fear and can enable the artist to experience emotional release.

5. Let your child decide what to do with his "fear drawing": he can throw it away, burn it, keep it in a closed box or talk to it. Anything goes so long as it's the child's own idea.

6. Invite your child to draw himself "now", and after overcoming his fear. These drawings will enable him to envision his life without the object of fear, and perhaps also to find a true path to overcome it.

7. Use your child's drawings to understand his subjective experience. When analyzing his drawings, pay particular attention to severe regression in drawing level and extreme trends evident in graphic indicators, since these suggest fear and other emotional difficulties in your child's life.

8. After identifying your child's fear, continue using his drawings as a projective tool to deepen your understanding and expand your dialog. Any dialog based on drawings can expand your discourse of fear and resolve issues that may not have been otherwise discussed in the first place. It is often easier for a child to discuss fears as they appear on the page than to describe them with reference to real-life situations. Drawings offer some protection, like a mask which allows the child to articulate fears, while experiencing emotional release and relief of symptoms. Therefore, you should encourage your child to talk about his fears as they appear in his drawings, and together, find ways to relieve his stress.

9. Often, the trigger for the child's fear is not immediate or sudden, but is actually a sequence of events. Examples are a wartime incident or an encounter with a strange dog. Children often find it difficult to understand how their fear was born, which makes them feel the event is not under their control and therefore that they cannot cope with it. They will often say that they heard a sudden siren or that the dog suddenly lunged at them. To resolve this, you must talk to the child, explain the sequence of events and his role in them, why the incident started and ended, and so on. Your child's realization that he can change reality by going to a safer place, or avoiding a certain dangerous place, will make him feel safer and contribute to alleviating his symptoms.

11 ANXIETIES AND TRAUMAS

The Dark Side of Colorful Drawings

Violence and aggression are basic to human existence, and children encounter them at a very young age, even before they become exposed to violence on TV. In classical legends, children are told about predators (Little Red Riding Hood), abusive parents, (Snow White and Rapunzel), dangerous adults (Hansel and Gretel), and continuous physical and mental abuse (Cinderella). The end of the story is happy, but the way there is fraught with fears and anxieties (Zipes 2002).

Whatever the source of violence, it always leaves the environment surprised and agape. This is doubly true when it is indiscriminate and directed at little children as well, when it occurs within the family and perpetrated by people who are familiar or even closely related to the victim, and when it is systematic and occurs over a prolonged period of time.

In such cases, drawings can help adults who wish to promote the child's well-being to understand something about an experience that may be too difficult to put into words. The drawings become the child's mouth, expressing what cannot be voiced as yet.

Children under the Threat of Terrorism – A Study

In areas subjected to military and terrorist threats, children and teenagers are inevitably exposed to media reports about terrorist attacks, and are preoccupied with death from a young age. Suicide bombings and attacks by helicopter gunships and UAVs, missiles and rockets – all of which are liable to occur without sufficient notice – leave children in conflict areas uncertain and anxious throughout the day.

As part of a larger study, I collected drawings made by children after rocket attacks in a conflict area. I discovered that their reactions may be grouped into three main types. One group includes children who refuse to draw. Some of them have found other media to express their anxieties and do not need this nonverbal medium. Other children who refused to draw said they had no fear of the rockets, and therefore had no need to draw. In these cases, as in most, I recommended continued conversations with the children in order to make sure their avoidance was not really an attempt to cover up their fears.

The second group included children who used drawings as media to express emotions nonverbally. These children accepted my invitation to draw, and used their drawings to externalize their anxieties. The following example is by a six year-old boy, who spent several weeks in a shelter due to rocket attacks on his community.

Figure 11-1:   Omitting the entrance door as an indication of distress

This child chose to omit the entrance door – a common phenomenon among children for whom staying at home has become associated with anxieties (Erford 2005). The door symbolizes access to the house and the child's inner world. Naturally, the reality faced by this six year-old involves the sense of invasion into his protected space, and this reality is depicted in the drawing above.

Nevertheless, note that omissions can often be interpreted positively. In this case, for example, the boy used the drawing to create an alternate, more desirable reality – the house drawn cannot be invaded because it has no door, it is protected and safe.

As for the tree on the right, the bottom of the trunk is swollen. The trunk is the basis for the tree's canopy. When something is broken or stuck in this area, this may symbolize a burden that is hard to put into words but is continually there, inside, a cause for concern. This interpretation suggests the drawing is indicative of the six year-old's stress and misery as a result of the conflict. Relatedly, the quality of the lines used in the drawing indicates his sensitivity and consideration for his social environment. Perhaps he does not wish to burden others around him and therefore chooses to remain alone with his thoughts and fears rather than to share them.

In order to help him in such difficult times and in their aftermath, it is better to accept his preference for drawing. To use indirect communication channels rather than address him verbally and directly. So long as he likes to draw, it is best to let him express his inner world that way.

Above all, it is essential to make it clear to the child, using whatever approach, that his feelings in such a situation are real and legitimate. He must be made aware of the various developmental rhythms of children – how children acquire reading in different ages, run in different speeds and also cope with the bombings differently. Remember, if the situation deteriorates and affects the child's daily functioning, you must seek emotional therapy.

The third and last group includes children who have agreed to draw, but what is revealed in their drawings requires immediate intervention. In these cases, drawings can easily identify children who require immediate counseling and support, as opposed to others who feel relatively supported.

The next drawing shows that even when children experience difficult life events, they interpret and cope with them in very different ways. Although the subject is a rocket strike, the general tone of the drawing is positive. The girl who made this drawing, aged eight and 8 months, is seen as tall and dominant, giving the impression of strength and control. To a certain degree, she even protects the houses around her. She does not ignore the rockets, and even darkens the sky after originally painting them blue. However, the drawing is made in a confident and consistent line. When I spoke to her after making it, she expressed confidence despite the situation, and optimism for the future.

Figure 11-2: Self-confidence in the face of adversity

Indeed, drawings give some children the sense that they control events around them. However, you must never rush to conclusions. Children do not always draw in order to cope or because they are not coping. Does their choice of subject, with blood and other horrific images, indicate distress or the need to overcome it? Not necessarily. In fact, in conflict areas many children show interest in these subjects simply because they are constantly on the news and on the adults' mind. They are not necessarily anxious at all. When analyzing drawings, you must therefore attend to the quality of the line and pressure, as well as to other graphic indicators and the color combinations. Moreover, to support any conclusion you must analyze a wide variety of drawings from different periods in the child's life.

The next drawing by a 13 ½ year-old illustrates that the choice of subject in itself does not necessarily indicate any personality characteristics. The boy chose the subject after watching *Lord of the Rings*. Examining other drawings he had made clearly showed that there was no cause for concern, and that he mainly wanted to depict the images he had seen in the film from a critical and sarcastic perspective.

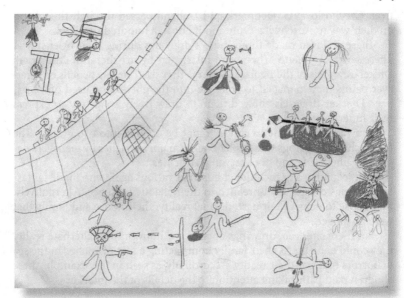

Figure 11-3:   The subject of an individual drawing does not necessarily indicate distress

As opposed to children such as the ones described above, children may find themselves faced with extreme situations called chronic traumatic conditions (Reyes 2008). The psychological definition of chronic traumatic condition refers to systemic mental injury. For a long period, and in a way that affects many areas of his life, the child is required to cope with a situation he is completely unable to.

The new situation is interpreted by the child, with some justice, as a total collapse of his familiar reality and worldview, affecting his objective prospects in life and the emotional support he needs from his environment. The dangers he is exposed to are real, this is no passing fear of any imaginary being. These threats scar the child deeply, for a long time (Eysenck et al. 1972).

As a result, the child experiences symptoms of distress on various levels: at first, increased stress and anxiety following the exposure to the event, followed by deeper distress due to the sense of helplessness experienced in trying to prevent it.

Children's Drawings in Theresienstadt Ghetto

One of the most traumatic events in human history, the Holocaust exposed millions of children to difficult situations and death. In a little Czech town called Terezin, the Germans created a ghetto they named Theresienstadt, after the town's German name. From 1941 to 1944, some 15,000 children from Czechoslovakia, Denmark and Holland passed through this ghetto on their way to Auschwitz. Only about one in a hundred survived.

These children made thousands of drawings during their brief stay at Theresienstadt Ghetto. They were instructed by art therapist Ms. Friedl Dicker-Brandeis of the Bauhaus School. They used simple pencils or whatever paints they managed to smuggle into the ghetto and used office papers. Diecker-Brandeis allowed them to draw freely, so as best to express their inner world.

Drawings by the ghetto children may be divided into two groups. The first includes drawings that depict reality, mainly sketches by teenagers describing ghetto life and documenting atrocities.

The second group includes children of various ages, who made fantastic drawings completely unrelated to their chaotic presence. Alternatively, they chose to depict their past, normal reality: their house and family that were no longer.

For these children, drawings opened a window into an alternate reality they could hang on to, their family home acting a sort of anchor in the sea of horrors that was their reality. Accordingly, as seen in this example, these children paid painstaking attention to the details of the interior.

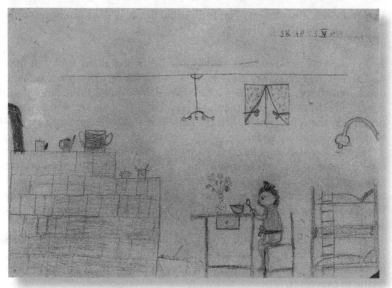

Figure 11-4:   Attempt to reconstruct the previous way of life

In many drawings, these children try to reconstruct their former way of life, drawing familiar objects with meticulous accuracy. However, most drawings, such as the one shown here, ultimately fail at reconstructing the safe atmosphere of the past. This drawing gives a cold and distant impression. In many houses, such as this, there is no entrance door. This omission is common in drawings by children from Theresienstadt Ghetto, and should be identified with children's natural desire to prevent invasion of their home.

Figure 11-5: Omitted door indicating a desire to prevent it from being invaded

In other drawings, you can see children emphasizing the familiar, safe and calm environment of the previous home compared to their present surroundings. As in previous drawings, steps are taken to protect the home. In the drawing in figure 11-6, a rainbow powerfully blocks sunlight, preventing it from lighting the home and protecting it against all invaders.

Figure 11-6:   A rainbow protecting houses against invaders

As in many other drawings from Theresienstadt, the floor in the next example is black-and-white. Although this could be a realistic depiction of reality, graphically the impression is of a sharp transition and unsettling conflict, creating an atmosphere of disquiet, instability and stress.

Figure 11-7: Black-and-white floor giving the drawing a conflictual quality

Other recurring images have to do with food. Disturbingly, the next drawing shows preparations for a large meal, but the dishes lack food or drink.

Figure 11-8:   Family dinner as depicted in the ghetto

Graphically, the drawings of Theresienstadt children are characterized, among other things, by angular emphasis of the shoulders, giving the impression that the figures are powerful and cannot be trifled with.

This is particularly true of the red-shirted figure seen in this playground drawing. She is drawn without a face, with her emphasized shoulders and tough posture communicating strength.

Figure 11-9:   Figures with angular shoulders making them seem powerful

The colorfulness of the last drawing in this series creates a misleading impression of joie de vivre. It also seems to have been painted with a free and confident hand. But in fact, due to the child's age, the picture is totally different. Since he is eight, he is within the age range where drawings typically tell a story and create quality integration of the various items depicted.

In the present drawing, however, despite its colorfulness, the overall impression is that of isolation and alienation: each figure is separate from the others, the play carts are untouched, and nobody approaches the food vendor depicted on the right.

Figure 11-10: A colorful drawing communicating loneliness and alienation

Some of the drawings seen above were made after the children had already lost their parents. However, they still kept on drawing their past lives, and used their drawings to represent a self-perception preserved despite the horror.

Child Abuse Victims

Drawings made by victims of psychological, sexual and physical abuse often provide indications of their distress (Fink 2000). Victims of psychological abuse often also suffer from physical neglect, including lack of access to appropriate medical treatment when sick or injured. These children are often left alone with no adult present, underfed, or forced to stay alone outside for hours. The need for emotional support is not met, and they often witness severe violence, drug use, etc.

Victims of physical abuse suffer repeated beatings completely unrelated to their behavior. In some cases, their victimizers use objects that cause particularly severe injuries.

The category of sexual abuse includes all cases that expose children to or involve them in sexual acts that violate societal or family taboos.

In drawings by abused children we find a broad range of manifestations, including total refusal to draw or express themselves at all. This is typical of children who have been victimized over a long period of time, and are afraid to share their secret. Another typical reaction to the request to draw is "flashlight drawings", designed to get rid of the task as soon as possible. Finally, some drawings do provide indications of the actual abuse.

The eight year-old who made the next drawing suffered physical and psychological abuse by her parents. This was concluded from her drawings after a comprehensive analysis and a personal interview with the family and case worker. The indicators discussed below may not suggest a similar conclusion in drawings by other children. When in doubt, always refer the case to professional and comprehensive diagnosis before arriving at any conclusions.

Figure 11-12: Regressive drawing level and omission of facial organs in the self-figure

First, the overall level is age-inappropriate. Most drawings by girls her age are rich in details and graphically well-developed human figures. They like drawing flowers, butterflies, hearts and figures decorated with various ornaments and accessories for their hair and clothes. On the other hand, this girl draws tiny "match-like" and identity-less figures. This drawing level at her age is often interpreted as a desire to avoid exposure to adults, and to remain dissociated and inaccessible to any form of communication or contact.

Since she hardly spent any energy on drawing her figure it also seems that she does not like herself or her body, or would prefer to shrink and disappear rather than face her parents' reactions. Victims of child abuse often draw their image so as to arouse rejection, maybe because they perceive themselves as flawed, thereby justifying their abuse. In any case, the way the victim draws himself is highly significant to future treatment.

The father and mother (the larger figures to the right and left, respectively) are drawn disproportionately to the girl and her siblings (which are titled "boy and girl", but do have facial features, unlike her image). The size of the parent figures creates a particularly threatening impression. Her father holds an angular tool in his hand, and on the other side you can see an angular scribble whose meaning is obscure. Her mother, also disproportionately large, is handless and feetless, and also looks threatening. However, it is difficult to determine based on this drawing alone whether the mother is partner to the abuse, or a helpless observer.

Another important issue related to this drawing is the lack of connectedness. Each family member is placed on the page as if by accident, and remains relatively distant from the other family members, who seem to be such by name only.

In this case, I was fortunate to also look at the girl's handwriting, which contained similar indications of distress.

A fascinating study of children's drawings (Ben-Natan 2001) found 44 significant indicators of general abuse, 38 of which were found significant for particular types of abuse. Children suffering from emotional neglect, for example, were found to draw flying figures or head-only figures eight times as frequently as non-abused children. Note that these indicators are relevant only above age six.

Children suffering from physical abuse tend to make drawings with violent content repeatedly, with the facial area massively shadowed. These indicators are relevant only above age eight. Indicators related to arms (armless figures or figures with long, overshadowed arms) were not found significant among this group.

Finally, children subjected to sexual abuse often drew phallic symbols, emphasized genitals by blackening or grotesque enlargement, and often drew the figures' legs clenched together, or drew them without legs at all. This indicator is relevant only above age nine.

To reiterate, no conclusions may be drawn based on a single indicator. Conclusions are only valid when based on dozens of indicators that repeat themselves in multiple drawings. I have often seen drawings in which children (mainly teenagers) depicted grotesque sexual organs and were amused by the concerned reaction of those around them. Also, children often copy from others. This is another reason why you should analyze a large number of drawings. This is the only way to control for the possibilities of copying, whim, or provocativeness. Moreover, you must also take the developmental issue into account, because some phenomena that require urgent attention at a certain age may be considered completely normal at another.

Drawings by a victim of severe abuse

The drawings presented below were submitted for my analysis by a daily national newspaper. I was asked to diagnose them within several hours, and was not told who had made them. Each drawing was scanned and sent to me separately, together with one picture of all drawings on a refrigerator.

At first, they seemed typical of a 3½–4½ year old. Beyond the indications from the drawings themselves, I could not ignore the fact that they had been photographed hanging on the home refrigerator. This was the writing on the wall par excellence.

After several hours of analysis and cross-reference, I sent my diagnosis back to the newspaper. I had only few drawings to look at, so the diagnosis took longer. Although it is always recommended, particularly when trying to detect distress, to analyze several dozens of drawings, this is not always possible. Sometime you have to rely on a narrower database which nevertheless contributes something to understanding the child's situation, particularly in difficult cases argued in court.

Overall, the drawings indicated that this girl was under real and present danger. The blackened areas and the deformed body line, particularly in the head area, suggested severe physical violence against her. The deformation in the head area is particularly worthy of attention given what was discovered later.

Figure 11-13: Blackened areas in the torso and a deformation in the head area

Emotionally, the drawings indicate such consistent neglect that it seems the victim hardly knew any adult family member who truly loved and supported her. She drew figures with unstable legs and other indicators that suggested she experienced the world around her as unsafe.

Although it is unclear how old exactly she was when she made those drawings, I assume she made them at least a year before, or, if they were drawn at a time nearer to my examination, they were definitely age-inappropriate, suggesting emotional regression in development and social functioning, so that her issues also included social difficulties, problems with daily functioning at home, and the like.

Figure 11-14: Unstable legs indicating perception of the world as un-safe

The drawings tell us this girl was living in a masquerade. Everything looked nice on the outside, but within there was a real sense of sadness, rejection and humiliation. Indeed, the figures were empty, one-dimensional and lacking in age-typical expressions of liveliness and laughter. Drawings such as these are common among children with low self-image, who feel alone in a world where they really have to fight for attention, let alone love.

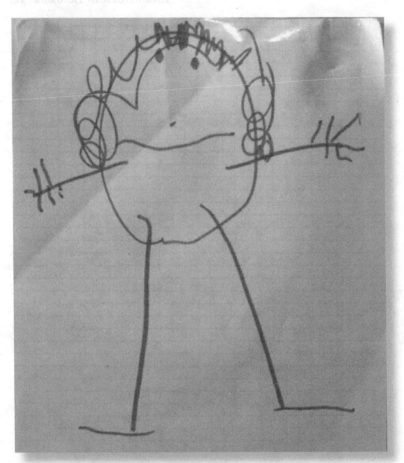

Figure 11-15: Regression in drawing level typically associated with emotional and social difficulty

In this case, the 4½ year-old girl suffered head injury before being thrown in the river. After the story was published in the newspaper, many concerned parents asked me if it was the victim's human figure drawing style – namely, figures with one-dimensional arms and legs jutting out of their head – that indicated her distress in my analysis. As mentioned earlier in the book, in Chapter 1, this style is called "tadpole" and is typical of drawings by children aged 3½–4½. Thus, distress is indicated not necessarily by the subject of the drawing, but by the way each child chooses to draw. This means that even drawings of innocuous subjects can have significant diagnostic value.

Figure 11-16: Example for a tadpole figure

Children who Lost Family Members in Terrorist Attacks

In many families who have lost a member prematurely, due to such causes as military service, traffic accident, disease or terrorist attack, the casualty lives on in the family memory in different ways. Even if the casualty is a parent and the remaining parent starts a new family, the child is very much aware of past events.

The girl who made the next drawing, aged five and 2 months, lost her father, grandfather, grandmother and great grandfather when a terrorist entered their home three years before this drawing was made. Her mother and her hid under a table and later managed to escape.

About 18 months after the tragedy the mother remarried. When drawing her family, the girl first drew a mother, a father and a girl. When she turned to the parent figures, she ran into difficulty, because she was not used to call her mother's new husband "daddy", but used his first name instead. Eventually, she wrote "daddy" near the sky at the top of the drawing. This may indicate where the girl believes her father to be, and chooses to refer to him accordingly.

Figure 11-17: The location of the deceased father's name indicating his assumed whereabouts

The boy who made the drawing in figure 11-18 – aged nine and 10 months – lost his father to a drive-by shooting attack. The reference to the father figure in the drawing is clear and concrete. Although several years have passed since his death, this is the boy's response to the request, "draw a family".

At the bottom of the drawing, the father is seen lying on a stretcher either during evacuation from the scene or during the funeral. It seems as though the boy clings to this concrete moment as the only way of adding the father figure to the family drawing. To the left, you can see a ladder rising to heaven, with the father climbing it. Thus, the boy has chosen to refer to various aspects related to the memory of his father, while showing impatience with drawing the rest of the family, and even omitting one of his brothers.

Figure 11-18: Topical reference to the father's death

Naturally, requesting children to draw home and family produces emotionally laden responses among some of those who lost parents or other close relatives to terrorist attacks, with their powerful images and deep lingering sense of injustice. One girl I studied refused to draw a house, and one boy adamantly refused to draw his family after trying several times and tearing up the page angrily at the end.

Coping with loss evokes emotional responses as diverse as depression, anger, fears, hyper-vigilance and distractedness. These can be experienced to a similar degree both by children who have actually witnessed the traumatic incident and those who have heard about it and are coping with grief.

Obviously, children experience other, more normative kinds of loss as well, as when a beloved grandfather dies of old age or when a pet dies. In these cases as well, children may undergo similar emotional experiences that will be articulated similarly in their drawings.

A study made on anxieties and traumas in children's drawings noted several typical trends that include repeating details, using a narrow color range and general atmosphere of grief, loneliness and self-destruction (Steele et al. 1995).

Children at Risk

In recent years, there has been a disturbing rise in reports of children at risk in industrialized countries, among other things as a result of the economic crisis. In Ireland for example, there were 218,000 children at risk of poverty in 2009 – 35,000 more than in 2007 (http://www.socialjustice.ie). Children at risk are defined as children growing up in a setting which involves neglect or does not provide for their basic needs (for example, when the parents are addicted to alcohol and other drugs), or physical, sexual or emotional abuse. These children are taken away from their homes by court order and transferred to a boarding school, often without their parents' knowledge since they might hurt them again. In less severe cases, at risk children stay in special daycare centers where they stay until the evening and receive physical and emotional nurturing they cannot receive at home.

Particularly due to their complex and problematic background, asking at risk children to draw a house can tell us much about their subjective experience at home. My first example was drawn by an 11½ year-old girl, who has been busy drawing houses ever since she arrived at the boarding school.

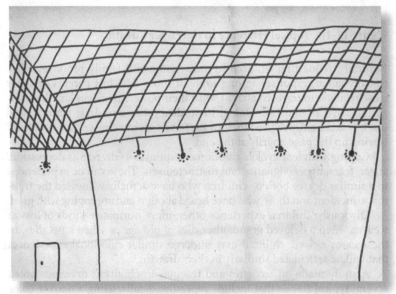

Figure 11-19: Poorly detailed and regressive drawing symbolic of the subjective experience of home

In her first day at the boarding school, this girl drew a house while murmuring, "I hate home". Her move into the boarding school involved sudden abandonment of her parental home and several transitions among foster families. Now, at her "new home", she refuses to communicate verbally and prefers drawing. The way she drew the house in figure 11-19 is considered poorly detailed and regressive for her age. She also seems to invest considerable energy in drawing the roof – a symbol of protectiveness. The crisscrossing lines of the roof burden the entire picture. This impression is only reinforced by the omission of the windows which represents social withdrawal. Finally, the excessive number of lamps in the drawings, which is completely atypical of house drawings, may represent her search for some heat source (Jolles 1971), or an attempt to "shed light" on her life.

The girl who made the next drawing, aged seven and 8 months, arrives at a daycare center every day after school. Her mother is a former drug addict who is now treated with psychiatric medicines. Like the first girl, she also invests considerable energy in coloring the protective roof, and omits the windows as well. The door, symbolic of emotional expression (Leibowitz 1999), is drawn in a twisted and unstable line, and the overall coloring style suggest profound stress and disquiet.

Figure 11-20: Stress and disquiet in the family as articulated through this house drawing style

The third drawing in this section was made by a girl aged eight and 4 months who usually arrived at the daycare center looking particularly neglected. The social workers at the center suspected she was being sexually abused and neglected. The house she drew is also inaccessible, with the windows and even the door completely missing. Indeed, it was found that inaccessibility is four times as likely to appear as a motif in drawings by at-risk children compared to drawings by non-at-risk children (Ben-Natan 2001).

Figure 11-21: Inaccessibility as protection

At the time the next drawing was made, the parents of the 8½ year-old who made it were addicted to alcohol, and he used to live mainly with his grand-mother. We can see that the walls are emphasized, symbolic of protection against what may be happening outside. This phenomenon has been found to be ten times as common among children at risk (ibid), suggesting the extent to which they feel unsafe in their own home, and perceive external reality as something that needs to be protected against and hidden from.

Figure 11-22: Reinforced walls indicating a desire for protection

The study (Ben-Natan, 2001) found that children at risk are ten times as likely to overburden the house with a large number of tiny details, representing their anxieties and fears. They also tend to frame their own figure, thereby perhaps expressing their desire for a personal, protected place inside their home. Emphasizing the walls is mainly typical of children suffering from emotional neglect, while collapsing or unstable walls are typical of physical and sexual abuse victims.

Surprisingly, perhaps, drawing bars on windows has not been found to be significantly related to abuse or distress among at-risk children, compared to non-at-risk children, who also draw bars quite often. This finding shatters another myth related to children's drawings.

Ten Questions You Can Ask to Identify Fear in Children's Drawings

1. **How does the child approach the drawing?** The older the child, the more he wants to create a beautiful and unique drawing in which he will be proud. When the child treats his drawing with anger or shame, check for other signs of emotional distress.

2. **Does the child refuse to draw?** After refuting physiological explanations, it is likely that the reason is emotional, and related to an intervention the child has experienced while drawing or to an avoidance strategy he has developed?

3. **How does the child approach the drawing materials?** The way the child approaches the drawing represents an emotional condition. For example, a hesitant approach and fear of expressing herself on the page represents low self-image; a rigid drawing represents rigid reaction patterns, etc.

4. **How does the child treat the finished product?** Children who "encounter" in the drawing emotions they have trouble expressing will express anger towards it: they will draw impatiently, grind their teeth, swing their leg nervously and even throw away the drawing in the end.

5. **Is there regression in the child's drawing development?** Such regression characterizes children who have fears, and acts as a defense mechanism – return to a previous, more familiar and less threatening stage of development.

6. **Is their use of intensive pressure on some of the organs?** Stressing expressive organs by applying strong pressure on the drawing instrument – more so than on other parts of the drawing – is indicative of fear or distress related to those organs.

7. **Are the figures "framed?"** Surrounding figures with arches or other frames is designed to buffer and protect the self figure against external threats.

8. **Are certain elements in the drawing "shrunk"?** When we are afraid, our internal organs shrink. It is the same in drawings – when a child is afraid, we will see shrinking and downsizing of distinct elements in the drawing.

9. **Is the source of fear blown up in the drawing?** Sometimes children who are afraid of something will spend considerable energy drawing it, and maximize its size relative to the page or the other elements in the drawing.

10. **Is there identification with or projection on the self figure?** Children often interpret information in a way that scares them and make them project the inaccurate information on themselves. Accordingly, in drawings we may evidence irrational situations, that have never happened, and which go to the roots of the child's fears.

12 COGNITIVE PERFORMANCE

Cognitive performance or mental ability is a blanket term for all functions related to acquiring, processing and using information. As such, it represents perceptive and mnemonic abilities including the ability to receive new information, attend to new stimuli, express oneself verbally, draw conclusions, make decisions and solve problems.

Children's cognitive performance is inseparable from their other mental functions. However, there is some disagreement regarding the causal role of the child's cognition relative to other mental functions. In other words, some argue that due to certain cognitive difficulties the child will also suffer emotionally and socially, while others argue the exact opposite – that emotional difficulties are the cause of cognitive difficulties.

This starting point significantly affects the way the child's overall performance is viewed, as well as the messages communicated to parents receiving parental guidance, and the course of treating the child himself. The mother of the 5 year-old who made this drawing contacted me asking about her son's feelings about himself and the quality of his social relationships, noting that he had just started out in a new kindergarten.

Figure 12-1: Regression in the design of human figures

Analysis of his drawings led to the conclusion that he was an intelligent and sensitive child. His drawings indicated that his cognitive level was high compare to his age group, with high concentration and persistence. His spatial perception ability was highly developed; he had a large vocabulary, impressive expressive ability and musical talent. His mother also reported that he had a rich and intricate inner world, so that he knew how to occupy himself with games or other interests. Moreover, at his early age he already showed real interest and ability in writing in two languages.

Socially, he appeared to be a quiet and pensive child, who tried to be nice to everybody and who was popular among his peers. Moreover, he also knew how to create intimacy and play with one friend only, without too many external stimuli.

Emotionally, however, perhaps as an outgrowth of his social style, I did identify some difficulties in his drawings. His coloring and drawing level, which did not match his age and high cognitive level reported by his parents, suggested high sensitivity. Recently, probably due to his move to the new kindergarten, he has been experiencing stress.

In his case, when experiencing social difficultly, like entering a new kindergarten and having to reestablish his social status, he used his emotional energies to compensate for his reduced social credit rating. This caused an emotional overdraft.

In drawings, "emotional overdraft" is evident in regression. Indeed, this boy's drawings regressed, among other things, in figure design. Five year-olds usually draw figures with two-dimensional arms and shoulders.

In this child's drawings, however, you see match-like figures. This child connects to certain children emotionally through gut feelings, and in other cases, whenever he runs into difficulty this is immediately expressed in the abdominal area. Since he relies on his "gut feelings", regression in complex emotional situations is more keenly articulated in the areas where he requires reinforcement.

In the cognitive area as well, this boy seems to show sensitivity that is affected by other aspects in his life. Therefore, it is important to follow up on this child's achievements, because although he is advanced compared to age group, he might run into difficulty when he is not the best in class. It is important to guide him to be tolerant with regard to his mistakes and understand that as a "big boy" he will continue to make mistakes and remain "little", just like everyone else. This issue is especially important, because this child is very sensitive to every nuance and tone of speech and knows when he does not meet adults' behavioral expectations.

In order to strengthen his emotional abilities, I recommended taking him to classes which focus on the physical aspect, such as baseball, basketball, soccer and so on. I also suggested combining age-inappropriate games in his daily routine, games that are more suitable for younger children, like hide and seek and catch, and ball games which involve bodily contact. This boy needs more of the wild childish part in his life, which will allow him to grow slowly and peacefully.

Indeed, once the emotional aspect was reinforced, the boy felt confident enough to express himself in "childish" ways as well. Social or cognitive crises no longer forced him to withdraw emotional energy and he remained more complete and happy inside.

To conclude, this case helps us understand why it is better not to attend to cognitive functioning in its own right. The degree to which every child realizes his cognitive potential is directly related to his emotional and social performance. These feed one another and negotiate for limited mental resources.

Emotional Intelligence

Today's children live in a different reality than their forefathers'. It is clear that today's media and society in general neglects certain unquantifiable values that are extremely important to psychological development, including emotional management, self-awareness, empathy and social skills.

EI, or emotional intelligence, is a term coined by Howard Gardner as part of his Theory of Multiple Intelligences (1983). Gardner divides intelligence into several sub-constructs, including verbal intelligence, logical/ mathematical intelligence, spatial intelligence, musical intelligence, kinetic intelligence and interpersonal intelligence.

These groups are also evident in children's drawings. In my recent studies I discovered that regardless of age, drawing analysis may be used to identify children who are quick to abandon drawing for writing (verbal/

linguistic intelligence); those who draw diagrammatically as though preparing an engineering plan (logical/mathematical intelligence); those who create detailed perspectives and maps (spatial intelligence); those who form original and artistic variations (musical intelligence); those who draw with a tempestuous but not uncontrolled movement (kinetic/physical intelligence); and finally, those who tend to draw human figures and various interpersonal situations (interpersonal intelligence).

The term EI has been further popularized by Daniel Golemen (1995), who offered his interpretation to an older model by Salovey and Mayer (1990). To them, emotional intelligence had nothing to do with high grades in schools. They defined it as the person's ability to monitor his own and other people's feelings, distinguish among various emotions and use that information to direct their thoughts and actions.

More recently, Reuven Bar-On (2006) proposed a model combining emotional and social intelligence. He defined it as the "totality of emotional and social traits that determine how effectively we understand ourselves and others, express ourselves, communicate with others and deal with daily demands".

Talented children with emotional difficulties

When there is regression in drawing level, this is often a manifestation of regression in coping ability, which has to do with EI. To the general drawing level I add the graphic indicators in the drawings: the more you can detect signs of balanced pressure and flowing movement, the higher the child's EI. A child who can adjust to stressful situations and solve emotional problems will not overemphasize accuracy and produce original variations on his drawing style.

The mother of the seven year-old and first-grade graduate who made the next drawing described him as extremely talented academically. Emotionally, he was "age appropriate", while sometimes behaving "less maturely" for his age. Among other things, she wanted to know whether he could advance academically and develop his abilities, and whether this would not affect him emotionally. She also told me that both she and her husband were careful to respond to his requests for further studies, rather than "push" him on their own initiative.

Figure 12-2:   Precision in coloring areas in the drawing

This child's drawings show that he is particularly talented. First of all, his drawing level is indeed high for his age, more typical of girls' than of boys' drawings. The high precision in coloring areas in the drawing and in general suggests high cognitive ability in the exact sciences and disciplines related to language and mathematics.

Nevertheless, you must always be aware of the thin line between cognitive intelligence – which develops quickly and naturally for this boy as well as in a more easily quantifiable way – and emotional intelligence to which you must devote extra attention since it is more difficult to assess. This is true for many of us – we find it easier to read an encyclopedia and memorize its contents than to hone our social skills, enhance our self-awareness, regulate our emotions, etc.

In this child's case, for example, his parents could tell me that when asked which games he prefers, he answers "board games". This is no coincidence. These games are highly cognitive games, and unlike socio-dramatic games, they allow less room for emotional processing. In order to develop and strengthen this child's emotional side, I recommended the following.

First, in the *intra-personal abilities* area, it seemed very important for this child to meet the expectations of his environment: this was evident in the precise and well-structured nature of his drawings. Although his parents denied "pushing" him, I was certain that he was well aware of his environment's expectations, given his past achievements. He therefore set a very high standard for himself. There's no need to "push" such kids, because they do it on their own...

One of the basics of EI is the child's own awareness of his feelings. In order to develop this awareness, it is important to ask daily questions such as, How did you feel? What did you want to happen? Why did you feel that way? At the same time, I recommended that his parents allow him to tell about situations in which he had succeeded less, and to deliver a clear and consistent parental message that it is OK to err and fail, and to accept yourself even if you got it wrong, and that it is important to express your authentic wishes and work to realize them.

Second, in the *inter-personal abilities* area, this boy's high achievements can cause his peers to feel threatened, and therefore keep a certain distance from him. Nevertheless, his drawings – particularly the high line qualities – clearly demonstrate that he is highly sensitive and can communicate with his peers pleasantly and without condescendence. The flexible line and accurate, but not rigid or over-structured coloring tell us that this boy can empathize with others, detect emotional subtleties, and above all, regulate his emotional expression. In other words, this is a socially capable child with a pleasant temperament. When having a dialog with such children, it is very important to allow them to express their feelings more freely, without fearing the environment's response. In the case of this child in particular, I cautioned his parents that wanting to "be OK" with everyone could make him give in to social pressure and yield too much of himself. In order to enhance his ability in this area, I recommended to his parents to play less board games and more dramatic games with mannequins. Such role-playing games are perceived by children as less "risky". Mannequins can lose their temper, use violence, curse and express a broad range of emotions. I told his parents that it wouldn't be easy to make him express negative emotions through the mannequins, but that if they persist, he would reap significant emotional benefits.

A third key area in my interpretation was *adjustment to new situations*. As already mentioned, despite his young age, this child knows to delay gratification; he can regulate his emotions and emotional reactions and shows good judgment. He graduated from first grade successfully without any particular difficulties. Nevertheless, as the school years go by, he will be faced with new challenges that will require him to deal with stressors, accept less than excellent academic achievements and suffer an occasional failure. His accurate and well-structured drawing style reflects his need for precise and unambiguous expression – life is not always that simple... In order to help him in that area in the future, I recommended to his parents to talk to him about failures, expand his problem-solving repertoire and mainly not rush into solutions but allow him to experience the difficulty and realize that it is not the end of the world... Later on, he will be able to provide his own solutions.

We all want to raise happy, optimistic kids, who manage to realize themselves and believe in their abilities. This isn't always simple. Sometimes we are too critical ("in order to prepare him for what's waiting for him out there"), sometimes we don't devote enough time to emotions ("so that he wouldn't grow up to be a sissy, so that he'd be able to take it"), and often we are simply not there ("because who has the energy for it after a crazy day at work"). Nevertheless, so long as we are aware and stop to think and reorganize our routine now and then, we can certainly manage to raise happy children.

Pre-School

In many schools nowadays, kindergartners and first-graders study in combined classes. The idea behind this model is to enable a learning environment in multi-aged groups. Since cognitive development in the relevant ages – 5–7 – is not uniform, the combined class enables children to be grouped by their achievement levels. Thus, a five year-old with high cognitive abilities is able to study in a group together with first-graders. The concept of multi-grade learning enables each child to be exposed to diverse levels of emotional development, and often experience learning experiences facilitated by older children (mentorship).

Another rationale for the combined class is to minimize the stress involved in moving to first grade by placing the combined classes within the school compound (albeit with a separate playground) and enabling the children to be gradually and less artificially exposed to formal schooling, through frequent visits in lessons, for example. As opposed to the drastic move from the kindergarten to the school environment with all its disadvantages, this model enables a certain transition phase, with direct continuation of kindergarten curriculum combined with the potential for adjusting to the school environment, with more cognitive demands and more children playing around.

Those who oppose combined classes point to the gaps between different schools in terms of their management. Thus, while some combined classes are mainly designed to integrate the children "geographically" in the school building (getting to know the system, the staff, and the class format), others emphasize academic achievements and pressure the five year-olds to acquire early literacy. Another perceived downside to combined classes is that often, "redshirting", or leaving the child one more year in the combined class becomes problematic. As opposed to the transition from an external kindergarten to first grade, the child has already been integrated in the school system and would have difficulty understanding why all his friends are studying in a different class, while he remains in the combined class.

Given the emotional complexity involved in the decision to have a child go to a combined class, many parents are unsure. The purpose of drawing analysis in the context of this decision would be to predict how capable the child is – emotionally and cognitively – to become effectively integrated in the combined class, and later in second grade.

The parents of the 5½ year-old girl who made the next drawings contacted me following a significant behavioral change she experienced immediately after joining the combined class. Indeed, my examination of her recent drawings and comparison with earlier drawings indicated an absolutely clear trend: this girl was indeed in the midst of a crisis, and this was not the ordinary crisis many children experience at the beginning of the school year, only to forget about it once they have adjusted to the new situation.

Analyzing dozens of drawings from various periods in this girl's life suggested several key insights. Apparently, she had well-developed concentration ability and patience for learning new subjects. She also evidenced several artistic talents, including musical hearing with the potential for a relatively early start in instrument classes, dancing and drawing skills.

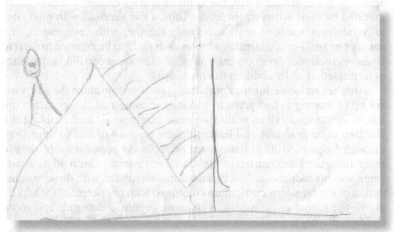

Figure 12-3: **Weak pressure, poor organization and poorly detailed human figure**

From the moment she started attending the combined class, this girl's drawings changed completely. As you can see in the example above, her drawings became age-inappropriately poor in details, particularly when compared with her own pre-transition drawings. All her recent drawings were made with weak pressure and some of them were poorly organized; her drawing level was also regressive compared to previous drawings, with undeveloped figures such as in this example. The combinations of all these indicators clearly pointed at a significant difficulty experienced by the girl.

Another example, shown below, adds further details related to the symbolic meaning of drawing two skies, with the bottom one seeming to crush the flowers.

The reality arising from the drawings is very similar to the reality in the combined class. From the very first day, this girl was included in a study group which spent many hours of the day together. Whenever she completed a task successfully, she received a positive reinforcement sticker, and when she didn't, it was taken away from her. Every day, kindergarteners received homework in arithmetic and literacy. Since she started writing at age four (naturally and at her initiative), she did well in all tasks, but the intense pressure she experienced was keenly felt, both in her drawings and in her handwriting.

Figure 12-4:   Intense pressure and tense movement

From the moment of crisis, as identified by her parents, she refused to go to kindergarten, cried every morning and would not cooperate throughout the day. My conclusions from the drawings convinced her parents to transfer her to an ordinary kindergarten which did not stress first-grade-level academic content. After two weeks, her behavior improved. At the same time, I instructed her parents to work with her using various games which made the transition straightforward and natural.

Figure 12-5: Balanced organization and well-regulated pressure

As you can see in this example, after the move her drawings were once again clear and well-developed, with well-regulated pressure on the drawing tool and the overall conduct on the page leaving the impression of confident presence. In other drawings as well, as the next one, the improvement is also evident in terms of color use.

Figure 12-6: Positive trends indicated by color use

To conclude, during their lives children experience crises that are sometimes part of their growth process. Having overcome the crisis, it is clearly evident that they have matured and drew a significant lesson from the very fact that they have coped with a major difficulty. Nevertheless, in some cases the difficulty has little to do with the normal course of development, and more to do with something in their environment that's not suitable to their character. I do not mean to say that the girl discussed above was victimized or mistreated in any way. However, the way the combined class was managed and the messages she received from her teachers were out of keeping with her emotional development, so she found herself lost and mainly deeply frustrated: although she completed her cognitive tasks successfully most of the time, there was not enough emotional space for her. The parents' attentiveness and decision to consult me at early in the school year enabled us to find an educational program more suitable to the girl's character, and enabled me to instruct the parents on how to communicate with her – facilitating an effective and rapid change. Having successfully coped with this transition, the parents needed to follow developments closely so that their daughter arrives in first grade well prepared.

First-Grade Preparedness

It all begins in one exciting day – the first day in first grade. The parents are swept with emotion as their little baby finally enters school: a big bag on his shoulders, with a pair of tiny legs peeking underneath, and many tasks waiting on the way to discover the world.

The decision to enroll the child in first grade, however, is not simple for many parents, mainly because it is almost irreversible. The decision involves concerns, because the child is not always prepared for first grade in all areas. The most common case involves a gap between the child's cognitive and emotional abilities: the child may be very skilled cognitively, but would still burst out crying whenever he runs into difficulties.

The objective of drawing analysis in the context of first-grade preparedness is to assess whether the child is mature enough to perform adequately at school. Reviewing the child's drawings prior to making this critical decision can equip the parents with tools that will help their children integrate in the school system.

Physical preparedness

When assessing first-grade maturity and preparedness, several areas are at the focus of attention. The first is physical preparedness. This includes mainly fine motor skills – the ability to button a shirt, to thread beads together, use scissors, etc. I would also check the ability to separate movements. That is, move the drawing tool using the wrist, rather than by moving the shoulder and lifting the elbow. In terms of gross motor skills, I would check the child's posture, equilibrium when climbing ladders or jumping on one leg, adequate muscle tone, ability to ride a bicycle, etc. Finally, I will make sure the child's visual perception and distinction are age appropriate (Haber 2001).

Since drawing requires the child to use the body on several levels, all these issues will be manifested indirectly in drawings through the way the child draws various elements, the quality of his line and pressure on the drawing tool. In the following drawing by a girl aged five and 7 months, for example, manual control of the drawing tool is impressive, as is the accuracy of rendering the multilinear arch on the house roof.

Figure 12-7: Elements characterizing multi-step and symbolic thinking

This girl has an ability to attend to little details within the general picture, and use abstract graphic signs to create a form with a new meaning. For example, the way she draws the grass is unlike the way grass grows in real life, but observers can clearly see that this is "grass" in the symbolic sense. This ability brings her closer to learning to read and write, where she will be required to combine abstract symbols (letters) made of familiar lines and geometric shapes into a new meaning (word).

Another aspect of cognitive development is the ability to separate the wheat from the chaff, combined with the ability of using generalization and conceptualization to draw conclusions. Later, these abilities promote reading comprehension, arithmetic ability and other important subject areas. In drawings, there are several indicators of these abilities. A good example is the flower in this drawing: the girl who made this drawing selects only the most essential "ingredients" of the flower: for her, the petals and stalk are sufficient to represent the concept of "flower".

The following drawing, by a 6½ year-old girl, is also a good example for manual control of the drawing tool (around the door), as well as for precocious ability to create perspective in drawing the house stairs. These are related both to her motor and to her cognitive readiness, as discussed below.

Figure 12-8: Multi-step thinking in coloring the door area and use of perspective in rendering the stairs

When it comes to motor readiness, both disruptions in brain-eye-hand co-ordination and motor disruptions are reflected in drawings.

In the following example, for instance, made by a 6 year-old, you can see age-inappropriate drawing level, as well as the use of impulsive and tense lines alongside weak lines and shaky movement. Ultimately, the impression is that of inaccuracy. Moreover, unlike his peers, this boy finds it difficult to cross lines, as evident in the green figure to the left.

Figure 12-9:   Age-inappropriate drawing level, with weak and impulsive lines

This is a good example for motor skills related among other things to poor coordination. It is important to treat such difficulties professionally; doing so before first grade may prevent difficulties in concentration and learning, and consequent loss of motivation to learn.

Cognitive preparedness

Assessing cognitive preparedness includes assessing the child's perception of quantities and various arithmetic concepts, visual perception and attention to details and differences, aural memory, sound recognition, vocabulary and the ability to invent a plot based on a picture. The child's ability to sort objects based on two dimensions such as color and form will also be assessed, together with various aspects related to attention, concentration, etc. To do so, I recommend analyzing both spontaneous drawings made on a blank page and specific drawing tests in which the child is asked to deal with a certain given situation.

This spontaneous drawing is a good example. Despite the general messy impression, the girl who made it honestly tried to organize it by creating distinct categories. The various elements in the drawings are sorted and organized, sometimes around a number and sometimes around a letter.

Figure 12-10: Organizing the page by creating distinct categories

In school, children are required to apply multi-step thinking and use previous planning. At home this ability may be promoted through simple actions that involve several stages, such as preparing a cake or setting the table. In drawings, this ability is naturally evident form age four, when you can see that the child takes time to plan his drawing.

The drawing in figure 12-11 is an extraordinary example for early cognitive maturity. Unlike other four year-olds who plan their drawing before actually making it, this girl demonstrates well-organized planning and thinking at a level typical of children approaching six years. Her early ability to organize the coloring stages systematically, as well as the schematic level she manages to attain, both suggest high cognitive ability, perhaps even giftedness.

Figure 12-11: Organization and method in coloring style

The next drawing, which was made by a four year-old, illustrates a well-organized system of elements that repeat themselves in a pattern. Thus, each triangle has two sides decorated with circles and one side decorated with extra coloring. Each time it is a different side, and each time the color is different. The elements recur in a pattern, with only slight visual differences. The ability of combining the graphic elements each time in a different order relies on the same logic required for acquiring literacy – the ability to combine graphic signs into various letters by using different combinations. Despite his tender age, this boy is mature and curious enough to start acquiring literacy.

Figure 12-12: Well-patterned drawing indicating the use of logic required for future literacy

Emotional maturity

The emotional world develops in the child's natural environment, and the parents naturally have a key role to play in this development. Therefore, it is essential for parents to be deeply involved in the child's emotional world, which is usually not expressed verbally but in other, indirect ways, one of which is drawing.

Emotional maturity is central to first-grade preparedness, because when the child feels confident in himself and his abilities this constitutes the most fruitful basis for learning. Any difficulty in this area may affect the child's performance in other areas. In the emotional area, you need to assess the child's ability to function independently, delay gratifications, identify and express emotions, cope with frustration and uncertainty, be able to accept authority, understand schedules and operate accordingly, store acquired knowledge and use it in new situations, etc.

Various afternoon activities can help your child acquire these basic skills. For example, group sports such as football or basketball, may contribute to delay of gratification and coping with frustration.

In drawings, emotional maturity is seen mainly through the colors and combinations of various elements, the child's confident or hesitant movements in the page area, line qualities such as shaky and insecure line, or poorly detailed human figures with some omitted organs as you would expect from a child about to enter first grade, and as seen in this example.

Figure 12-13: Poorly detailed human figures

In Figure 12-7, on the other hand, the graphic picture is more positive, mainly due to the use of impetuous lines that are full of presence, which attest, among other things, to the emotional maturity of the girl who made that drawing.

Social maturity

The fourth area that requires attention is social maturity. This includes how the child adjusts to new social situations, communicates and cooperates with his peers, plays with several children at the same time, listens to others, compromises and acts considerately, respects the rules of the game, etc.

In drawings, we observe the style of organization over the page area and the degree of cognitive flexibility that is manifested in line quality, as well as in recurring exploration of a certain element, which appears each time in a new and original style – indicating curiosity and motivation for novel experiences. For example, the girl who drew Figure 12-7 paid considerable attention to the roof, which is rendered differently in her other drawings.

An opposite example is shown in figure 12-14. Here you can see that despite the schematic understanding of the house and flower elements, the human figures are not drawn at a level appropriate for first-graders. This fact, combined with other elements, is a common indicator of difficulties in social skills.

Figure 12-14: Age inappropriate human figure

The parents of the 5½ year-old who made the next drawing wanted to see whether she was mature enough to enter first grade. My impression from her drawings was that she was an active child, sometimes impatient when asked to focus on small details. This did not result from a difficulty involving fine motor skills, because you can see how accurately she crosses lines, but from her emotional need to quickly arrive at an outcome you can show others.

Cognitively, she is attentive to everything around her. She is quick to grasp, and her thinking flows from one idea to the others, although she sometimes seems preoccupied with other things. Nevertheless, she needs an activity space with clear boundaries set by the parents. She loves to compete, and becomes motivated when comparing her abilities to others.

Emotionally, this girl is sensitive and alert. She tries to please others, and therefore often accepts considerable responsibility and is afraid to fail (this issue will be significant for her throughout her school years). This need for perfection, evident in her intense pressure on the drawing tool, makes it difficult for her to express her emotions and weaknesses at kindergarten. On the outside, she smiles, but on the inside a storm is brewing. These repressed emotions are expressed indirectly by a regressive behavioral pattern, with sudden temper tantrums (mainly when she is with the family) or loss of patience for tasks to which she used to devote much time.

My analysis of other drawings by the same girl convinced me that I should not recommend leaving her in kindergarten for an extra year. She had adequate cognitive skills and was well aware of her environment. As is often the case, emotionally she was not as well prepared, but in this case, given appropriate ongoing guidance, it could be attended to as she entered first grade.

Figure 12-15: Intense pressure and impulsive movement

The transition from unpreparedness to preparedness can take between several weeks and several months. It is therefore important to follow your child's development over the critical months from February to June. In addition to the aforementioned criteria, you must take into account the girls' future sexual development: if your child enters first grade when she's older, she will mature sexually earlier then her peers. Other factors to be looked into are the child's height and build, handedness and other physiological characteristics, whose combination with the other criteria may affect the final recommendation.

Deciding to leave the child in kindergarten for another year is a significant decision for him; it must not be viewed as a personal failure by the parents. For some children, "red-shirting" can be quite beneficial, as it enables them to improve their social skills. In any case, I recommend, in addition to drawing analysis, consulting with several professionals – kindergarten teachers and psychologists, as well as external consultants – before making any decision.

I also recommend that you start preparing for first grade at an early age, and not during the months leading up to the new school year. Involving your child in an emotional therapy process may also contribute to his ability to cope with the emotional difficulties involved in the transition and help him face the school systems' challenges.

Coping with Academic Difficulties and Challenges

School poses a broad range of challenges for children:

- *Motor challenges* – Students are required to complete tasks involving fine and gross motor skills, from writing to sports.

- *Social challenges* – Students are required to become socially integrated in the peer group and collaborate with other children on various tasks.

- *Cognitive challenges* – Students are required to understand and conceptualize various knowledge areas.

Every child faces these challenges subjectively, with his own emotional and cognitive coping abilities. Naturally, these are not uniform, and neither are the solutions that will help each child cope. Drawing and handwriting analysis can help parents and practitioners understand the child's difficulties when facing school challenges.

When a child runs into difficulties, he experiences a gap between himself and the environment and mobilizes various forces and solutions to remedy the situation. These solutions may be positive or negative to varying extents. When the child feels his intuitive solutions "work", his self-perception becomes more balanced and his drawings and handwriting will be age appropriate and lacking in indications of distress.

Lies

When children feel unable to find positive solutions to a given situation, they choose other solutions. One of the most common solutions in the early school years (more common than in other ages) is lying.

Lies, white or otherwise, fantasies, fabrications and exaggerations are all part of normative human behavior. Studies have found that nearly every adult utters a white lie at least once a day… While this common phenomenon is considered acceptable, when it comes to children, many parents are terrified by the very idea that their child is lying.

Therefore, it is first important to distinguish between exaggerations and fantasies and lies. Young children will often tell you wonderful stories about their superhuman powers or exciting worldwide adventures that happened yesterday afternoon... Lies, on the other hand, are more "modest" and used in a variety of situations.

In most cases, children lie when under pressure. This could be social pressure: when the child feels socially uncertain, he will use lies to narrow the gap. In doing so, he will seek to paint a different picture of reality that shows him in a better light. This is why you must not underestimate the significance of lying – in many cases the lie is the child's solution for an ongoing, stressful problem.

In this context, drawing analysis will try to assess the stressors operating on the child, how he experiences his environment and why he chose lies as a way of coping with it. The parents of the 6 year-old who made the following drawing contacted me because they were very concerned with her behavior. They said she kept lying, fabricating and making things up, giving them the sense that she could not be trusted at all. They were particularly concerned by the fact that she was about to enter first grade: if she continued to behave that way, they would not be able to trust her with her homework and in other areas related to school work.

My analysis of her drawings revealed many positive aspects: she can focus on and invest in tasks, as apparent from her tendency to focus on little details in the drawings and from her perfectionistic approach.

Figure 12-16: Focus on little details and accurate, rigid line style

This girl's parents are very involved in their children's lives. They said it was important for them to be good parents, as well as to equip their daughter with a wide variety of tools that will help her later on in life. This is why they were concerned – they believed that today's lie did not portend well for the future.

I had to qualify this perspective, however. As already mentioned, lies are a kind of social code. Sometimes children lie because reality is too tough for them, too demanding. It is therefore important to refer to the content and intensity of the lie. In other words, does the lie actually trans-forms reality – "I was born in a faraway land and I have no parents" – or is it just an attempt to give reality a facelift, as in claiming to have done homework when in fact this is not the case.

When the lies are frequent and "intense", this may indicate that the child is experiencing stress. In drawings, you will see this manifested in intense pressure on the drawing/writing tool. This is evident in the two drawings made by this girl: in the condensed rainbow area (Figure 12-16), and in the little girl's blackened hair and legs (Figure 12-17).

Figure 12-17: Hair and legs blackened with intense pressure

Lies related to school tasks are particularly common. In fact, you can treat those lies as another manifestation of social pressure, mainly because the child and often also the teacher do not always separate cognitive from social performance.

Parents often find themselves helping their children with their schoolwork in the afternoon, or sending them to private lessons. Consequently, many parents such as those who contacted me find themselves stressed by their tasks. On the other hand, if the parents eventually decide to push their child forward beyond curriculum requirements, it is important to assess the child's own motivation, and tailor their plans accordingly.

To conclude, lies in childhood should never be treated strictly as such. They are often caused by the child's feeling that too much is expected of him, and that therefore reality must be twisted in order to meet those expectations. In the case presented here, despite the parents' involvement and goodwill, they still truly feared that their daughter was a liar – bound to fail in her future as such. It was important to dissolve that fear by analyzing her drawings. The findings of this analysis enabled the parents to look at her lies from a more emotional perspective, and through it, understand what had made her lie.

Perfectionism

Another solution adopted by children coping with school challenges is perfectionism. Perfectionism and high achievements in school are often regarded as a source of strengths, but a deeper analysis often shows that behind this solution there's a child who's afraid to err and fail at school. In order to avoid this unpleasant experience, he mobilizes internal abilities to focus on his learning and make a continuous, unrelenting effort to avoid any mistake.

Perfectionism is related to one of the central myths about children's drawings. Perfectionist children will produce carefully rendered drawings as a relatively high level for their age. Some go even further and claim that such drawings are a clear indication of first-grade preparedness, but it would be wrong to assume that these pretty, accurate drawings are not a cause for concern..

The next drawing by a five year-old illustrates this. Her mother contacted me in order to better understand her emotional and social world and assess her first-grade preparedness. I analyzed both her recent drawings and drawings made when she was three and four. Her mother said that everything used to be OK in school, until one day, she suddenly began behaving erratically for no apparent reason.

When she was just four years old, she drew the tree shown here. Her kindergarten teacher drew the branches, but she was responsible for all the rest. My examination of other drawings clearly suggested a tendency for perfectionism and social desirability. Her level of coloring at age four (note the trunk) is typical of older children, so that at her age, it testifies to the intense emotional pressure she is subjected to or subjects herself to in order to attain such results.

By the way, an accurate and well-structured drawing does not necessarily indicate artistic talent. When I identify such talent, I do so not only on the basis of precocious coloring ability alone; it has to be combined with other indicators (such as line quality, drawing human figures in profile, shading and perspectives) to support the conclusion that the child has a special talent. Such indicators were not found in this case, so the intense pressure in coloring the trunk was considered indicative of her extreme stress.

Figure 12-18: Rigid and condensed coloring in the trunk area

When I compared the older with the more recent drawings, I became aware of her recurrent vomiting. When I asked her mother about it, she told me that every morning when she enters kindergarten, the girl goes to the bathroom and vomits. Afterwards, she says goodbye to her and starts her day. This behavior was highly significant and suggested that the child was under extreme stress (probably for emotional reasons, since the physiological angle had already been ruled out by medical examinations). Apparently, the child was willing to hurt herself on the way to the coveted objective of becoming a perfect girl. She found separation difficult and her parents asked for tools to deal with this behavior, in order to stop it or channel it into more verbal and less self-destructive directions.

How does such a "perfect" child grow? In most cases, such a child does not grow up in an environment lacking in messages of perfection, and guidance talks with parents can reveal this broader picture. One possibility is that his parents and families expect the child to succeed and talk about their own lives in terms of success and failure. They perceive their child as a key source of self-realization, such that each achievement by the child is for them evidence of their success as parents, as perfect parents. Whenever the child shows them his achievements, they are filled with pride and mention this over and over again. I do not mean to say that parents must not be proud of their children's achievements; the problem is that in these cases, attention is focused on the success per se, rather than on the process which led to it.

According to the same logic, when the child fails, it is failure that captures the parents' attention, rather than the curiosity which motivated the child to dare and try.

"Perfect" parenting is exhausting. Usually, the parents find themselves rushing from one activity to the next in order to enable their child to acquire more and more knowledge, more and more skills. They are preoccupied with comparing his achievements to others', and if they find that he does not draw as well as another kid, they immediately consider this a personal failure and a cause for concern.

In other cases, "perfect" children are raised in liberal, permissive families. In these cases, the child's perfectionism and attendant rigidity grow out of his need for clear boundaries. Since no such parental model is available, he adopts his own system of behavioral rules and prohibitions.

When such a "perfect" or too-good-to-be-true child starts drawing, he treats this as another task in which he must succeed. First, he will find out what is "required" for the drawing to be perfect. His approach to the drawing will be slow and cautious, and he would rather look at his friends' drawings before starting his own, in order to minimize any errors. Thus, as in other areas in life, the most important thing to him is to "be OK" and please the environment rather than freely express his inner world. While drawing, he will pause several times and seek the others' opinion and approval by saying things like, "don't I draw nicely?" Typically, he will repeat rather extreme self-praises such as "my drawing is the *most* beautiful, I draw better than everybody", and express a constant need to compare his drawings with others, and thereby evaluate his work.

Should such a child encounter failure, however negligible, this will be a terrible and unforgivable thing for him. He could respond by saying things like "I'll never draw again... I don't know anything", screaming and crying. This child is liable to tear up the entire drawing for a tiny error. In some cases, it is enough for him not to receive the attention he wanted for the drawing to make it completely meaningless for him – this is because from the very start, the drawing was designed to please others, rather than to express the child's feelings.

Generally, perfectionist children find it difficult to express their emotions, both negative and positive, in an authentic way. They would rather adjust themselves to the reactions of those around them, and are therefore focused on it rather than on themselves (Solberg 1996). Consequently, their drawings often include indirect indications of emotional repression, as in the rigid style used to color the trunk in Figure 12-18. In most cases, the reason for this repression is the misguided view that every failure threatens the child's safe place as beloved and accepted by his family and friends. Such misconception is typical of many children, but does not necessarily lead to such extreme acting out as in the case described above.

Importantly, not all families provide justifications or support for such misconception. Moreover, in many cases, changing the parents' attitude towards the child's behavior – e.g., using the simple sentence, "I see it is important for you to succeed", instead of "Why do you always have to win? Why are you so afraid to lose?" – can facilitate positive change.

When drawing, it is important to enable the perfectionist child to undergo safe experiences that include the option of "withdrawal", such as using pencils or other erasable utensils (Solberg 1996). The choice of such drawing tools is motivated by the child's fear that freestyle drawing might deliver a message that is unacceptable to adults, on whom the child is dependent for survival. Therefore, the child makes an effort to obtain their approval and thus mobilize their support so that he will not have to cope with the immense challenges facing him all on his own.

In my own experience as a therapist, I found it beneficial to invite the child to try painting in water colors. The experience of gouache painting necessarily involves "fluidity" and imprecision and invites the child to cope with this challenge. Apart for lying and perfectionism, there are many more coping patterns adopted by children facing cognitive and social challenges. These include aggression, social avoidance and other patterns described in previous chapters.

How to Help Children Cope with School?

At Home

- **Don't try to fix the child!** Let him get to know his academic difficulties as part of his personality. When he comes to terms with the difficulties rather than try to make them go away, you will be able to find ways of coping with them, together.

- **Align your educational approaches.** Spend some time to talk together about the appropriate educational approach for your child and come up with a uniform and consistent approach that does not confuse the child.

- **Look for opportunities for positive reinforcements.** Self-esteem is built on success experiences, even the smallest ones. If you show your child that you notice her successes, she will not add low self-esteem to her learning and attention difficulties.

- **I have to win!** When your child throws a tantrum every time he loses a game, reflect the difficulty of losing and let him win, while explaining: "I see that it is difficult for you to lose. Therefore, today we will play by your rules, and not by the rules of the game". The next day, play as usual – by the rules.

- **Help the child maintain narrative continuity.** Children with ADHD or learning disabilities sometimes have trouble understanding how it all began and why they became upset or violent. Search together for the reasons for their anger and let them understand that they can control and change their behavior.

- **Family task.** Plan the next week according to family needs, in order to form a clearer framework that is easier to manage. As part of the planning, create a division or rules and let the child who may be experiencing difficulties play a role of his own.

- **Break tasks into smaller units.** When the child needs to perform a task with several stages, give her the instructions for the first, and only then for the second and so forth. Children with attention and learning difficulties find it difficult to perform multistage tasks.

- **Give a thought to how you talk at home.** If you want your child to be serious and industrious at school, notice how you talk about the teachers at home, or what you tell everyone about your work. If you tell them your work is tiresome and exasperated, there's no reason for your child to treat her school experience differently.

- **Order and organization.** Help the child acquire tools and methods that help you when you need to get organized: tidying up the desk before making homework, planning for the school trip – How will the day look like? When will there be breaks? What is the route? All these will make it easier for the child to orientate and function.

- **Reduce the amount of stimuli.** People with attention and learning difficulties may get lost inside a huge playroom with lots of toys. Organizing the toys in boxes by subject (assembly, imagination, creation) will improve the child's play experience and make it easier for her to tidy up herself.

- **Give your kids a chance.** Even if yesterday was a bad day, tomorrow is a new one. Sentences such as, "Why do you never listen? Why do you never help out at home?", communicate lack of truest in the child and his ability to change. If your child has ADHD, ask yourself when your child is more attentive – some children with learning and other difficulties listen better during physical activity such as walking.

In Class

- **Have the child sit next to the wall** rather than next to the aisle to prevent distractions.

- **See if attention improves when you use contact.** Some children listen better when you put a hand on your shoulder or when they hold a sponge ball.

- **Let the child go outside for short breaks during the lesson.** Together with the educational staff, see if walking around outside improves the child's attention and concentration, enables him to go back to class more attentive.

- **Ask the teacher to report positive things as well.** Work on your relationship with the homeroom teacher and stress that the child has the right to also receive positive reinforcements and caring. Call it "the compliment notebook".

- **Comments in the notebook.** A child's relationship with his teacher has a strong effect on his achievements. Sometimes, a little smiley, a heart, or even a verbal comment next to the evaluation can help the child feel the teacher believes in him, despite the difficulties.

EPILOGUE

Over the years, my students have been asking me many complex questions. Every question has an answer, because there is nothing mysterious about interpreting children's drawings – it is a science grounded in robust studies. One of the most common questions is, How do you know everything is OK? How can you tell the child is happy? This question always makes me smile. It is really important, on both a practical and a philosophical level.

In recent years, various writings refer increasingly to happiness: happiness recipes, happiness genes… People seem to feel that absolute happiness is "out there" somehow, and if you only follow a certain blueprint you will get there. Consequently, I believe many people nowadays walk around feeling they have somehow stumbled on their way to happiness and lost sight of the Holy Grail.

Is there really a child who's happy every single moment in his life? Surely you would agree that the answer to this question is elusive and complex, and may not necessarily be related to any gene or mathematical formula.

I believe that you can only find happiness on the move, on a constant search. In other words, parents must constantly ask themselves questions and observe their child anew each day, wondering what he needs. The child should also look inside, be curious to make new discoveries, show interest in the world and ask questions.

What does all this have to do with children's drawings?

There is no drawing where everything is "OK" – there is always some difficulty, something else to do… Thank God for that, because in some deep sense, this is the engine of life. Nevertheless, I would like to emphasize that you can certainly find drawings that indicate that the child is in a good place. Perhaps not everything is "OK", and there are things that need to be worked on, but these are minor, perhaps not even necessarily requiring adult intervention – something that the child can deal with using his own natural skills. Often, all you need to do is simply let go…

The drawings presented here have been made by a boy aged six and 9 months during a huge forest fire. As a result of the fire, his father, a firefighter, had to work around the clock and was hardly at home. These were times of uncertainty and stress, with constant TV reports heard at home. If you notice well, you could even notice the TV channel number at the top corner to the right.

During such critical periods, right in the thick of things analyzing draw-ings contributes immensely to understanding a child's emotional situation.

Despite the obvious stress, however, this child's drawings include a va-riety of positive indicators. The dominant line quality is good and continu-ous throughout, and the drawing is spread very well over the page surface. The subject corresponds to the issues preoccupying the child. Moreover, there are no indicators of any regression to age-inappropriate drawing lev-el. Specifically, the fire seems to be under control – it is in fact a bonfire drawn in a quite orderly manner, changing its hues without straying from the area allocated to it by the artist. Finally, and perhaps most important-ly, the water also seems to be orderly and under control, drop by drop, particularly in the second drawing where you can see a clearly delineated firewater pump that actually protects the father figure like a wall.

The combination of all those indicators led me to conclude that this child was coping effectively, and was emotionally held and contained. This may have had to do with the conceptualization and emotional mediation provided by his mother in real time. It could also be ascribed to his character and ability to conceptualize reality. In this case, the drawings seem to have made it possible for him to create a different reality, a desirable one. At a time when news reports constantly talked about the fire being out of control, and about how the firefighters failed in their attempts to control the fire with their inadequate firefighting equipment, the drawings painted a different picture. This is an example of positive coping, which is very common among children. Such children do not skirt the painful issue, but rather "mend" it and tailor it to size.

When all these are combined with positive graphic indicators, the final conclusion is to let the child be just as he is right now, because instinctively, his parents seem to be doing a great job with their explanations and emotional mediation. There is no need to intervene.

I hope that reading this book has opened another window for you, a new way of looking into the child's world, his character and talents. My purpose has been to enhance your relationship with your child and help him realize his potential in a way that suits him best. On a more personal note, as I always tell my students, beyond all the academic knowledge and studies, I always recommend leaving something uninterpreted in every drawing, from which – I guarantee it – something very interesting is bound to find its way into the next one…

References

Adler, A. (1964). *Problems of neurosis*. New York: Harper and Row.

American Psychiatric Association (2000). *Diagnostic and Statistical Manual of Mental Disorders*. Fourth Ed., Washington DC.

Avtgis, T. & Rancer, A. S. (2010). *Arguments, Aggression, and Conflict: New Directions in Theory and Research*. Routledge

Bandura, A. (1977). *Self-Efficacy: Toward A Unifying Theory Of Behavioral Change*. Psychological Review, 84, 191–215

Barkley, R. A. (2004). *Taking Charge of ADHD: The Complete Authoritative Guide for Parents*. Guilford Press.

Barness, R.; Parish, T. S. (2006). *Drugs' Versus 'Reality Therapy*. International Journal of Reality Therapy, 25(2), 43–45.

Bar-On, R. (2006). *The Bar-On model of emotional-social intelligence (ESI)*. Psicothema, 18 , 13–25.

Bell, R. & Peiper, H. (2006). *The ADD & ADHD Diet!, A Comprehensive Look at Contributing Factors and Natural Treatments for Symptoms of Attention Deficit Disorder and Hyperactivity*. Square One Publishers.

Ben-Natan, S. (2001). *The Use Of Projective Drawing In Identifying The Type Of Abuse In Young Children*. Bar-Ilan University, The School Of Social Work.

Berger, R. (1995). Children Draw Their Stepfamilies. Journal of Family Psychotherapy, 5, 33–48.

Carter, E.A & McGoldrick, M. (1981). *Family Life Cycle*. Psychology Press Ltd.

Cohen, O. & Ronen, T. (1999). *Young Children's Adjustment to Their Parents' Divorce as Reflected in Their Drawings*. Journal of Divorce & Remarriage, 30, 47–70.

Cordova, J. (2003). Behavior Analysis and the Scientific Study of Couples. The Behavior Analyst Today, 3 (4), 412–419.

Cox, M. (1996). *Drawings of People by the Under-5s*. Routledge.

Cox, M. et al (2001). *Childrens Human Figure Drawing In The UK & Japan: The Effects Of Age, Sex & Culture*. The British Journal Of Developmental Psychology, 19, 275–292.

Craft, M. J. & Denehy, J. A. (1990). *Nursing Interventions for Infants & Children*. W.B. Saunders Company.

Di Leo, J. H. (1973). *Children's Drawings As Diagnostic Aids*. Routledge

Di Leo, J. H. (1983). *Interpreting Children's Drawings*. Bruner & Mazel.

Dreikurs, R. (1986). *The ABC's of guiding the child*. North Side Unit of Family Education Association.

Dreikurs, R. (2000). *Children: The Challenge: The Classic Work on Improving Parent-Child Relations–Intelligent, Humane & Eminently Practical*. Plume.

Duke, M. P., Martin E. A. & Nowicki S. (1996). *Teaching Your Child the Language of Social Success*. Peachtree Publishers.

Dunn, J., G. O'Conner T. and Levy I., (2002). *Out of the Picture: A Study of Family Drawings by Children from Step-, Single-Parent, and Non-Step families*. Journal of Clinical Child and Adolescent Psychology, 31 (4), 505–512.

Ehrensaft, D. (1999). *Spoiling Childhood: How Well-Meaning Parents Are Giving Children Too Much – But Not What They Need*. The Guilford Press.

Eno, Elliott& Woehlke (1981). *Koppitz Emotional Indicators in the Human-Figure Drawings of Children With Learning Problems*. The Journal of special education.

Epstrin, J. N. et al (2000). *Familial Aggregation of ADHD Characteristics*. Journal of Abnormal Child Psychology, 28 (6), 585.

Erford, B. T. (2005). *Counselor's Guide to Clinical, Personality, And Behavioral Assessment*. Wadsworth Cengage Learning.

Erikson, E. H. (1993). *Childhood and Society*. W. W. Norton & Company.

Eysenck, J., London, H. & Arnold, W. Meili Berne, W. (1972). *Encyclopedia Of Psychology*. Search Press: London.

Fink, G. (2000). *Encyclopedia of Stress, Three-Volume Set*. Academic Press.

Freud, A. (1971). *Ego and the Mechanisms of Defense (The Writings of Anna Freud, Vol. 2, 1936)*. International Universities Press; Revised edition.

Freud, S. (1954). *The Origins Of Psychoanalysis*. New York: Basic Books.

Frick, P. J., Barry, C. T. & Kamphaus, R. W. (2009). *Clinical Assessment of Child and Adolescent Personality and Behavior*. Springer, 3rd edition.

Gabriels R. L. (2000). *Children's illness drawings and asthma symptom awareness*. The Journal of asthma 37(7), 565–74.

Gardner, H. (1983). *Frames of mind*. Basic Books.

Gardner, R. A. (1977). *Children of divorce: Some legal and psychological considerations*. Journal of Clinical Child Psy., 6(2), 3.

Gillis, J. J. et al (1992). *Attention Deficit Disorder in Reading-Disabled Twins: Evidence for a Genetic Etiology*. Journal of Abnormal Child Psychology, 20 (3), 303–315.

Goethe J. W (1970). *Color Theory*. Van Nostrand Reinhold Co: New York.

Goleman, D. (1995). *Emotional intelligence*. Bantam Books.

Goode, W. J. (1971). *Social systems and family patterns: A propositional inventory*. Bobbs-Merrill Co.

Goodenough, F. L. (1926). *Measurement Of Intelligence By Drawing*. Yonkers-On-Hudson, World Book.

Green, R. et al (1986). *Lesbian Mothers And Their Children: A Comparison With Solo Parent Heteosexual Mothers And Their Children*. Archives Of Sexual Behavior, 15, 167–184.

Greene, R. W. (2010). *The Explosive Child: A New Approach for Understanding and Parenting Easily Frustrated, Chronically Inflexible Children*. Harper Paperbacks.

Gulbro-Leavitt, C., & Schimmel, B. (1991). *Assessing Depression In Children And Adolescents Using The Diagnostic Drawing Series Modified For Children*. The Arts In Psychotherapy, 18, 353–356.

Hallowell E. M. & Ratey, J. J. (1995). *Driven to Distraction: Recognizing and Coping with Attention Deficit Disorder from Childhood Through Adulthood*. Touchstone Books.

Hechtman, L. (2000). *Assessment and diagnosis of attention deficit/hyperactivity disorder*. Child and Adolescent Psychiatric Clinics of North America, 9(3), 481–498.

Heimberg, R. G. Turk, C. L. & Mennin, D. S. (2004). *Generalized Anxiety Disorder: Advances in Research and Practice.* The Guilford Press.

Hetherington & J. Arasteh, Eds. (1988). *Impact Of Divorce, Single Parenting, And Stepparenting On Children.* Hillsdale, NJ: Lawrence Erlblum Associates.

Hodgetts, R. M. & Hegar, K. W. (2007). *Modern Human Relations at Work. (with InfoTrac),* South-Western College Pub.

Hoffman, M. L. & Hoffman, L. W (1964). *Review of child development research.* Society for Research in Child Development. Russell Sage Foundation.

Hurlock, E. B. (1977). *Child Development (McGraw-Hill Series in Psychology).* McGraw-Hill Companies.

Huston, A. C (1983). *Sex Typing. Handbook Of Child Psychology.* Wiley, 4, 387–467.

John, O. P., Robins, R. W. & Pervin, L. A. (2008). *Handbook of Personality, Third Edition: Theory and Research.* Guilford Press.

Jolles, I. (1971). *A Catalog for the Qualitative Interpretation of the House-Tree-Person (H-T-P).* Western Psycho Services.

Jolley, R. P. (2009). *Children and Pictures: Drawing and Understanding (Understanding Children's World).* Wiley-Blackwell.

Joseph, J. (2004). *The Gene Illusion – Genetic Research in Psychiatry and Psychology Under the Microscope.* Algora Pub.

Kaiser, D. H. (1996). *Indications of attachment security in a drawing task.* The Arts in Psychotherapy, 23 (4), 333–340.

Kandinsky, W. (2010). *Concerning the Spiritual in Art.* CreateSpace.

Kellogg, R. (1969). *Analyzing Children's Art.* Mayfield.

Klein, B. S. (2003). *Not All Twins Are Alike: Psychological Profiles of Twinship.* Praeger.

Klepsch, M. & Logie, L. (1988). *Children Draw And Tell: An Introduction To The Projective Uses Of Children's Human Figure Drawing.* Routledge

Kluger, J. (2007). *The Power of Birth Order,* TIME magazine, Oct. 17.

Koch, E. (2003). *Reflections on a Study of Temper Tantrums in Older Children.* Psychoanal. Psychol., 20, 456–471.

Koppitz, W.J. (1990). *Human Figure Drawing.* Prentice Hall Professional.

Kramer, E. (1975). *Art As Therapy With Children.* Schocken Books.

Krampen, M. (1991). *Children's Drawings: Iconic Coding of the Environment (Topics in Contemporary Semiotics).* Springer.

Kubler-Ross, E. (1969). *On Death And Dying.* London: Collier-Macmillan Ltd.

Lansdown, R. (2004). *Your Childs Development from Birth to Adolescence.* Frances Lincoln

Leibowitz, M. (1999). *Interpreting Projective Drawings: A Self-Psychological Approach.* Routledge.

Lev-Wiesel, R. & Al-Krenawi, A. (2000). *Perception Of Family Among Bedouin – Arab Children Of Polygamous Families As Reflected In Their Family Drawings.* American Journal Of Art Therapy, 38, 98–105.

Lowenfeld, V. & Brittain, W. L. (1987). *Creative and Mental Growth.* Prentice Hall, 8th Edition.

Lüscher, M. (1972). *The Lüscher Colour Test*, Pan Books

Madigan, S., Ladd, M. & Goldberg, S. (2003). *A picture is worth a thousand words: Children's representations of family as indicators of early attachment.* Attachment & Human Development, 5, 19–37.

Malchiodi, C. A. (1993). *Medical Art Therapy: Contributions To The Field Of Arts Medicine.* Journal Of Arts Medicine, 2(2), 28–31.

Malchiodi, C. A. (1998). *Understanding Children's Drawings.* The Guilford Press.

Malchiodi, C. A. (2002). *Handbook of Art Therapy.* The Guilford Press.

Mathers, D. (2001). *An Introduction to Meaning and Purpose in Analytical Psychology.* Routledge.

Matthews, J. (1988). *The Young Child Early Representation And Drawing.* In G.M Blenkin, and A.V. Kelly (eds.) Early Childhood Education: A Developmental Curriculum, London: Paul Chapman, 83–163.

McNeil, C. B. & Hembree-Kigin, T. L. (2011). *Parent-Child Interaction Therapy (Issues in Clinical Child Psychology).* Springer; 2nd Edition.

Mills, J. C & Crowley, R. J (1986). *Therapeutic Metaphors For Children And The Child Within.* Brunner & Mazal.

Minuchin, S. (1974). *Families and Family Therapy.* Harvard University Press.

Moschini, L. B. (2004). *Drawing the Line: Art Therapy with the Difficult Client.* Wiley.

Muir, E. (1992). *Watching, waiting and wondering: applying psychoanalytic principles to mother-infant intervention.* Infant Mental Health Journal, 13 (4), 319–328.

Nadeau K. G. & Dixon E. B. (1997). *Learning to Slow Down and Pay Attention: A book for Kids About ADD.* Magination Press.

Nathan, S. (1973). *Body Image In Chronically Obese Children,* Journal Of Personality Assessment, 37, 456–463

Oppawsky, J. (2000). *Parental bickering, screaming, and fighting: Etiology of the most negative effects of divorce on children from the view of the children.* Journal of Divorce & Remarriage, 32(3–4), 141–147.

Palkovitz, R. J. & Sussman, M. B. (1989). *Transitions to Parenthood.* Routledge.

Peterson (1995). *American Psychological Association: Lesbian and Gay Parenting.* pub. by A.P.A.

Piaget, J. (1968). *Six Psychological Studies.* Vintage books.

Piaget, J. (2007). *The Child's Conception of the World.* Rowman & Littlefield Publishers.

Piaget, J. & Inhelder, B. (1971). *Mental Imagery in the Child.* N.Y: B. Books.

Rathus, S. A. (2007). *Childhood and Adolescence: Voyages in Development.* Wadsworth Publishing.

Restak, R. (2009). *Brain: The Complete Mind: How It Develops, How It Works, and How to Keep It Sharp.* National Geographic.

Reyes, G.; Elhai, G. D. & Ford, J. D. (2008). *The Encyclopedia of Psychological Trauma.* Wiley.

Ritberger C. (2009). *What Color Is Your Personality: Red, Orange, Yellow, Green.* Hay House.

Ronald, M.; Kahn A. P. & Adamec, C. A. (2008). *The Encyclopedia of Phobias, Fears, and Anxieties.* Library of Health & Living.

Salovey, P. & Mayer, J. D. (1990). *Emotional intelligence*. Imagination, Cognition, and Personality, 9, 185–211.

Salter, S. (2006). *When A Child Becomes the Four Year Old Parent...Trouble Don't Last Always*. Infinity Publishing.

Schick, A. (2002). *Behavioral and emotional differences between children of divorce and children from intact families: Clinical significance and mediating processes*. Swiss Journal of Psychology, 61(1), 5–14.

Shapiro, L. A. (1998). *How to Raise a Child with a High EQ: A Parents' Guide to Emotional Intelligence*. Harper Perennial.

Shapiro, L. A. (2010). *Embodied Cognition (New Problems of Philosophy)*. Routledge.

Spigelman, G., et al (1992). *Analysis of family drawings: A comparison between children from divorce and non-divorce families*. Journal of Divorce & Remarriage, 18(1–2), 31–54.

Steele, B. Ginnes-Gruenberg, D. & Lemerand, P. (1995). *I Feel Better Now!: Leader's Guide*. Grosse pointe Woods, MI: Institute For Trauma And Loss In Children.

Tasker, L. & Golombok, S. (1997). *Growing Up In A Lesbian Family: Effects On Child Development*. New York: Guilford Press.

Terman, L.M. (2009). *The Measurement of Intelligence*. BiblioLife.

Timimi, S. & Taylor, E. (2004). *Adhd is Best Understood As A Cultural Construct*. British Journal of Psychiatry. 184, 8–9.

Uhlin, D.(1979). *Art For Exceptional Children*. Dubuque, IA:William Brown.

Van Cleave, J. & Leslie, L. K. (2008). *Approaching ADHD as a chronic condition: implications for long-term adherence*. Journal of Psychosocial Nursing and Mental Health Services, 46 (8), 28–37.

Waska, R. T. (1999). *Projective Identification, Countertransference, and the Struggle for Understanding Over Acting Out*. Journal of Psychotherapy Practice and Research , 8, 155–161.

Weingartner P. L. (1999). *ADHD Handbook for Families: A guide to Communicating with Professionals*. Child Wellfare League of America.

Wesolowski, K. L.; Nelson, W. M., III & Bing, N. M (2008). *Relationship components and nature of postdivorce parenting responsibilities among individuals going through a divorce*. Journal of Divorce & Remarriage, 49(3–4), 258.

Wilde, J. (1996). Treating Anger, Anxiety and Depression in Children and Adolescents: A Cognitive-Behavioral Perspective. Accelerated Development.

Wilens, T. E. (2004). *Straight Talk About Psychiatric Medications for Kids (revised edition)*. Guilford Press.

Winnicott, D. W (1971). *Therapeutic Consultation In Child Psychiatry*. New York: Basic Books.

Winnicott, D. W (1992). *The Child, The Family And The Outside World*. Perseus Publishing.

Zipes, J. (2002). *The Brothers Grimm: From Enchanted Forests to the Modern World*. Palgrave Macmillan, 2nd edition.

Travel across Alexandria and discover the artifacts, buildings, gravestones, waterways and landscapes that have been shaped by diverse peoples over 9,000 years. The Alexandria Heritage Trail is a 23-mile loop from the Mount Vernon Trail, a segment of the Potomac Heritage National Scenic Trail, which can be explored in one day or in 10 segments over many visits. There are eight Detours, which go to streetcar suburbs, presidential homes, cemeteries, churches, a botanical preserve, a historic mill, and a seminary. And seven off-trail treks take you through the history of Jones Point, the center of the historic district around Market Square, the town cemetery complex, the first 18th-century suburb by the King Street Metro Station, and neighborhoods associated with the Lee family and George Washington.

The Alexandria Heritage Trail uses designated street and offstreet bike routes across the city, so the entire Trail is accessible to cyclists. Walkers can transverse all of the Trail on foot, or travel along individual segments. Most of the Trail is handicapped accessible. Skaters will enjoy the Trail too, but some of the treks and detours are not paved. Boat tours, and bike and kayak rentals are available; those in water craft will learn much about maritime heritage.

The Alexandria Heritage Trail links Alexandria's many stream valleys, parks, historic museums and charming neighborhoods, which are often tucked away from the major thoroughfares. Discover woodlands, waterways, wildlife, cemeteries, and architecture from three centuries, while appreciating Native American craftsmanship, free African American streetscapes, infamous slave pens, colonial founders' aspirations, Civil War forts and hospitals, and women's history. Go below the surface of everyday life and discover how much of the past is still present in Alexandria, Virginia.

Trail Segments:

1. Canal Trail - *1.43 miles*

2. Bay Trail - *0.77 miles*

3. Shipyard Trail - *0.62 miles*

4. Hayti Trail - *1.33 miles*

5. Baron of Cameron Trail - *3.21 mi.*

6. Mill Race Trail - *2.94 miles*

7. Preservation Trail - *3.45 miles*

8. Campaign Trail - *3.05 miles*

9. Sugar House Trail - *0.74 miles*

10. Friends Trail - *0.72 miles*

FRONT COVER: *Historic Alexandria was a town of brick buildings, particularly along Washington St., where many of the elite lived near new industries, such as the Mt. Vernon Cotton Mill (right foreground). The Lee family homes are grouped around the second intersection, at Oronoco St. The Potomac River is in the background.*

1853, E.SACHSE AND COMPANY, BALTIMORE, MD.

COURTESY ALEXANDRIA LIBRARY, SPECIAL COLLECTIONS

Artist's rendition of Duke St. and public wharf at the southern end of the original bay, ca. 1760 (opposite; also see pages 20–21).

ART BY ELIZABETH LUALLEN, AAM;

COLOR ADDED BY ADELE DUNNE, AAM

ILLUSTRATION CREDITS:

BACK COVER MAP OF MOUNT VERNON BICYCLE TRAIL, COURTESY OF NATIONAL PARK SERVICE.

ALL OTHER MAPS, ON COVERS AND THROUGHOUT BOOK, BY SHANE KELLEY,

KELLEY GRAPHICS, CENTREVILLE, VA.; LINE ART ON MAPS BY ELIZABETH LUALLEN.

UNLESS OTHERWISE NOTED, ALL ARTWORK AND PHOTOGRAPHS COURTESY

OF THE *ALEXANDRIA ARCHAEOLOGY MUSEUM*, OFFICE OF HISTORIC ALEXANDRIA, CITY OF

ALEXANDRIA, VA, HEREINAFTER REFERRED TO AS **AAM**.

Walk and Bike
the Alexandria Heritage Trail

A Guide to Exploring
a Virginia Town's Hidden Past

by Pamela J. Cressey, Ph.D, RPA

For the *Friends of Alexandria Archaeology*

CAPITAL
BOOKS, INC.
Sterling, Virginia

Library of Congress Cataloging-in-Publication Data

Cressey, Pamela J.
    Walk and bike the Alexandria Heritage Trail : a guide to exploring a Virginia town's
hidden past / by Pamela J. Cressey for the Friends of Alexandria Archaeology
        p. cm.
    Includes index.
    ISBN 1-892123-89-4 (alk. paper)
        1. Walking--Virgina--Alexandria--Guidebooks. 2. Cycling--Virginia--Alexandria--
Guidebooks. 3. Alexandria Heritage Trail (Alexandria, Va.)--Guidebooks. I. Friends
of Alexandria Archaeology (Alexandria, Va.) II. Title.

GV199.42.V82 A33 2002
917.55'2960444--dc21   2001058221

*Medallion (opposite) on English stoneware
pitcher excavated from Gadsby's Tavern block in 1967 by the
Smithsonian Institution. The image symbolizes
friendship, abundance and health—optimistic expressions
celebrating the end of the War of 1812.*

ANDREW FLORA, AAM

STAFF FOR THIS BOOK

David H. Chisman   *Project Manager*
Pamela J. Cressey   *Author*
Viviane Y. Silverman   *Designer*
Mary E. Downs   *Editor and Writer*
Laura M. Heaton   *Researcher and Writer*
Hope Johnson   *Writer*
William H. Tabor   *Marketer and Researcher*
Jennifer Hembree   *Production Assistant*

Acknowledgments

Among the people who have contributed to this project, special thanks are due to: The City of Alexandria—the Alexandria Archaeological Commission, the Office of Historic Alexandria, Alexandria Archaeology, Alexandria Library Special Collections, Alexandria Commission for Women; Gerald R. Ford Library, the Richard Nixon Library and Birthplace, Virginia Department of Historic Resources, *Don Cope* from Radian Incorporated, *Don Briggs* from the National Park Service; *Mary Downs, Laura Heaton, Adele Dunne, Andrew Flora, Bill Tabor, Hope Johnson, Ruth Reeder, Steven Shephard, and Francine Bromberg* from Alexandria Archaeology. *Ben Brenman* must be credited as the originator of the concept of trails as a major vehicle for bringing archaeology to life for the public. *Chan Mohney* created the first "Tour de Digs" bike rides, which continue today with the support of the Alexandria Bicycle Committee. Information in the book comes from the excellent research provided by many, including: Alexandria Archaeology, *T. Michael Miller, James Munson, Wesley Pippenger, Ruth Lincoln Kaye, Timothy Dennee, Anna Lynch, Sara Revis, Andrew MacDonald* and archaeologists employed by Alexandria developers. We give special thanks to *Dr. Pamela Cressey, City Archaeologist,* for the authorship of this publication. Without her vision and advice, this guide would never have come to life. Thanks also to our many friends for their feedback, support and patience.

David H. Chisman

Friends of Alexandria Archaeology

ontents

Native Americans (left) in the Powhatan Confederacy predated Europeans who designed an urban grid (below left) around the bay in 1749; Africans provided much of the 18th-century work force, leading to Alexandria's prosperity and 19th-century free African American households (below right).

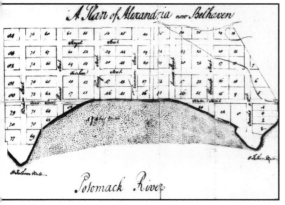

Introduction: Alexandria's 9,000 Year Heritage

Alexandria is unique. It is a community that preserves its heritage while keeping pace with the modern world. Situated on the Potomac River, the area has attracted people for thousands of years. Alexandria's inhabitants have carved their needs and values into the landscape. We can discover what they left behind and preserve these places and artifacts for decades to come.

The first Alexandrians came to this area more than 9,000 years ago. Small groups of Native Americans hunted big game during the last Ice Age. With a warmer climate, people turned to seasonal hunting and gathering along the river terraces. They collected an array of resources near the many waterways—plant, animal and marine foods, as well as stone cobbles for making tools. After founding Jamestown in 1607, John Smith traveled up the Potomac and recorded a nearby village of the Tauxenent, an Algonquian-speaking group. The English established land patents, and the native population was forced west. Mistress Margaret Brent of

*Wharves and warehouses, used for shipping
hogsheads of tobacco to Europe, characterized the Potomac
waterfront of the early town. Wharves and ship hulls
were buried when the bay was filled in by the 1780s and discovered
by archaeologists 200 years later.*

Maryland was the first to receive a patent for this area in 1654. Fifteen years later, John Alexander bought 6,000 acres for six hogsheads of tobacco (6,000 lbs). The land passed on to his sons, and in 1749 a small portion of the family's holdings became the town of Alexandria.

The town was founded on a crescent bay with the Hugh West tobacco warehouses and wharf at the north end; it was the best place for ocean-going ships to drop anchor before the Potomac Falls. Enterprising merchants were drawn by opportunities for exporting agricultural products from the hinterlands and importing goods from the West Indies, Europe and Asia. Other modes of transport were developed in the 19th century: the Alexandria Canal in 1843, and the Orange and Alexandria Railroad in 1851.

A variety of linguistic, cultural and religious groups— English, Scots, Welsh, West Africans, French, Irish, Germans, Jews, Catholics, Episcopalians, Baptists, Quakers, Methodists, Presbyterians—built the town into an active port and regional center. About one-quarter of the residents at any time have been African American. They constructed many of the town's buildings, streets and wharves. While more than 90 percent of the black population was enslaved in the 1790s, a small

9

After the Revolution, the town expanded, and Washington Street, as seen bordering Christ Church cemetery (above), was designed as a grand thoroughfare to commemorate the local hero, George Washington (right). He attended Christ Church, owned property and conducted business and politics in town.

number of free African Americans established neighborhoods. As the number of free blacks increased, the neighborhoods grew; many continue today.

Alexandria was incorporated into the District of Columbia but retroceded to Virginia in 1847. At the outbreak of the Civil War in 1861, Union troops occupied the town. Residents, soldiers, medical personnel, escaped slaves (freedmen), and abolitionists here to assist African Americans endured four years of hardship in Alexandria, a center for federal hospitals and supply routes. In the 20th century, the town annexed suburbs, which grew around new modes of transportation—rail, electric trolley, automobile and subway.

Research from archives, archaeological sites and oral interviews has rediscovered 9,000 years of Alexandria's past. As you travel the Alexandria Heritage Trail, experience the town's charm and centrality. View the buildings, appreciate the landscapes, and touch the objects associated with those often forgotten—the first Alexandrians, African Americans, women—as well as the famous— George Washington, Robert E. Lee, Richard Nixon, Gerald Ford, and rock music icons Jim Morrison and Mama Cass Elliott. ■

Archaeology: Discovering Our Common Ground

Archaeologists explore the past by excavating sites and then linking artifacts, ecofacts and human remains to past peoples' behavior and beliefs. Each excavated item is more than an interesting object; it is a fragment of a larger story about families, events, or even global processes, such as urbanization.

Excavations are undertaken methodically. Archaeologists take careful measurements and notes, since an artifact's position and its relationship to other data in the soil divulge more meaning than any one item alone. All soil is sifted through mesh screens to recover everything of importance. The laboratory is the central place in the archaeological discovery process. It takes longer to wash, identify and catalogue the materials than to excavate them. The sheer volume of materials —millions of artifacts, bones and seeds for large sites— requires a computer database to

Clockwise from left: archaeologists measure the location of an artifact using a grid system; a volunteer thrills at finding an unbroken wine bottle; oldest Alexandria artifact, ca. 9,000-year-old stone tool; American Eagle plate discarded about 1810 at McKnight's Spread Eagle Tavern.

ALL ILLUSTRATIONS, AAM; (ART, ABOVE LEFT) ADELE DUNNE ; (ART, ABOVE RIGHT) RUTH REEDER

analyze results. The materials are studied along with other available information, such as written records, oral history, and geologic data, to interpret the meaning of the site.

Contemporary archaeology also includes a stewardship ethic: protection of sites which have not been excavated and curation of excavated collections in proper climate-controlled facilities.

Community Archaeology in Alexandria is a partnership of the City arch-aeologists, volunteers, developers and educators who create a shared heritage— a common ground. ■

AAM, KAREN MAURLEY

The Alexandria Archaeology Museum— History at the Cutting Edge

The museum is dedicated to preserving and studying Alexandria's rich archaeological heritage and fostering a connection between the past and present while inspiring a sense of stewardship and adventure. The City archaeologists work with hundreds of volunteers to discover and bring meaning to Alexandria's buried treasures. Archaeological resources are preserved by a City code, so private developers partner in the exploration of Alexandria's multi-layered history.

Archaeology has been conducted in Alexandria since 1961, and the Alexandria Archaeology Collection is one of the largest and best maintained in any American city. Adventure Lessons and Public Dig Days invite people into the laboratory and onto the site for hands-on experience. The museum seeks to use the discovery process and findings to increase the presence of the past in town, as well as heighten the sense of community identity and collective ownership of the material heritage still held underground in trust for future generations.

The museum is located in the Torpedo Factory Art Center (see Sites 8 and 9), and is owned and operated by the City of Alexandria.

Friends of Alexandria Archaeology

The Friends of Alexandria Archaeology (FOAA) is a nonprofit organization that promotes archaeological exploration and education. FOAA sponsors many public events and produces a monthly newsletter. Call the Alexandria Archaeology Museum for information (see page 79).

How to Use This Guide

This book is intended to help you peel back the layers of time to reveal 9,000 years of human history in Alexandria. Whether you only travel one trail segment or the entire 23-mile Trail, with its interesting treks and detours, you will enjoy reading about the historical and archaeological sites. Many of these places are still visible; some, no longer visible, will stimulate your imagination.

Special features in this guide include: **a foldout map** of the Trail inside the front cover and **a close-up map of Old Town** inside the back cover. Both maps may remain open for reference while you read about

(ABOVE) C. T. WASHBURN, 1963, THE CITY OF ALEXANDRIA, VIRGINIA

each site. The Trail is a loop divided into **ten trail segments**, each one with its separate chapter and **an enlarged segment map** with site locations and welcome visitor features, such as parking and restrooms. There are **special boxes with BIO, ECO, GEO** and **ARTIfacts** that disclose "down to earth" discoveries. For readers with specific interests, **symbols identify important historical periods and peoples.**

Symbols Used Throughout This Guide

Open to the Public
The pineapple is a colonial symbol of welcome. Contact places for specific hours of operation; see pages 79–80.

Native American
Sites documented by archaeological studies which span from 7,000 B.C. to A.D. 1,000

Civil War
Places associated with American Civil War heritage (1861–65).

Colonial and 18th Century
Sites related to the history of Alexandria's earliest years.

African American
Sites related to enslaved or free peoples before the Civil War, "freedmen" who had escaped slavery during the war, postbellum and 20th-century residents.

United States Presidents
Presidential sites associated with U.S. presidents George Washington, Gerald Ford and Richard Nixon.

Women's History
Sites with information about women's roles and activities.

Archaeological History
Places associated with archaeology—excavations, exhibits and preserved sites.

National Register
Sites that are currently on the National Register for Historic Places or that have been determined to be eligible.

(NOT VISIBLE) Physical evidence of the site cannot be seen.

SYMBOLS ABOVE, ADELE DUNNE, AAM

About the Trails

The Alexandria Heritage Trail consists of 10 trail segments totaling 17 miles. There are six additional miles included in seven treks and eight detours which allow you to explore "off trail" sites. The Trail is designed to give the biking and walking enthusiast a flavor of the rich and varied history of Alexandria. A large portion of the Trail is on level ground, particularly in Old Town and along the Potomac River and Cameron Run; however, some Trail sections have challenging hills. You can also use this guide while traveling on the water. Much of the trail is car and wheelchair accessible.

Safety, Parking and Local Traffic

Since some of the routing is on public roads, care must be taken when bicycling these sections of the Trail. Bike defensively, observe rules of the road and wear a helmet. Always yield to pedestrians on paths and sidewalks. Dismount from your bicycle on paths where bicycling is prohibited, such as Jones Point, Fort Ward and along the Potomac River. Old Town has narrow streets, which are busy at rush hours; parked cars can obstruct views. The Campaign and Preservation Trails have heavy traffic most of the time. If you arrive by car, parking is available on City of Alexandria streets, but note zones with two or three hour limits; parking regulations are strictly enforced. Many parking facilities are available (locations shown on Old Town and segment maps).

What to Bring

In the summertime, Alexandria can be hot and humid, so sufficient water or another suitable drink is essential. A snack, a bandanna (to wet and use on forehead if needed), and sunscreen are other useful items. Winter days often start out cold, warming up later in the day, so layered clothing is a good idea. A bike lock is needed if you intend to stop anywhere along the Trail to eat or to explore the surrounding area.

Metro Access

There are four Metro stations convenient to the Trail: Braddock Road, Ronald Reagan Washington National Airport, King Street, and Eisenhower Avenue stations. Bikes are allowed on the Metro 10 A.M. to 2 P.M. and 7 P.M. to closing, Monday through Friday, and all day Saturday and Sunday.

(ABOVE) C. T. WASHBURN, 1963, THE CITY OF ALEXANDRIA, VIRGINIA

The Washington Area Metropolitan Transit Authority may be reached at (202) 962-1116, or www.wmata.com.

Sources for Maps and Bike/Boat Rentals

The City of Alexandria "**Recreation Facilities Trails Map**" is available at all Alexandria libraries, recreation centers, City Hall, and the Alexandria Visitors Center. It is also available online at **ci.alexandria.va.us/rpca/bikemaps/**. There are several bike shops within the vicinity of the Heritage Trail where maps, rentals, repairs, and other biking needs can be obtained:

Big Wheel Bikes, 2 Prince St. Located near the Potomac River along the Bay Trail; (703) 739-2300.

Spokes, Etc., 1506 Belle View Blvd. Located off the Mt. Vernon Trail, south of Jones Point Trek; (703) 765-8005.

Spokes, Etc., 1545 N. Quaker Lane. Convenient to the Preservation and Campaign Trails and the Parkfairfax Detour; (703) 820-2200.

Wheel Nuts, 302 Montgomery St. Located one block west of the Canal Trail; (703) 548-5116.

The history of the Canal, Bay and Shipyard trails can also be enjoyed from the perspective of the Potomac River:

Atlantic Kayak Co., 1201 N. Royal St. Rentals on the Canal Trail; (703) 838-9072.

Potomac Riverboat Co. Boat tours and private charters, on waterfront behind Torpedo Factory Art Center; (703) 684-0580.

Now your exploration of the hidden past begins. Enjoy the Alexandria Archaeology Adventure.

Canal Trail

Length:
1.43 miles

Terrain:
Predominantly flat trail,
bike and walking trails diverge;
some street
and pedestrian traffic

Highlights:
- Potomac River Views
- Alexandria Canal Tide Lock

Alexandrians sought to restore prosperity by constructing the Alexandria Canal in 1843, (the tide lock, right) thus linking the town to the C & O Canal. Drained during the Civil War, it finally ceased operation in1886.

Take the Mt. Vernon Trail, or the George Washington Memorial Parkway, to Daingerfield Island, just north of Alexandria. Parking is available straight ahead near the Washington Sailing Marina. Go south on the bicycle trail.

1. Pearson's Island (*now* **Daingerfield Island**)   The island played an important role in property ownership of the Virginia elite from the mid-17th through late 18th centuries. Early records show that John Alexander purchased a part of the island in 1669. He bequeathed a 6,000-acre patent to his son, Robert, who in turn, leased the entire island to Thomas Pearson III in 1696. The southeastern part of the patent—willed to Robert's nephew, Philip—became the new town of Alexandria in 1749. To his son John, Robert left Pearson's Island and the land south of Four Mile Run. Another son, Gerrard, received the plantation to the north and built a home, Abingdon, by 1746.

The land owned by the Alexander children and by Thomas Pearson III came to figure in the estates of the families of George and Martha Washington. Robert's son, John Alexander, married

*For information on symbols used in this book, turn to page 13.

Pearson's granddaughter, George Washington's cousin. Abingdon was bought by John Parke Custis, Martha's son and George Washington's adopted stepson, in 1778. It was here that Nelly Parke Custis, Washington's adopted granddaughter, was born. Although Abingdon burned in 1930, its ruins can be seen on a knoll between Parking Structures A and B/C at Ronald Reagan Washington National Airport. (*See the Archaeology Exhibit in Terminal A.*)

Proceed south; at fork, bear left to follow the bike path along the river's edge. Proceed until you reach the power plant.

2. Bellevue Plantation *(NOT VISIBLE; area to your right [west])*

A 17-acre plantation once covered these grounds. Some time before 1789, a mill and a home were built; in 1801, the land was leased by the English merchant, William Hodgson, and his wife, Portia Lee, to set up a dairy farm. In 1841, Bellevue was bought by John Slater, who added greenhouses for his floral business, which he had learned from William Yeates (see Site 56).

17

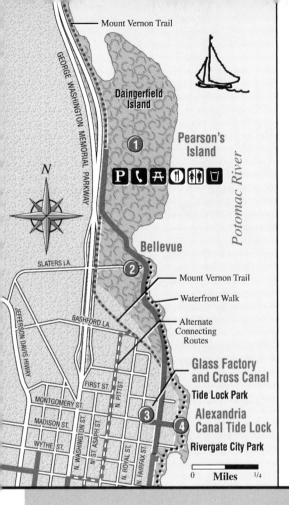

Mount Vernon Trail

GEORGE WASHINGTON MEMORIAL PARKWAY

Daingerfield
Island

Pearson's
Island

Potomac River

①

P (🔥 🏕 🍴 🚻 🚻 🚻

Bellevue

SLATERS LA.

JEFFERSON DAVIS HWY.

②

BASHFORD LA.

Mount Vernon Trail

Waterfront Walk

Alternate
Connecting
Routes

Glass Factory
and Cross Canal

Tide Lock Park

FIRST ST.

N. PITT ST.

MONTGOMERY ST.

③

Alexandria
Canal Tide Lock

MADISON ST.

④

WYTHE ST.

N. WASHINGTON ST.

N. ST. ASAPH ST.

N. ROYAL ST.

N. FAIRFAX ST.

Rivergate City Park

0   Miles   ¼

N

Canal Trail

1. Pearson's Island:
Purchased by John Alexander, the southeastern part of this patent became the new town of Alexandria in 1749.

2. Bellevue Plantation:
Once the site of a gracious home and gardens.

3. Old Dominion Glass Factory: Made functional and decorative objects. **"Cross Canal":** During the Civil War, many African Americans seeking freedom settled here.

4. Alexandria Canal Tide Lock: One of four locks, it was built in 1845 to link the port to the C&O Canal.

Continue south until path splits. Walkers may take Waterfront Walk to left; bikers must follow bike path to right onto N. Fairfax St.

3. Old Dominion Glass Factory and "Cross Canal"

(NOT VISIBLE; area to your right between First and Montgomery Sts.)
The land on which a hotel now stands *(901 N. Fairfax St.)* was once on the outskirts of town. The Alexandria Canal cut through this area: there was a "pathway for horses that pulled the barges [with coal] down the canal." During the Civil War, freedmen settled across the canal from town in the area known as "Cross Canal."[*] One of these was Emily Lomax Washington, whose granddaughter, Virginia Knapper, worked in the Old Dominion Glass Factory, which opened here in 1901. One of four glass factories in town, it employed 250 people in 1920 and made bottles and novelty items.

AAM

18   [*]AAM, 1982 Oral History of Virginia Knapper.

The Tide Lock could be filled or drained, thereby lowering or raising the canal boats. They discharged and took on cargos at wharves or piers at the mouth of the Lock. Commerce on the canal decreased after the Civil War, and it was abandoned in 1886.

4. Alexandria Canal Tide Lock *(River's edge, foot of Montgomery St.)*   The canal opened a route to the interior by connecting the town with the C&O Canal at Georgetown in 1843. It fueled an economic recovery following the recession of the early 19th century. This lock, completed in 1845, was one of four which lowered and raised the boats 38 feet from the N. Washington St. canal elevation to the Potomac level. The lock and gates are protected beneath a reconstruction based on archaeological evidence. Stones removed during its construction are located in Windmill Hill Park **(see Site 19)**.

BIOfact: Time in a Bottle

Virginia Knapper grew up in Cross Canal and told of her grandmother's *(left)* work cutting fish on the wharf. At the factory, Virginia said, glass was made "in something like a furnace. It was runny . . . more like the dough you make pancakes from. . . . The molten glass looked like a stone. . . . They rolled it up and down and there'd be two of us sitting at the molds. . . . I was a snapper: when it came out of the mold, I'd be right there with my gadget and snap it off." Shears, tongs, a blow pipe, molds and irregular finished glass were excavated from the factory site and are now in the Alexandria Archaeology Museum (see Site 9). AAM, 1982 ORAL HISTORY OF VIRGINIA KNAPPER

*Walkers continue south through Tide Lock Park to reach the blue boathouse on the left. Bikers continue south to Madison St. The **Bay Trail** begins here at Oronoco Bay Park.* ■

2 Bay Trail

Length: 0.77 miles

Terrain: Flat trail on Old Town streets near Potomac
River; Waterfront Walk for pedestrians

Highlights:

● *Market Square Trek (History Museums)*

● *City Marina; Torpedo Factory Art Center,
Alexandria Archaeology Museum*

Begin at the Madison St. entrance to Oronoco Bay Park.

5. Ralph's Gutt *(Oronoco Bay Park between Madison and
Pendleton Sts.)*   The bay here is a remnant of a large marsh, Ralph's
Gutt, that dominated the landscape of the northern end of the original
town. According to the 1748 map, a "rolling road" skirted the southern
edge of the "gutt" over which tobacco was conveyed to the West's
warehouses for export. Many ships were scuttled in the original bay
and may remain under the landfill used to make the park.

*Continue to right on the walking or bike path through the park, turn left
onto Pendleton St., then right onto N. Union St., until you reach Oronoco St.*

6. West's Point Warehouses and Founders Park
(NOT VISIBLE; foot of Oronoco St.)   From the park, you can see two
metal warehouses. They stand near the site of the first Fairfax County
tobacco warehouse, which was constructed in 1732 on Simon Pearson's
land (see Site 1). As one of the last upstream anchorages on the
Potomac River, this was a convenient point for shipping. Hugh
West saw the potential for the development of an international port.

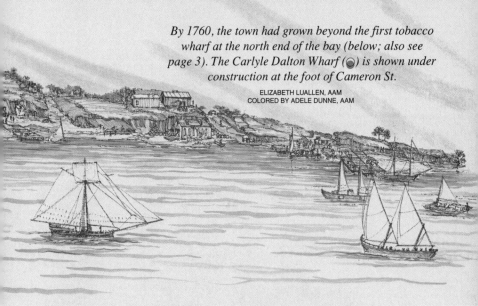

By 1760, the town had grown beyond the first tobacco wharf at the north end of the bay (below; also see page 3). The Carlyle Dalton Wharf (◕) is shown under construction at the foot of Cameron St.

ELIZABETH LUALLEN, AAM
COLORED BY ADELE DUNNE, AAM

He was also one of the prime movers in establishing a town here in 1749, rather than at Cameron (see Site 33). His family's burial vault was discovered by archaeologists (see Site 33); West's wife Sybil, who died at age 83, and others were buried inside the vault.

*Follow the path paralleling the river through Founder's Park. At Union and Queen Sts. you enter the **Old & Historic Alexandria National Landmark District**.*

7. Alexandria Seaport Center *(0 Thompson's Alley)*
A floating museum with a marine science laboratory and a boat-building school, the center maintains Alexandria's 250-year maritime craft tradition by making longboats. *Open to the public.*

*Continue along marina boardwalk. Enter back door of **Art Center** to right.*

8. Torpedo Factory Art Center *(105 N. Union St.)*
Construction did not start until after armistice was declared for World War I, but the factory did produce torpedoes during World War II. It was transformed by artists in the 1970s into a popular and innovative art center. Now, nearly 200 artists work here. Visit the studios and galleries, and learn at the Art League School. *Open to the public.*

9. Alexandria Archaeology Museum *(Go to 3rd floor of the Art Center; elevator available in center of waterside of building)*
The museum offers a public laboratory, hands-on discovery kits, exhibits and computer kiosk. The City archaeologists and part of the two million

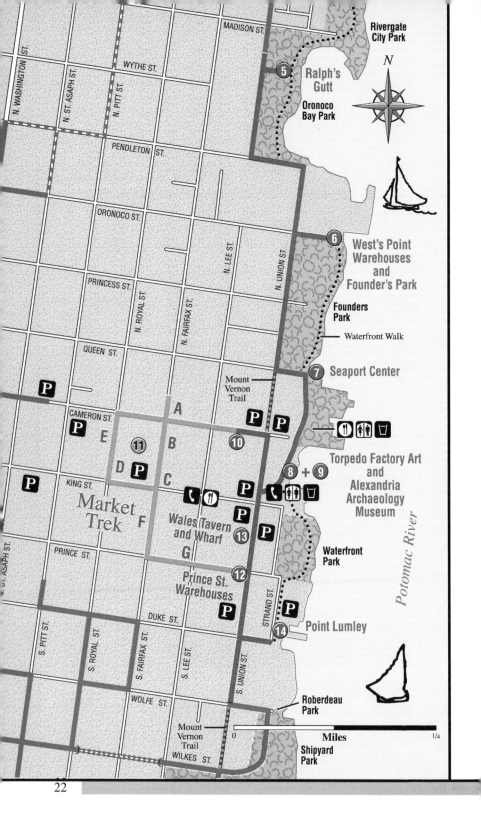

MADISON ST.

Rivergate
City Park

WYTHE ST.

⑤

Ralph's
Gutt

N. WASHINGTON ST.
N. ST. ASAPH ST.
N. PITT ST.

Oronoco
Bay Park

N

PENDLETON ST.

ORONOCO ST.

⑥

West's Point
Warehouses
and
Founder's Park

N. LEE ST.
N. UNION ST.

Founders
Park

PRINCESS ST.

N. ROYAL ST.
N. FAIRFAX ST.

Waterfront Walk

QUEEN ST.

⑦ Seaport Center

Mount
Vernon
Trail

P

P **P**

CAMERON ST.

P

A

E

⑪

B

⑩

🍴 🚻 🥤

D **P**

C

⑧ + ⑨

Torpedo Factory Art
and
Alexandria
Archaeology
Museum

P

KING ST.

📞 🚻

P

☎ 🚻 🥤

Market
Trek

F

Wales Tavern
and Wharf
⑬

P

P

G

Waterfront
Park

PRINCE ST.

Prince St.
Warehouses

⑫

S. ASAPH ST.
S. PITT ST.
S. ROYAL ST.
S. FAIRFAX ST.
S. LEE ST.
S. UNION ST.
STRAND ST.

P

P

DUKE ST.

⑭ Point Lumley

Potomac River

WOLFE ST.

Roberdeau
Park

Mount
Vernon
Trail

0   Miles   1/4

WILKES ST.

Shipyard
Park

Bay Trail

5. Ralph's Gutt: A remnant of a large marsh at the north of the early town.

6. West's Point Warehouses and Founders Park: Stand near the site of the first tobacco warehouse in Fairfax County.

7. Seaport Center: Maintains Alexandria's 250-year boat building tradition.

8. Torpedo Factory Art Center: World War II torpedoes have been replaced by a popular art center.

9. Alexandria Archaeology Museum: Offers a public laboratory, hands-on discovery kits and a collection spanning 9,000 years of Alexandria's heritage.

10. Carlyle-Dalton Wharf: A large timber wharf extended into the bay, which has since been filled in.

11. Market Square Trek: The heart of the historic district. Includes:

(A) Dalton House: *(207 N. Fairfax St.)* Built in the mid-1700s by merchant John Dalton.

(B) Carlyle House and Park: *(121 N. Fairfax St.)* Restored Georgian mansion built in 1753 by local merchant John Carlyle.

(C) Ramsay House Visitors Center: *(221 King St.)* The reconstructed home of William Ramsay now serves as an excellent source of tourist information.

(D) Market Square: Center of early Alexandria, it once included the schoolhouse, town hall, food market, prison and fire company. Still in active public use.

(E) Gadsby's Tavern and Museum: *(134 N. Royal St.)* ca. 1785 inn that hosted George Washington, among other notables, for meals and lodging.

(F) Stabler-Leadbeater Apothecary Shop: *(105 S. Fairfax St.)* Established in 1792, it was owned and operated by the same Quaker family for 141 years.

(G) Athenaeum: *(201 Prince St.)* The Bank of the Old Dominion in 1851–52, it now houses a museum operated by the Northern Virginia Fine Arts Association.

12. Prince St. Warehouses: Built in the 1780s, the Shreve–Lawrason and Harper buildings are some of the oldest warehouses in town.

13. Wales Tavern and Wharf: River water flowed through pipes to Andrew Wales' nearby 1780s brewery.

14. Point Lumley: Formed the southern end of the crescent bay around which Alexandria was established in 1749.

items in the Alexandria Archaeology Collection, spanning 9,000 years of Alexandria heritage, are here. *Open to the public.*

Go out front door, turn right (north) on N. Union St. and left on Cameron St.

10. Carlyle-Dalton Wharf *(NOT VISIBLE; 100 block of Cameron St.)*

Alexandria's waterfront was originally a bay extending between present-day Oronoco and Duke Sts., and as far west as Lee *(originally Water)* St. In 1759, two of Alexandria's founders, John Carlyle and John Dalton, built a large timber wharf extending out into the bay. The timbers of the wharf are still preserved below the sidewalk on the south side of the 100 block of Cameron St. In the 18th century, the bay was filled to make more city blocks.

To take the Market Square Trek, continue west on Cameron St. until you reach N. Fairfax St. To continue on the Bay Trail, backtrack south on N. Union St., cross King St., and proceed to 125 S. Union St. (see Site 12).

11. Market Square Trek *(Fairfax, King, Royal and Prince Sts.)*

At auction, merchants purchased the best lots in the new town, so that they could build family homes as well as wharves to control access to the waterfront. Three family homes of the merchant town founders can be seen along N. Fairfax St. John Carlyle and John Dalton formed the longest corporate partnership in northern Virginia, although their homes are quite different. The **Dalton House** (A) *(to your right at 207 N. Fairfax St.)* is similar to the Ramsay House in its size and placement on the street, though the façade is not original. A large domed brick icehouse was discovered in the basement; it may have held Dalton's perishable products until time for resale. *Backtrack and visit the* **Carlyle House Historic Park** (B) *(121 N. Fairfax St.)*, an imposing restored Georgian mansion built in 1753. It was designed according to the traditions of the landed gentry in John Carlyle's ancestral home in northwestern England. Set back from the street, this was a country manor removed from the commerce of the town. Perched on the bluff, the Carlyles would have seen the broad view of the Potomac, as did the Washingtons at Mt. Vernon. *Turn left and continue south to the* **Ramsay House Visitors Center** (C) *(221 King St.)*, a 1956 reconstruction, based on early photographs, of the home of merchant William Ramsay. It now serves as the visitors center. *Carlyle and Ramsay houses open to the public.*

Turn right (west) on King St. and cross N. Fairfax St.; go up steps to town square and fountain. Visit **Market Square** (D), center of early Alexandria, and the heart of the **Old & Historic Alexandria National Landmark District**. In the original town plan, public space was demarcated on the 300 block of Cameron, stretching south to Market

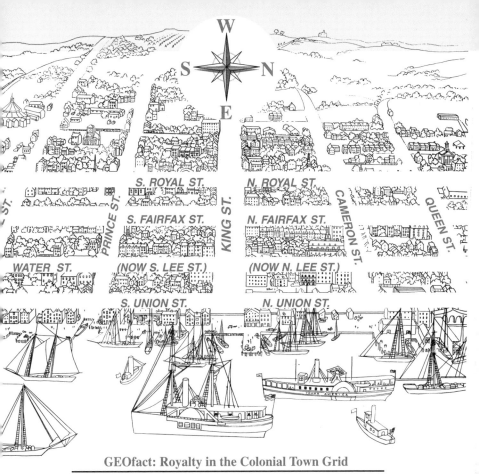

W
S   **N**
E

S. ROYAL ST.   N. ROYAL ST.

S. FAIRFAX ST.   N. FAIRFAX ST.

PRINCE ST.   KING ST.   CAMERON ST.   QUEEN ST.

WATER ST.   (NOW S. LEE ST.)   (NOW N. LEE ST.)

S. UNION ST.   N. UNION ST.

GEOfact: Royalty in the Colonial Town Grid

Fairfax and Cameron Sts. were designed as the geographical
center of the colonial town.* The intersection is a symbol of the colonists'
loyalty to the British hierarchy. It recognizes Lord Fairfax, Baron of
Cameron, the sixth in his family with proprietary rights
granted by the Crown over millions of acres in northern Virginia. The
Fairfax family was the only one honored by name in the early town grid.
Note the symmetry of the names of the first streets, which pay
homage to royalty. King and Queen Sts. were placed on either side of
Cameron St.; the next streets were Prince and Princess. Masculine titles
occur south of Cameron St., while feminine titles are to the north.
Finally, to preserve the descending hierarchy, came Duke and—Oronoco.
Oronoco? What happened to Duchess? In the only deviation from regal
titles, the founders selected the name Oronoco for the street leading from
West's Point (see Site 6), the first tobacco warehouse and shipping port.
Oronoco was the name commonly used for the tobacco grown here, which
came originally from the Oronoco River Valley in Venezuela.
Fairfax St. ran along the bluff overlooking the river; only one other north-
south street was established in the early town: Royal St.

C.T. WASHBURN, 1963, THE CITY OF ALEXANDRIA, VIRGINIA

*By the late 1800s, King St. was used as the center of town and as the north/south divider for streets
parallel to the river (e.g., Fairfax St.); the 100 blocks north and south start at King Street.   25

Alley. Before 1776, the market house, jail and schoolhouse/town hall all stood on Cameron St., while the Fairfax County Courthouse, watchhouse and prison were on N. Fairfax St. **The Sun Fire and Friendship Company** (see Site 51) engine houses sat on Market Alley *(near the current fountain)*, along with the pillory and stocks. By 1817, a new market house, containing butcher stalls, town hall, library, coffee house and museum, had been built along Royal St. In 1871, a fire destroyed the market structures, and a new City Hall of Second Empire design was built. The police and fire office signs can still be seen on the Fairfax St. side of **City Hall**. The market continues every Saturday morning on the square.

Cross Market Square to west; then cross and turn right on N. Royal St., *to visit* **Gadsby's Tavern Museum** (E) *(134 N. Royal St.),* composed of two buildings (ca 1785 and 1792) that hosted George Washington for meals and social occasions. Under the management of John Gadsby (1796–1808), it became famous for the luxury of its accommodations and hosted a variety of distinguished guests including John Adams, Thomas Jefferson, James Madison and James Monroe. *Open to the public.*

Gadsby's is one of the few preserved tavern buildings in town. During the 1960s, urban renewal brought the need for rescue archaeology. Thousands of English artifacts were excavated at Gadsby's and at other nearby taverns. Tall ale tankards, large and small punch bowls, and teacups show which drinks were consumed. Artifacts, such as white clay tobacco pipes, snuff bottles, toothbrushes, hairbrushes, medicine bottles and chamber pots (precursors of indoor plumbing) also testify to the clientele's needs. Much of the service work was performed by African Americans; more blacks were enslaved by tavern keepers than by other business owners. *Turn left when leaving the tavern, then left again on Cameron St. Step down on your left to see* **Gadsby's Ice Well**— definitely large-sized for commercial, not domestic, use. *Across Cameron St. and down to the right is* **315 Cameron St.**, one of the few black-owned eating establishments. Dominick Bearcroft operated his oyster house from 1817, but he was known for his crab specialties. After gaining his own freedom, he purchased his wife, Esther, and then emancipated her in 1804.

Backtrack to King St., turn left (east) and then right onto S. Fairfax St. to reach the **Stabler-Leadbeater Apothecary Shop** (F) *(105 S. Fairfax St.).* The shop was established in 1792 and was owned and operated   by the same Quaker family for 141 years (see Site 54). After closing in 1933, the shop became a time capsule; dried herbs, bottle labels, pharmaceutical equipment and business records are preserved. Now a private museum. *Open to the public.*

Continue south on S. Fairfax St, then turn left onto Prince St. until you reach the **Athenaeum** (G) *(201 Prince St.).* This is one of the few examples of Greek Revival architecture in town. It was built for the Bank of the Old Dominion in 1851–52. After the occupation of Alexandria by Union forces during the Civil War, the bank closed. The cashier buried the assets of the bank until peace was declared, keeping the bank solvent and enabling it to reopen. Today, it houses a museum, operated by the Northern Virginia Fine Arts Association. *Open to the public.*

Look left along S. Lee St. (originally called Water St.) to see how the elevation declines to King St., which was in the original Bay. Behind the Athenaeum is one of the many alleys in town. High brick walls encircled elite homes and controlled the movements of slaves; alleys also provided places for African Americans to socialize. *Continue east on Prince St. to its intersection with S. Union St.*

12. Prince St. Warehouses *(100 Prince St. and 125 S. Union St.)*

Built in the 1780s during Alexandria's post-Revolutionary heyday, the Shreve-Lawrason and Harper warehouses once held exotic cargo, such as mahogany desks, West Indian rum and Rhode Island cheese. During the town's less prosperous period, in the late 1800s, the Harper warehouse on Union St. held more staple stock like fertilizer. Note the painted advertisement on the side of the building, one of the few to survive. *Turn left onto S. Union St., and proceed a half block.*

13. Wales Tavern and Wharf *(NOT VISIBLE; 115 S. Union St.)*

Andrew Wales opened a tavern here in the 1780s; his brewery stood at the other end of the alley. Pipes carried water from the river to the brewery two blocks away. Before the new commercial building and garage were constructed, Alexandria Archaeology discovered the burned tavern basement and artifacts including mugs, oyster shells and sharks' teeth. *Proceed south on S. Union St., turn left onto Duke St.*

14. Point Lumley *(foot of Duke St.)*

This point formed the southern end of the crescent bay around which the first town of Alexandria was established in 1749. While other wharves were built by private merchants, Point Lumley served as the public wharf, and was also the site of the first shipyard; the two points (see Sites 6 and 14) were the first wharves for transatlantic trade. Today they continue as Alexandria's international port, even though they no longer were points of land after the bay was finally filled in by the 1780s.

Return to S. Union St. and turn left. Then turn left onto Wolfe St. to begin the **Shipyard Trail.** ■

The Alexandria Marine Railway and Shipbuilding Company, shown c. 1880, was one of many shipyards that thrived in Alexandria from the 1750s into the 20th century. Robert Portner started the shipyard, where three-masted schooners were built, but then focused on his prosperous beer-brewing business.

WILLIAM FRANCIS SMITH COLLECTION

Shipyard Trail

Length:
0.62 miles

Terrain:
Flat trail on
Old Town streets;
Waterfront Walk for pedestrians

Highlights:
● Jones Point Trek
● Keith's Wharf
● Potomac River Views

The trail begins at the intersection of S. Union St. and Wolfe St. Proceed east on Wolfe St. to the river.

15. Roberdeau Distillery *(NOT VISIBLE; at foot of Wolfe St.; park is open)* Daniel Roberdeau, a Revolutionary War general, operated a distillery complex on his wharf, which included granaries, a sail loft and a cooper's (barrel-maker's) shop. Born in the West Indies and educated in Philadelphia, Roberdeau imported products from the islands: rum, wines, sugar and molasses. He lived at 418 S. Lee St., in a house which, it is said, had a "great key" from France to open the door.

Continue on Waterfront Walk south along the river (bikers dismount).

16. Hunter's Shipyard *(NOT VISIBLE; see Shipyard Marker on Potomac River, between Wolfe and Wilkes Sts.)* Three generations of Hunters operated the shipyard here. Many vessels were built, including, in 1815, the first Potomac longboat, a low-slung, schooner-rigged boat that carried cordwood.

Continue south on S. Union St. At foot of Gibbon St., turn left; follow the Waterfront Walk along the river's edge and behind the townhouses.

17. Keith's Wharf *(area to right occupied by townhouses, foot of Franklin St.)* In the 1780s, three Alexandria merchants built a wharf at this location, intending it to be the primary shipping point of the town. Franklin St. was laid out to be 100 feet wide so as to encourage trade. In the standard historic grid of 66-foot-wide streets, only Washington St. was built as wide as Franklin St. By 1849, the Alexandria Marine Railway Company established a shipyard here to refit and repair ships. During the Civil War, the wharf was used by the Union forces. In 1931, Ford Motor Company built a service plant here. Archaeologists in 1989 uncovered the remains of the marine railway, a huge shipway, the wharf and the hulls of eight vessels, now preserved under the new townhouses. *Note the six historic markers near the river.*

To TAKE THE *Jones Point Trek,* continue south on the Waterfront Walk and bear left into Jones Point Park. To CONTINUE ON THE *Shipyard Trail,* follow path straight ahead to rejoin S. Union St. Turn right, and proceed north to Site 19 in Windmill Hill Park (formerly Potomac View Park).

18. Jones Point Trek *(near Woodrow Wilson Bridge)* **Jones Point** was a boot-shaped "point" of land and formed the southern tip of **Battery Cove (A)**, between **Keith's Wharf** and the **Lighthouse (C)**. In 1911, Battery Cove was filled in. The **Virginia Shipbuilding Corpora-**

Shipyard Trail

15. Roberdeau Distillery:
This complex on a wharf included granaries, a sail loft and a cooper's shop.

16. Hunter's Shipyard:
Three generations of Hunters built ships here.

17. Keith's Wharf: 18th-century merchants built this wharf to be the primary shipping point of the town.

18. Jones Point Trek: Includes:

(A) Battery Cove: Historic bay once filled area to right of line (A).

(B) Site of Virginia Shipbuilding Corporation

(C) Lighthouse: Dates from 1856.

(D) District of Columbia South Cornerstone: Erected in 1794.

(E) Site of Josiah Davis' Ropewalk

(F) Native American Site

19. Windmill Hill: Once a site of a windmill, the hill's base also sheltered the numerous shanties of freedmen during the Civil War.

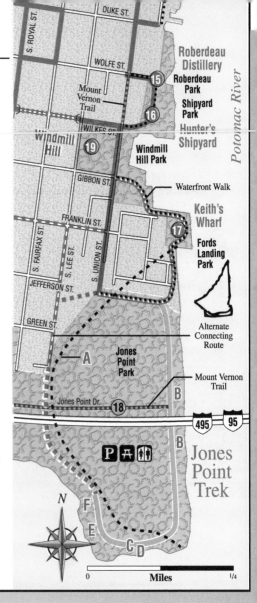

tion (B), established on the landfill, constructed World War I merchant ships. The metal-hulled vessels were constructed on concrete shipways and launched into the river. The shipways remain near the shore.

The 1856 **Lighthouse** (C) is one of the earliest existing inland waterway lighthouses. Inside the picket fence, note the **memorial marker to Margaret Brent** (1601–76). Mistress Brent was an extraordinary woman of colonial America; she acted as a lawyer and politician, and was the first woman landowner in the colonies. She added to her estates in

St. Mary's City, Maryland, with the grant of a 700-acre plot of land encompassing Jones Point and extending north to present-day Queen St. With this 1654 acquisition, she became the first European owner of land which became part of Alexandria in 1749.

Visit the **District of Columbia South Cornerstone** (D) *(found in the seawall, facing the river, near the Lighthouse).*
George Washington included the prosperous port of Alexandria in the 10-square-mile area of Virginia and Maryland, which became the District of Columbia. As the Federal District survey team laid out the boundary, they placed markers every mile along the perimeter; the first stone was placed in 1791. This stone was erected in 1794 on dry ground; the rising sea level has submerged the end of the point.

Ropewalks were long buildings in which workers walked backwards the length of the structure, spinning raw fiber into rope for ships. Remains of Josiah Davis' 19th-century ropewalk (E) were discovered here; it extended about 1,200 feet. Many rope makers were African Americans, both slave and free. A typical advertisement for runaways appeared in the "Alexandria Gazette" of June 10, 1784:

> **Runaway from Ropewalk.**
> Ishmael has worked at the rope making business for several years. Purchased from Norfollk, it is probable he'll make for that place or Baltimore and endeavor to pass as a freeman.

Native Americans lived on the point at least 9,000 years ago, judging from the age of the oldest stone tool discovered here (see page 11). Archaeologists also found pottery and evidence of 2,000-year-old houses (F).

Backtrack to S. Union St., and go north until you reach Gibbon St. and Windmill Hill Park on your left.

19. Windmill Hill *(S. Union St. between Gibbon and Wilkes Sts.)*
The bluff to the left of the tunnel was called Windmill Hill into the 20th century. It was here that a water-drawing windmill was built in 1843, much to the amazement of locals. African Americans fleeing slavery during the Civil War crowded into Union-occupied Alexandria; they lived in shanties at the base of the bluff and held religious services here. The amphitheater-like shape of the park was created for the town's 200th anniversary play in 1949.

*Continue north on S. Union St. and turn left onto the path into the Wilkes St. Tunnel to begin the **Hayti Trail**.* ∎

4 Hayti Trail

Length:
1.33 miles

Terrain:
Predominantly flat terrain
on Old Town streets; street and
pedestrian traffic;
ride with caution

Highlights:

● Church and Freedmen Detours

● Cemetery and West End Treks

　● Wilkes Street Tunnel;
　Hooff's Run Bridge

● African American Neighborhoods, Churches and Park

*Archaeological discoveries provided
the information from which the free
African American neighborhood
of Hayti, centered on the 400 block
of S. Royal St., is depicted, ca. 1850.*

*To begin the **Hayti Trail**, enter the
Wilkes St. Tunnel in Windmill Hill
Park. The park is found on S. Union
St. between Gibbon and Wilkes Sts.*

20. Wilkes Street Tunnel *(under the 200 and 300 blocks
of Wilkes St.)*　Completed in 1856, this tunnel gave direct access
to the busy Alexandria port along the Orange & Alexandria Railroad
tracks, which opened in 1851. The tunnel is one of the two oldest surviving
railroad structures in town (see Site 29). The tracks continued west on
Wilkes St., curving over to Wolfe St., and then proceeded out of town
parallel to Duke St.

*At the exit of the tunnel on S. Royal St. you enter the historic African Ameri-
can neighborhood known as "**Hayti**;" oral history rediscovered the name.*

21. Hayti *(pronounced hay-tie)* This free African American neighborhood once encompassed the area around the Wilkes St. Tunnel. As early as 1810, Hayti was a center for antebellum free black life where African Americans established homes and businesses. Quakers enabled the formation of Hayti. The area was named after the island of Haiti, where a successful slave revolution against French colonialism occurred in the early 1800s. Archaeological studies yielded thousands of Hayti artifacts, archival research and oral histories.

To take the D-1 Church Detour, turn right onto S. Royal St. and right

Hayti Trail

20. Wilkes St. Tunnel: Gave rail access to the Alexandria port.

21. Hayti: Was a large free African American neighborhood.

D-1 Church Detour: Area was a 19th-century religious hub to Presbyterians, Methodists and Catholics.

22. Wilkes St. Pottery: Made stoneware from 1813–76.

D-2 Freedmen Detour: Visit African American church and cemetery.

23. The "Bottoms" and Odd Fellows Hall: Early black neighborhood and meeting hall.

24. Alfred St. Baptist Church: Has provided African American spiritual and educational leadership for nearly 200 years.

25. District of Columbia SW Mile Marker 1: Placed in 1791 by the District of Columbia survey team to record one mile from the South Corner Stone (see Site 18 D).

26. Cemetery Trek: 12 cemeteries formed outside town limits.

27. Orange & Alexandria Roundhouse: Once was the rail hub for Union forces in the Civil War.

28. Franklin & Armfield Slave Office & Pen: Enslaved people were held here until they were shipped to the South for resale.

29. Hooff's Run Bridge: Alexandria's oldest surviving bridge.

30. Old West End Village Trek:

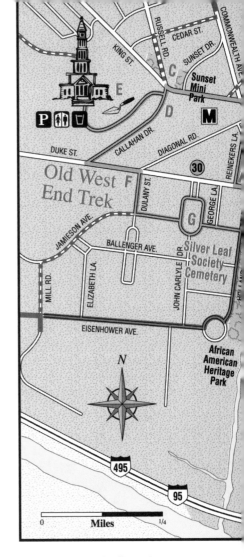

(A) Bruin & Hill Slave Pen

(B) King Street Gardens

(C) D.C. SW Mile Marker 2

(D) Union Station

(E) G. W. Masonic Memorial

(F) Shuter's Hill Brewery

(G) Virginia Glass Company

31. Silver Leaf Society Cemetery and **Alexandria African American Heritage Park.**

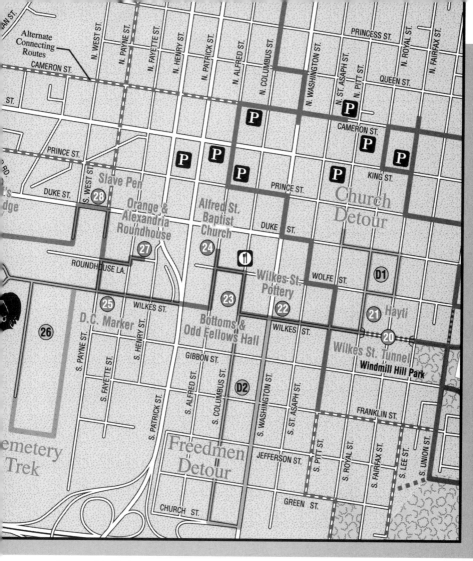

again onto Wolfe St.; proceed for one block, then turn left onto S. Fairfax St.
TO CONTINUE ON *the Hayti Trail, follow Wilkes St. from the end of the tunnel*
west to Site 22, *the 600 block of this street.*

D-1 Church Detour   The block on your left served as a religious hub at the turn of the 19th century to Presbyterians, Methodists
and Catholics. Visit the **Old Presbyterian Meeting House** *(321 S.*
Fairfax). A symbol of the town's Scottish heritage, it was first constructed about 1775; after a fire in 1835, the current building was
erected. Visit the adjoining cemetery and the "flounder" half-gable brick
building. This half-gable style was used when a structure was needed but
funds or time did not allow construction of a full-gabled home. The
flounder was placed well back from the street, so that it could serve as a

kitchen after the permanent home was built in front of it to conform to the urban grid. Other flounders are on S. Fairfax, S. Lee and S. St. Asaph Sts.

Proceed on S. Fairfax St. and turn left onto Duke St. Methodists built their first meeting house on Chapel Alley off Duke St. in 1791; the congregation continues today as Trinity United Methodist Church on Cameron Mills Rd. African American church members (about 35 percent of total) established their own chapel in 1832 (see **D-2 Freedmen Detour**).

Continue on Duke St., and turn left onto S. Royal St. Visit **St. Mary's Catholic Church** *(310 S. Royal St.)*. Until American independence, there were strict laws against practicing Catholicism. It was only with the adoption of the Virginia Bill of Rights in 1786 that public mass was permitted. The first church *(no longer standing)* was built in 1796 in St. Mary's Cemetery (see **D-2 Freedmen Detour**); the church was consecrated on this site in 1826, and then modified several times.

Backtrack to Duke St., turn left, and proceed one block. Turn right onto S. Pitt St. **St. Paul's Episcopal Church** *(228 S. Pitt St.)* was formed in 1809 due to a split between members of Christ Church (see **Site 49**). The building was designed by Benjamin H. Latrobe, America's first professionally trained architect, and was completed in 1818. Latrobe is well known for his work on the U.S. Capitol and the White House.

*To rejoin the **Hayti Trail**, backtrack to S. Royal St. and turn right (south). Turn right onto Wilkes St., and cross its intersection with S. St. Asaph St.*

22. Wilkes Street Pottery *(NOT VISIBLE; north side of the 600 block of Wilkes St.)*   Alexandria's longest operating pottery (1813–76) encompassed half of this block. The stoneware from this pottery is known for its distinctive blue cobalt designs. Free African Americans, including several women, were employed at the pottery. One of these artisans, David Jarbor, made a large stoneware jar *(right)* signed with his name and the date 1830. It is now at the Museum of Southern Decorative Arts in Winston-Salem, N.C. The Alexandria Archaeology Collection (see **Site 9**) includes thousands of fragments of stoneware made here and marked with the pottery owners' names, B. C. Milburn and H. Smith.

ANDREW
FLORA,
AAM

*To take the **Freedmen Detour**, continue on Wilkes St., and turn left onto S. Washington St. (which has heavy traffic; bike on the sidewalk for safety). To continue on the **Hayti Trail**, follow Wilkes St. across S. Washington St. Turn right onto S. Columbus St., and proceed to 411 Columbus St., Site 23.*

D-2 Freedmen Detour

Washington St. did not continue to Mount Vernon until 1932, when the **George Washington Memorial Parkway** was constructed over great Hunting Creek. The black neighborhoods of Hayti *(east of Washington St.)* and "The Bottoms" *(west of Washington St.)* expanded during the Civil War (1861–65), when thousands of enslaved African Americans escaped from Confederate-held areas and fled into Alexandria, a Union stronghold.

While runaways were not at first legally emancipated, they were accepted under "contraband of war" policy. Alexandria was impoverished as an occupied city during the war, and the new "freedmen" suffered miserable living conditions and high mortality rates.

Roberts Memorial United Methodist Church *(606-A. S. Washington St.)* is the oldest African American church structure in Alexandria. The black members of Trinity Methodist (see **D-1 Church Detour**) completed the building in 1834 and named it Davis Chapel; a new facade was added in 1894. The members changed the name when the white minister, Davis, supported slavery. The church has always provided education, except during the years when Alexandria returned to Virginia from the District of Columbia before the Civil War (1847–61).

Continue south four blocks on S. Washington St. until you reach
St. Mary's Cemetery *(at the east corner of Church St.)*, the oldest public Catholic cemetery in Virginia. Construction for the town's first Catholic church began in 1796 at the northwest corner of the cemetery. This place is now at the foot of Church St. It has been reported that it was a true ecumenical effort: people of different faiths formed and fired the brick used in this chapel.

Across S. Washington St. lies the **Alexandria Freedmen's Cemetery**, where the blacks who fled here during the Civil War were buried by the U.S. military. As many as 1,800 people, more than half children, may be buried here under the asphalt, sidewalks and on the bluff. The land was seized from Robert E. Lee's attorney, Francis L. Smith, and used from 1864 to 1869 for freedmen burials. After abandonment, the cemetery was forgotten until 1992. The Friends of the Freedmen's Cemetery began a campaign to commemorate the land in 1998. Archaeological remote sensing and excavations have identified many graves and ensured their protection.

*Rejoin the **Hayti Trail** by proceeding west one block on Church St. and turning right on S. Columbus St. Go five blocks until you reach Wilkes St.*

23. "The Bottoms" and Odd Fellows Hall *(411 S. Columbus St.)*

The earliest free African American neighborhood began forming in the 1790s and came to be known as "**The Bottoms**" from its location in a low-lying area next to a stream. Enslaved blacks were allowed to hire out and earn funds to purchase their own freedom. Some whites (often Baptists and Quakers) assisted by purchasing individuals and then freeing them, by sending them to a free state, or by filing a formal deed of manumission (see Site 54). Archaeology undertaken by the City of Alexandria into several blocks that were slated for redevelopment has discovered artifacts and food remains, as well as written documents and oral histories of free black households.

The **Odd Fellows Hall** was completed after the Civil War and housed several male and female secret benevolent associations. Prominent black builder, George L. Seaton, enlarged a small 1864 structure into this Second Empire–style meeting hall in 1870. Funded by the U.S. Freedmen's Bureau, Seaton also gained the Bureau's support for black education. The hall became a free space in which African Americans trained themselves in leadership and democratic principles.

Continue north on S. Columbus St., turn left onto Wolfe St. and then turn right onto S. Alfred St.

24. Alfred Street Baptist Church *(315 S. Alfred St.)* The

Colored Baptist Society, Alexandria's oldest African American congregation, first rented land here from James and Alice Lawrason (a founder of the First Baptist Church) in 1818. The date of the first church is not known, but this structure was constructed in 1855 *(note the cornerstone)* and renovated ca. 1880–90 and 1990. The congregation has provided spiritual and educational leadership for almost 200 years.

Backtrack south on S. Alfred St. Make a right to take the designated bike path west through the Old Towne West apartment complex. Cross busy Route 1, then take Wilkes St. west three blocks to S. Payne St.

25. District of Columbia SW Mile Marker 1 *(in front yard, southeast corner of intersection of Wilkes and S. Payne Sts.)* **Placed in 1791 by the District of Columbia survey team to record one mile from the South Corner Stone (at Jones Point; see Site 18).**

To TAKE THE *Cemetery Trek, continue west on Wilkes St. You are now leaving the Old & Historic Alexandria National Landmark District. To* STAY *on* THE *Hayti Trail, turn right on S. Payne St. to Site 27 on Roundhouse La.*

26. Cemetery Trek *(Please remember that some of these cemeteries are still used for burials and most are visited by friends and family. They are not public parks; be respectful, and please keep dogs out.)* Over time, Alexandrians were buried farther from their homes. In 1755, while accompanying Braddock's troops, a Mrs. Brown reported that people were buried in their gardens. By the 1780s, many churches had adjoining burial grounds. But soon, more space was needed. This area contains twelve cemeteries, which were started between 1795 and 1933. In 1804, the Common Council outlawed new cemeteries within the corporate limits. Many churches purchased land here in Spring Gardens Farm, just outside the town's boundary, for new burials.

Wander and read; look for family groupings and determine the ages of death. Many women died at childbirth, and it was not uncommon for half of a family's children to die. Yellow fever and small pox epidemics raged through town until new technology brought fresh water (see Sites 30 E and 33). Gravestones were carved locally by skilled masons, who often carved their names at the right base of the stone. Although these cemeteries have many gravestones, they do not equal the total number of people buried. **National Cemetery** is one of the oldest in the federal system; the **Colored Troop (C.T.) section** contains many soldiers interred here after being exhumed from Freedmen's Cemetery (see D-2 Freedmen Detour) because hospitalized black soldiers petitioned for the right to be buried with military honors (see Site 28).

Visit the **Home of Peace** (ca. 1860) and **Agudis Achim** (1933) cemeteries, where some of the town's Jewish population, which began to grow in the 1830s, are buried. **Douglas Cemetery** was considered to be the oldest black burying ground until two others were discovered by archaeological investigations (see D-2 Freedmen Detour and Site 31); only a few African American graves have been identified in other cemeteries. **Penny Hill Cemetery** was generally used to bury the poor, but most of the gravestones were discarded down a well. Not only are infants and the poor less likely to have permanent markers, but gravestones also have been lost to weather, vandalism and lawn mowers. Locate **Francis Hall's** marker. The "Old Bachelor" wrote in 1861 of the "thousand recollections of my early manhoood thronging my brain— called up by this humble man . . . . Frank Hall was . . . a 'barkeeper'. . . He had no office: he stood behind the counter at the bar, where he handed you the bill for meals . . . mixed you a glass of toddy, chatted with you."*

*To resume the **Hayti Trail**, backtrack to Wilkes St., and turn right (east). Go to S. Payne St., and turn left. Proceed, and turn right onto Roundhouse La.*

27. Orange & Alexandria Roundhouse *(NOT VISIBLE; area in front of you extending to the intersection of S. Henry and Duke Sts.)*
The Orange & Alexandria Railroad was in operation by 1851. Its complex of buildings, now demolished, once included a large brick roundhouse, surrounding a turntable, with garage-like alcoves in which locomotives were housed and serviced. When Union forces captured Alexandria in May of 1861, this yard became part of the U.S. Military Railroad system, serving as a hub for Union supply and hospital transit. The complex was expanded by freedmen to include laborers' quarters, a powder magazine, a commissary, a hospital and the headquarters for the U.S. Sanitary Commission. The architecture of the current building is reminiscent of the Roundhouse.

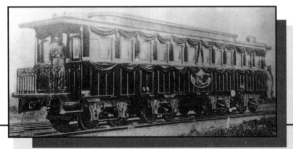

ARTIfact:
A One-way Ticket,
Please

One of this rail yard's most famous commissions was to design and build a coach to take President Lincoln to the front during the Civil War. But the coach was not completed until 1865. The only time it carried the president was in his funeral procession through seven states over 12 days to his hometown of Springfield, Illinois, for burial.

SMITHSONIAN INSTITUTION, NMAH

Backtrack on Roundhouse Lane to S. Payne St., turn right, then turn left onto Duke St. Cross to the other side of Duke St.

28. Franklin & Armfield Slave Office & Pen (now
Freedom House, *1315 Duke St.*) Here, enslaved African Americans were held in walled yards until they were shipped to the South for resale. This was one of the most infamous slave dealerships in America

*Manuscripts of an Old Bachelor" in "The Local News," November 16, 1861

before the Civil War. A Union black hospital also stood on this block; in addition to its providing medical services to soldiers and freedmen, thousands of coffins were made at L'Ouverture Hospital for Freedmen's Cemetery (see D-2 Freedmen Detour).

Proceed west to intersection of West and Duke Sts. Turn left onto S. West St. and go 1 1/2 blocks. Make a right onto the designated bike path and follow it to Hooff's Run.

29. Hooff's Run Bridge   This is Alexandria's oldest surviving bridge. Construction began in 1851 when the Orange & Alexandria Railroad began rail service. An original wooden structure was replaced by the stone bridge in 1856 and was widened in 1885–95. Built in sections, the north side (older) is gray sandstone, while the southern side is made of red sandstone (see Site 20).

Continue to Holland La. TO TAKE THE Old West End Village Trek, turn right (north) on Holland La. Proceed to, then cross Duke St. TO CONTINUE ON THE Hayti Trail, turn left on Holland La. and enter the park (see Site 31).

30. Old West End Village Trek   The area around the intersection of Duke St. and Holland Lane, known as West End Village, was the setting for early businesses and homes in Alexandria's first suburb. In 1796, John West subdivided the land into 33 half-acre residential lots to promote development. One of Alexandria's main arteries, Little River Turnpike (Duke St.), was incorporated in 1802. With only a few bad roads available, a wide turnpike was in great demand and made it easier to bring agricultural goods into town for processing and shipment. The turnpike also brought cattle to the West End for butchering, while numerous businesses, including hotels, saloons, breweries, blacksmith shops and slave dealerships, developed along its route. Barges traveled down Hooff's Run and Cameron Run (see Sites 29 and 32) transporting meat to the Potomac wharves for export. By creating Alexandria as the terminus of several turnpikes, the merchants made the town a major commercial center 200 years ago and laid the foundation for today's traffic problems. Duke St., King St. (Leesburg Turnpike) and Route 1 (Washington-Alexandria Turnpike) are still the major arteries into town.

The **Bruin and Hill Slave Pen** (A) *(1707 Duke St.)* was established along the Little River Turnpike by Joseph Bruin in the 1840s. Agents for the business scoured the countryside, and newspaper ads offered "top dollar" for slaves, who were then sent to the deep South for resale.

Continue west on Duke St., then turn right on Reinekers La. Turn right onto Prince St., turn left onto Daingerfield Rd. and proceed to King St.

At **King Street Gardens** (B) *(in the triangle formed by King St., Diagonal Rd. and Daingerfield Rd.)*, note the public art project, including a 35-foot metal sculpture symbolizing 18th-century Alexandria: a plow, tricorn hat and ship's prow. The design invokes the historic interface of the hard urban grid and the naturalistic hinterland west of Hooff's Run, which flows under the street. *Open to the public.*

Turn left (west) onto King St. Go under railroad bridge and proceed to the northeast corner of the intersection of King St. and Russell Rd. to see a replica of the **District of Columbia SW Mile Marker 2** (C), the second mile marker along the southwest side of the district. The original stone was placed here in 1791 by the District of Columbia survey team to record two miles from the South Corner Stone (see Site 18). Because the Constitution did not allow residents of the District of Columbia to vote in federal elections, Alexandrians were denied the vote for 48 years.

Cross King St. and go south on Callahan Dr. to visit **Union Station** (D). The building was constructed in 1905 by the Washington Southern Railway Co. at the crossroads of two historic turnpikes: the Little River Turnpike (Duke St.) and the Leesburg Pike (King St.). It was recently renovated, and many of the historic interior elements still survive. A transportation hub in the past and present, the station now serves three rails: Metro, Amtrak and the Virginia Railway Express. *Open to the public.*

Backtrack on Callahan Dr. and proceed up the service road to your left to the top of the hill. The topography of Alexandria is dominated by **Shuter's Hill** *(King St. and Callahan Dr.)*, which is made more dramatic by the massive **George Washington Masonic National Memorial** (E). Built between 1922 and 1933, the monument commemorates the life of the first president and his Masonic affiliation. *Stand at the entrance* for a spectacular panoramic view of Alexandria. *Inside,* visit the museum and the great hall, modeled on a Greco-Roman temple, with a colossal statue of George Washington. See the archaeology exhibit. *From the top of the memorial (look northwest),* you can see the outline in the grass of Fort Ellsworth, one of Alexandria's four Civil War forts. On the hill north of the memorial, City archaeologists have excavated a plantation laundry building occupied by slaves, as well as stone tools used by Native Americans in the prehistoric period. The Alexandria Water Co. (founded in 1852) pumped water from Cameron Mills (see Site 33) to a square reservoir, still in use, atop the hill. Pipes brought the water to homes, which reduced epidemics. *Open to the public.*

Backtrack downhill and turn right (south) on Callahan Dr. Turn left onto Duke St., and right onto Dulany St. **Shuter's Hill Brewery** (F) operated here from 1858 until fire closed it in the 1890s. The company of Strausz and Klein was the first in town to produce lager beer, a German-style malt liquor. As it requires colder temperatures for fermentation than other brews, a deep brick cellar was built where ice kept the barrels of beer cold throughout the year. The brewery was a success during the Civil War, when as many as 20,000 Union soldiers were camped in the vicinity. Remains of barrels, kegs and wooden beams were found by archaeologists in the cellar; they are still preserved under Duke St. near Dulany St. Plates and mugs used in Henry Englehardt's adjoining saloon were also excavated.

From Dulany St., turn left onto Jamieson Ave. and proceed to John Carlyle St. Under the grass circle, the ruins of the **Virginia Glass Co. (G)** (in operation 1894–1916) are preserved.

*To resume the **Hayti Trail,** proceed east on Jamieson Ave. to Holland La. Cross Holland La. and enter the park.*

31. Silver Leaf Society Cemetery and Alexandria African American Heritage Park *(Holland Lane)*

In 1885, a group of men known as the Silver Leaf Society of Alexandria incorporated and founded a small African American cemetery. Archaeological excavations discovered and protected 26 graves, most of which were unmarked. Four graves are identified by headstones. In 1995, the Heritage Park was dedicated with Jerome Meadows' bronze sculptures, which commemorated the lives of individuals buried in the cemetery, as well as local educational, business, civic and religious leaders. The wetlands in the park and the banks of Hooff's Run abound with wildlife.

ARTIfact: Gone, But Not Forgotten

This metal coffin handle came from one of the unmarked grave sites of the Silver Leaf Society's cemetery. While the burials here lacked large stone monuments, clam and oyster shells, and broken ceramics were sometimes placed above the coffins. These African American burial customs have been interpreted as symbolizing immortality (the durable shells and their association with water) and the spirit's break with life (the broken pottery).

STEVEN J. SHEPHARD, AAM

---

*To begin the **Baron of Cameron Trail,** go south on Holland La., bear right around the circle onto Eisenhower Ave., and proceed to Mill Rd.* ■

 ### Baron of Cameron Trail

Length:

3.21 miles

Terrain:

Moderately flat trail;
pedestrians and traffic

Highlights:

● Mill Detour

● Old Cameron Run; Views of Wildlife

● Phoenix Mill

*Thomas Fairfax, sixth Baron of Cameron, (opposite),
1693–1781, inherited more than 5 million acres in the Northern
Neck of Virginia. His name can still be found today in Cameron
St., Fairfax St. and the neighborhood of Cameron Mews.*

*The trail begins at the intersection of Eisenhower Ave. and Mill Rd. Turn
south onto Mill Rd. Proceed a short distance to find a wooded stream bank
on your left and right.*

*

32. Old Cameron Run *(Mill Rd. south of Eisenhower Ave.)*

This is a vestige of Cameron Run; in the 18th century it was a river as
wide as the Capitol Beltway and deep enough that European ships
could sail up from the Potomac River as far as the first ford (the
Old Colchester Rd., or today's Telegraph Rd.) to Cameron Village
(see Site 33). Tobacco was brought to the village on one of the
few roads leading to the ford, to then be transported to England.

*Backtrack to Eisenhower Ave., and turn left. The Metro Station will be on
your left. Look north, just left of the elevated track.*

33. Cameron Mills and Cameron Village *(NOT VISIBLE; area near
Eisenhower Metro)*   Near here, by the 1730s, the village of Cameron

developed as a trade settlement near the crossroads of southern and
western paths and near the first ford of Cameron Run. Cameron
competed unsuccessfully with West's Point (see Site 6) for
Virginia General Assembly approval of a new town, Alexandria, in
1749. Cameron Mills was constructed by 1791, and its foundations are
still preserved underground east of today's theater. In 1851, the Alexandria
Water Co. used one mill to pump water up to a reservoir at Shuter's Hill
(see Site 30 E). The flour mill continued in use until about
1920. Archaeologists unearthed the stone mill foundations in 1990–92; the mill race, the remains of the
Roberts family home, and the West family burial vault
and cemetery with 14 graves in 1998–2000. The human
remains were dealt with in accordance with the living
family's wishes (see Site 6 and page 47).

*Continue west on Eisenhower Ave. and
go over the Telegraph Rd. overpass.
Pass Cameron Run Regional Park, and bear
right when the path forks; go under
the Metro and railroad bridges. Continue
to Tarleton Park.*

*A water wheel provided
the energy to turn the
millstones which ground the
wheat into flour.*

STEVEN J. SHEPHARD,
AAM

*For information on symbols used in this book, turn to page 13.   45

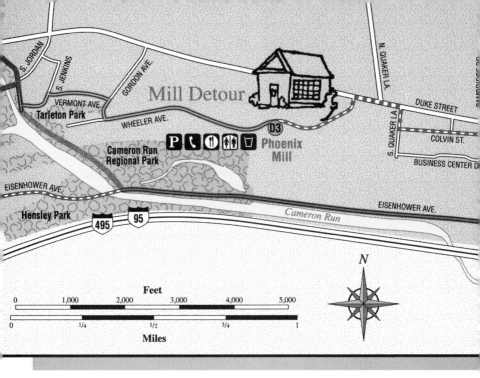

*To take the **Mill Detour**, follow the bike path to the intersection of S. Jenkins St. and Holmes Run Pkwy. Turn right onto S. Jenkins St., right onto Vermont Ave., and right onto S. Gordon St. Finally, turn left on Wheeler Ave. Proceed for one mile to 3642 Wheeler Ave., where the mill is still located.*
*To continue on the **Baron of Cameron Trail**, continue straight on the path.*

D-3 Phoenix Mill Detour

William Hartshorne, a Quaker merchant, probably constructed this four-story brick mill (see page 48) by 1812. It is the last surviving flour mill in town and one of several "merchant mills" that were opened near major roads to encourage Alexandria's flourishing flour trade. Hartshorne and Phinneas Janney (see Site 30) were instrumental in developing Little River Turnpike, which opened between Alexandria and Little River in Aldie, Virginia, in 1806. This major artery was conveniently located near their mills to facilitate the transport of wheat and ground flour. Wheat had usurped tobacco's primacy before the Revolution, and the town's merchants wanted to continue Alexandria's commercial dominance. Through their efforts, the town was designated an official flour inspection station. Alexandria's enterprising merchants, especially the Quakers, were responsible for Alexandria's economic boom in the late 18th century.

Although the mill produced 10,000 barrels of flour annually, a poor economic climate after the War of 1812 forced Hartshorne to sell his mill and his home, Strawberry Hill.

*To resume the **Baron of Cameron Trail**, backtrack to the intersection of*

46

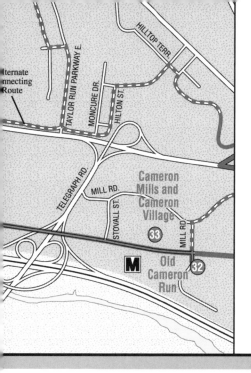

Baron of Cameron Trail

32. Old Cameron Run: A remnant of the historic river, surviving after siltation, flood control and beltway construction.

33. Cameron Mills and **Cameron Village:** The village preceeded Alexandria.

D-3 Phoenix Mill Detour: This four story brick "merchant mill" was opened near a major road to encourage Alexandria's flourishing flour trade.

Old Cameron Mill, as it looked during the Roberts family tenure.

*S. Jenkins St. and Holmes Run Pkwy. Turn right onto bike path and proceed a short distance to the steel bridge, where the **Mill Race Trail** begins.* ■

47

6 Mill Race Trail

Length:

2.94 miles

Terrain:

Flat with some short sections of incline; short sections of gravel trail in the forest preserve, which are easily passable (note that Holmes Run floods periodically onto the trail underneath I-395); some street and pedestrian traffic

Highlights:

● Winkler Preserve Detour

● Holmes Run

● Bicentennial Tree

● Cloud's Mill Race

The Phoenix Mill wheel (right) was powered by water in the mill race, a channel carrying water to and from a mill. Another race carried water from upper Holmes Run to Cloud's Mill.

The trail begins on the designated bike path that parallels Holmes Run Pkwy., between S. Jordan and S. Jenkins Sts. Cross over the steel bridge, and enter the park.

34. Camp California and Cameron Station *(NOT VISIBLE; Ben Brenman Park)* The confluence of Holmes Run and Backlick Run can be seen just before reaching the bridge; the area was once rich in wildlife and was a magnet for Native Americans for thousands of years. The level alluvial plain to the west was used as a military depot as early as 1818. The Union Army established Camp California here in 1861; Confederate troops were nearby. In November 1861, four regiments from New York and Rhode Island arrived on foot without maps or a

guide: "The march was more like advancing in the presence of an enemy than like ordinary marching." The raw recruits, in high spirits and whistling "I Wish I Were in Dixie" as they crossed the Potomac River from D.C., changed their tune after two wet days of walking through mud and tossed their belongings out to lighten their packs. One autobiographer noted: "The weather was so cold this winter that it was quite difficult at times to keep warm at night. . . . Braisers of hot coals were sometimes kept in the tent. . . . one morning a tent . . . was discovered

49

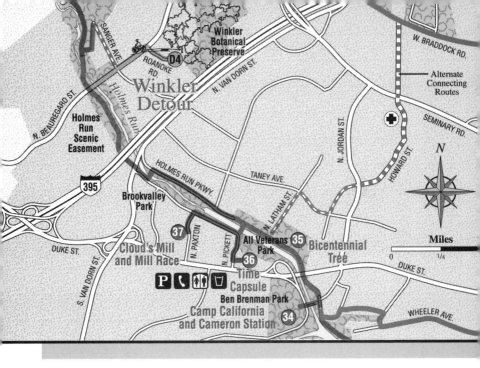

unopened and . . . its occupants were found to be stiff and unconscious from breathing coal gas."* Cameron Station did not receive its name until 1950, but the quartermaster depot and commissary functioned during World War II. The U.S. government deeded over the more than 160 acres in 1995 for homes and parks. Many species of waterfowl can be observed on the pond.

ECOfact: No Wood in Sight

During the Civil War, the Union's great demand for wood resulted in massive deforestation, as seen in this view from Shuters Hill (see Site 30 E). By the end of the war, troops stationed in Alexandria had to go as far as Vienna, Virginia, to find firewood. One soldier told of having to go without dinner because there was not enough wood to cook meals. Agricultural fields, pasture land and quarries prevented more trees from growing until well into the 20th century.

*Gilbert Frederick, *The Story of a Regiment being a Record of the Military Services of*

Mill Race Trail

34. Camp California and **Cameron Station:** Federal military installations were here for more than 130 years.

35. Bicentennial Tree: Thought to be the oldest tree in Alexandria. Willow oaks were introduced in the mid-18th century.

36. Alexandria's 250th Anniversary Time Capsule: Contains over 700 items; to be opened in 2099.

37. Cloud's Mill and **Mill Race:** A flour mill operated for most of the 19th century; portions of the race survive.

D-4 Winkler Preserve Detour: More than a mile of walking trails with 200,000 plants and trees focusing on species native to the Potomac Valley.

Backtrack over the steel bridge, and turn left (north) onto the bike path along Holmes Run Pkwy. Turn left at the children's park and follow bike path over Holmes Run bridge, then under Duke St. Stay left to follow trail north along Holmes Run until you come to the largest tree with a fence.

35. Bicentennial Tree *(located on east side of Holmes Run Park bike trail)* Believed to be the oldest tree in Alexandria, this willow oak was designated the "Bicentennial Tree" as part of the city's celebration of America's 200th birthday in 1976.

Continue along the path and turn left to go over the Charles E. Beatley, Jr. bridge across Holmes Run. Continue straight onto N. Pickett St. to library.

36. Alexandria's 250th Anniversary Time Capsule
(inside the Charles E. Beatley, Jr. Central Library, 5005 Duke St.)
The library was designed by Michael Graves. In the interior courtyard is an underground vault, marked by a 500-pound Maryland Bluestone cut block engraved by master mason Raymond Canetti, containing the time capsule. The stone was used to build the Alexandria Canal Tide Lock (see Site 4) in 1845. In 1999, the Alexandria Archaeological Commission placed over 700 items in an oxygen-free (argon gas) environment within a stainless steel cylinder in order to both undertake tests on the preservation of materials and to amuse and educate turn-of-the-22nd-century citizens about life in the late 20th century when it is opened in 2099.

the 1895 Fifty-Seventh New York State Volunteer Infantry in the War of the Rebellion 1861-1865. The Fifty-Seventh Veterans Association, page numbers 23-31.

Return to Pickett St., and turn right. Turn left onto Holmes Run Pkwy., then left onto Paxton St.

37. Cloud's Mill *(NOT VISIBLE)* **and Mill Race** *(Paxton St. across from Fire Station No. 8)*   Built in 1813, the flour mill was owned by James Cloud from about 1835 to 1863; operation continued into the late 19th century. It was fed by a mill race that channeled water from Holmes Run to power the wheel. A section of the race survives and is marked by a millstone.

WALKERS, return to Holmes Run Parkway, turn left, then proceed until reaching steps leading down to the path by the stream bank.   BICYCLISTS, return to Holmes Run Pkwy., backtrack to Pickett St., and turn left to go back over the bridge. Then follow path to the left along Holmes Run until you reach the crossing at the far end of the park, opposite Ripley St. Cross the stream, and take a right.   WALKERS AND BICYCLISTS both go through the tunnel under I-395. Follow bike trail through woodland area to intersection of N. Beauregard and N. Morgan Sts. Note the ditch on your left, another remnant of Cloud's Mill Race, which runs parallel to Holmes Run.

ARTIfact:
Rake and Bake

A hoe blade was found during excavations of a 19th-century rural homestead (see D-4 Winkler Preserve Detour). **Standard equipment for farms, hoes were also a common cooking surface for farm workers. While working the fields throughout the day, white tenant farmers and African American slaves would slip the hoe blade off its handle, place it over the fire, and cook cornmeal "hoecakes" directly on the hot metal. Every morning , George Washington enjoyed his hoecakes made of cornmeal, eggs, water and yeast with honey and butter. Hoecakes were a dietary staple for laboring folks, though they may have been made without the expensive yeast.**

ALEX J. WEDDERBURN, 1907, "SOUVENIR VIRGINIA
TERCENTENNIAL OF HISTORIC ALEXANDRIA,
VIRGINIA, PAST AND PRESENT"

**The Winkler Botanical Preserve is located within an old
coastal plain, which includes a forest of oak, hickory and chestnut
trees. The "terrace gravel" ecosystem is characterized by
quartzite pebbles that were deposited here, perhaps by the
ancient Potomac, during the glacial Pleistocene epoch (1.6 million
to 10,000 years ago). Groundwater flows through the hillside
terraces to nourish a magnolia bog on the hillside and to provide
fresh water to the streams that eventually flow into Great
Hunting Creek by Jones Point.**

CONTEMPORARY GLACIER PHOTO BY U.S. NAVY ALASKAN SURVEY PHOTO,
NATIONAL ARCHIVES; FROM AMERICAN GEOGRAPHIC SOCIETY COLLECTION ARCHIVED AT
NATIONAL SNOW AND ICE DATA CENTER, U.C.–BOULDER

*To go on the **Winkler Preserve Detour**, turn right onto N. Beauregard, then
turn right onto Roanoke Ave. To continue on the **Mill Race Trail**, cross
the intersection of N. Beauregard and N. Morgan Sts., and continue on the
designated bike path to the Jerome "Buddy" Ford Nature Center.*

D-4 Winkler Preserve Detour *(5400 Roanoke Ave.)*

*Due to sensitive plantings, no bicycles or pets are allowed. Please walk
only on the paths.* The 44-acre, privately owned Winkler Botanical
Preserve is located at the eastern terminus of Roanoke Ave. The
preserve features more than a mile of walking trails that pass through
reclaimed and rejuvenated oak hickory forest, and by wildflower meadows
and several constructed ponds. Since 1980, the staff has planted over
600,000 plants and trees, focusing on species native to the Potomac Valley.
Programs, especially for children, are held regularly at Catherine Lodge, the
visitor's center. Before development, Mark Center Properties' archaeologist
undertook the excavation of a rural cabin outside the preserve.
Tenant farmers or those enslaved by the Terrett family probably
lived here ca. 1800 to 1870, when the cabin burned down.

*Backtrack on Roanoke Ave. and make a left onto N. Beauregard St. At the
intersection of N. Beauregard and N. Morgan Sts., turn right onto the
designated bike path. Proceed to the Jerome "Buddy" Ford Nature Center
to begin the **Preservation Trail**.* ■

7 Preservation Trail

Length:

3.45 miles

Terrain:

Varied, with many hilly sections;
street and pedestrian traffic; ride with caution, especially
at intersections; note: no dogs are permitted within
the grounds of the park and sanctuary

Highlights:

● Dora Kelley Nature Park and Wildlife Sanctuary

● Jerome "Buddy" Ford Nature Center

● Fort Ward Museum and Historic Site

*The trail begins at the Jerome "Buddy" Ford Nature Center, located at the
back of William Ramsay School. The Dora Kelley Nature Park is accessed
through the wooden gate at the northern terminus of Sanger Ave.*

38. Jerome "Buddy" Ford Nature Center and Dora Kelley Nature Park and Wildlife Sanctuary *(both, 5700 Sanger Ave.)*

*   Visit the Nature Center to learn about the area's geological and ecological history. In Dora Kelley Park, visitors can see how Holmes Run may have looked when Native Americans began camping and hunting here several thousand years ago. Along the stream, which is a tributary of Cameron Run and Great Hunting Creek, metamorphic and igneous rocks form small rapids (a smaller version of the same kind of rapids that can be seen at Great Falls on the Potomac).

*Follow the trail through the park to its exit onto N. Chambliss St.
Go straight on N. Chambliss until it becomes Fillmore St. Follow Fillmore,
turn left onto N. Stevens St., then right onto Dawes Ave. Follow Dawes
across Seminary Rd. and through the campus of Northern Virginia
Community College. After the Bisdorf Building, turn right at the blinking
red light onto E. Campus Dr. and follow it to N. Beauregard St.
Cross N. Beauregard and continue on W. Braddock Rd. The Preserve
will be on your left, just before I-395.*

    *For information on symbols used in this book, turn to page 13.

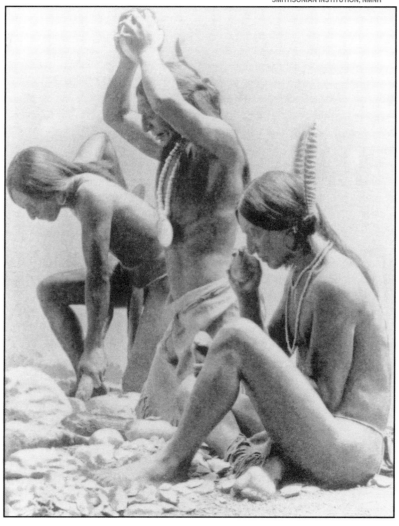

The plaster statues above were used in a
Smithsonian Institution exhibit 100 years ago to depict Native
Americans making tools from cobbles found in stream beds.

39. Stonegate Archaeological Preserve   Alexandria's first archaeological preserve. About 4,000 years ago, Native Americans occupied the ridge along both sides of Braddock Rd., where they selected cobbles from the stream beds and chipped off flakes to make spear points and other tools. Another Native American site—where pottery was found dating to about 3,000 years ago—is located to the north, on a low terrace adjacent to the floodplain. *Continue east on Braddock Rd. to Fort Ward Park on your left, at the top of the hill. Bike only on park road.*

55

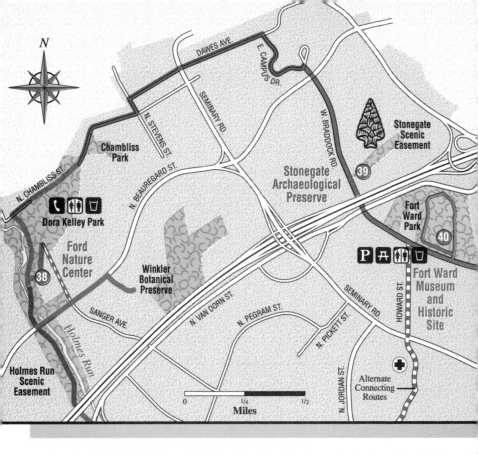

Preservation Trail

38. Jerome "Buddy" Ford Nature Center and **Dora Kelley Nature Park and Wildlife Sanctuary:** Woodlands and wildlife are preserved here; see what Holmes Run might have looked like when Native Americans were here thousands of years ago; hands-on learning.

39. Stonegate Archaeological Preserve: Native Americans sat on the terraces overlooking the stream while making tools from cobbles.

40. Fort Ward Museum and Historic Site: Civil War site withreconstructed bastion, exhibits and public progams.

Native Americans (opposite) collected the abundant marine life in the area's many waterways, which also had water-worn cobbles used for making implements.

DEBRY, DOVER PUBLICATIONS, INC

40. Fort Ward Museum and Historic Site *(4301 W. Braddock Rd.; follow loop road)*
This fort was one of 161 forts and batteries constructed to defend Washington, D.C. during the Civil War. Named for Commander James Harmon Ward, the first Union naval officer to die in the war, the fort was the fifth largest in the defenses of Washington. Following the war, the fort was dismantled and the property was purchased by African Americans who built homes, a school and a cemetery here; the neighborhood was called "Fort Hill." The Oakland Baptist Church Cemetery (see Site 41) is still in use. In 1961, the first archaeological excavation in the City was conducted here to assist in the reconstruction of the fort. *Open to the public.*

*Rejoin Braddock Rd and turn left (east). Continue across Quaker La. to King St. The **Campaign Trail** begins at this intersection.* ∎

8 Campaign Trail

Length:

3.05 miles

Terrain:

Some flat terrain with a very steep descent along Braddock Rd., where there is little to no shoulder; watch for cars and ride with caution

Highlights:

- Parkfairfax, Ivy Hill, Rosemont, and Town of Potomac Detours
- Seminary/Chinquapin Trek
- President Ford House
- Braddock Cannon

During the Civil War, Union troops used the Protestant Episcopal Theological Seminary as a campground, hospital and cemetery.

The trail begins at the busy intersection of Braddock Rd. and King St.

41. Fairlington Village Historic District *(north of intersection of King St. and Braddock Rd.)* and **Oakland Baptist Church** *(3408 King St.)*   This has been a crossroads for more than 200 years. Braddock Rd., Quaker Ln. and the Alexandria–Leesburg Turnpike (King St.) were central arteries to move products and people into the port of Alexandria. Even before the turnpike (1813) people complained about the difficulty of travel. Archaeological excavations and interviews with long time residents have provided another layer of history to this area. After the Civil War, several African American neighborhoods were established along Braddock Rd., Quaker Ln. and King St., including one neighborhood known as "Macedonia." T. C. Williams High School was built on another such site in 1965. The Oakland Baptist Church began as an outdoor site for religious services under an arbor. The congregation is more than 100 years old and continues to use its historic cemetery,

*

accessed through Fort Ward Park (see Site 40).

To tour one of Alexandria's oldest garden apartment complexes, go north on King St. and cross Quaker Ln. Go to brick entrance gates on right, and enter the **Fairlington Village Historic District**. Constructed between 1942 and 1944 in Alexandria and Arlington, it offered 3,439 units to families in close proximity to the Pentagon (which was completed in 1943). The complex was developed by the Federal Defense Homes Corporation Project and was the largest apartment project in America at the time, providing needed housing for the people pouring into the area during the New Deal and World War II. Developed from the English garden city and German superblock designs, the colonial revival–style multi-family units of Fairlington Village were considered a prototype of the new garden apartment concept, characterized by buildings clustered around open spaces and staggered for light. *See the replica of the* **District of Columbia SW Mile Marker 4** *near S. Wakefield and King Sts.*

Campaign Trail

41. Fairlington Historic District and **Oakland Baptist Church:** Crossroads marked by a historic church congregation and pre-WWII garden apartments.

42. Seminary/Chinquapin Trek: Visit buildings and grounds:

(A) Protestant Episcopal Theological Seminary.

(B) President Ford House.

(C) Chinquapin Park and Chinquapin Village

D-5 Parkfairfax Historic District Presidential Detour: Pre-WWII commuter suburb with homes of two presidential families.

43. Braddock Cannon: Marks the trail of Braddock's troops.

D-6 Ivy Hill Cemetery Detour: Resting place of local families spanning 190 years.

D-7 Rosemont Historic District Detour: A street-car suburb almost 100 years old.

D-8 Town of Potomac Historic District Detour: 20th-century town with strong identity.

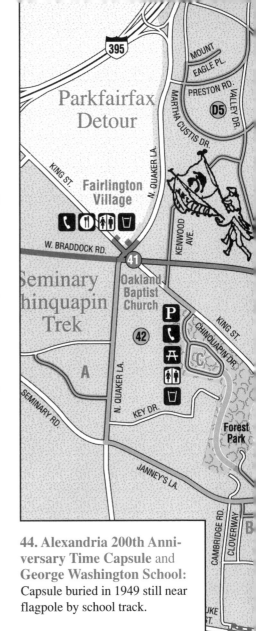

44. Alexandria 200th Anniversary Time Capsule and **George Washington School:** Capsule buried in 1949 still near flagpole by school track.

*Backtrack to N. Quaker Ln. and King St. TO TAKE THE Seminary/Chinquapin Trek, follow N. Quaker Ln. south 3/4 mile to **the Seminary** (A). TO CONTINUE ON THE Campaign Trail, turn left (east) on W. Braddock Rd., and proceed to the **D-5 Park Fairfax Detour**.*

42. Seminary/Chinquapin Trek   Visit the **Protestant Episcopal Theological Seminary in Virginia** (A), *(3737 Seminary*

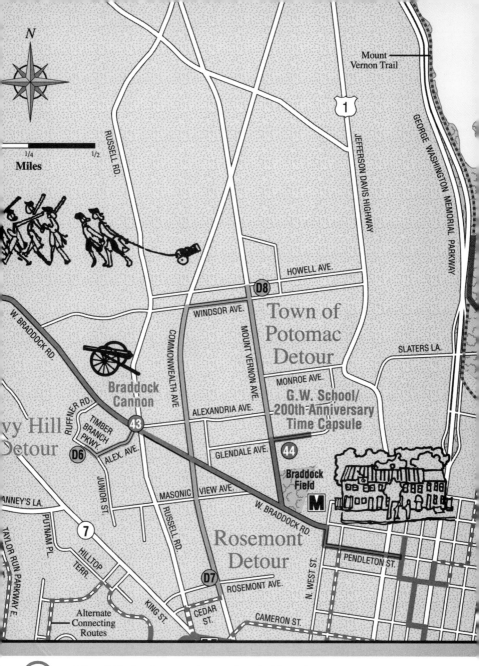

N

¼ ½
Miles

Mount Vernon Trail

GEORGE WASHINGTON MEMORIAL PARKWAY

JEFFERSON DAVIS HIGHWAY

1

RUSSELL RD.

HOWELL AVE.

D8

WINDSOR AVE.

COMMONWEALTH AVE.

MOUNT VERNON AVE.

SLATERS LA.

Town of Potomac Detour

W. BRADDOCK RD.

Braddock Cannon

RUFFNER RD.

TIMBER BRANCH PKWY.

43

ALEX. AVE.

ALEXANDRIA AVE.

MONROE AVE.

G.W. School/ 200th Anniversary Time Capsule

vy Hill Detour

D6

JUNIOR ST.

GLENDALE AVE.

44

Braddock Field

ANNEY'S LA.

PUTNAM PL.

MASONIC   VIEW AVE.

RUSSELL RD.

W. BRADDOCK RD.

M

7

HILLTOP TERR.

N. WEST ST.

PENDLETON ST.

Rosemont Detour

TAYLOR RUN PARKWAY E.

KING ST.

D7

ROSEMONT AVE.

CEDAR ST.

CAMERON ST.

Alternate Connecting Routes

Rd., off N. Quaker La.). It was founded in 1823 and moved here four years later. Numerous buildings have been constructed over the past 150 years; most notable is Aspinwall Hall, built in 1858. During the Civil War, the property was converted into a Union convalescent hospital, with female nurses supervised by Jane Woolsey. Excavations by Alexandria Archaeology in 1993 uncovered a Civil War hospital drainage system and foundations of a meat storage structure.

Backtrack to N. Quaker La., turn right, then left onto Janney's La. The Janneys were a prominent Quaker family in Northern Virginia for many generations. *Turn right on Cloverway, and make a left onto Crown View Dr.*

Visit the **house of former president Gerald R. Ford, Jr.** (B) and his family *(514 Crown View Dr.)*. Jerry and Betty Ford built this house in 1955, after having lived at Parkfairfax (see **D-5 Parkfairfax Detour**). The family lived here while Mr. Ford served in Congress as the representative of the 5th District of Michigan, as House minority leader and as vice president. The house was altered to accommodate his needs: the garage was refitted to be a command post for the Secret Service, bullet-resistant glass was installed in the master bedroom, and the driveway was enlarged for the vice-presidential Lincoln Continental.

BIOfact:
Resident
President

The Fords did not move into the White House until 10 days after Richard M. Nixon's resignation in August 1974. Gerald Ford continued his suburban lifestyle; the morning after being sworn in as president, he was seen in baby blue short pajamas on his doorstep looking for the newspaper.

1959, GERALD R. FORD LIBRARY

Return to Janney's La., turn right, and then left onto Francis Hammond Pkwy.; continue to the off-street trail in Forest Park. Follow the trail until you reach:

Chinquapin Park and **Chinquapin Village** (C) *(3210 King St.)*
Walk the trail to see Taylor Run, once used by Native Americans and by 19th-century African Americans. Oral histories recount that this area was a delightful recreation spot, where children played in the creek and collected chinquapin nuts to use in guessing games. The name of the park, Native American in origin, refers to the dwarf chestnut trees that once covered this place. The area with the circular road was the location of a World War II village for Torpedo Factory workers (see Site 8). Some foundations of Chinquapin Village can still be seen.

Exit Chinquapin Park, and turn left onto King St. Then turn right onto Kenwood Ave. Turn right on W. Braddock Rd., and continue until you reach Valley Dr. To TAKE THE *Parkfairfax Presidential Detour, turn left onto Valley Dr. and follow it seven blocks to its intersection with Martha Custis Dr.* To CONTINUE ON THE Campaign Trail, *proceed on Braddock Rd. to its intersection with Russell Rd. (see Site 43)*

D-5 Parkfairfax Historic District Presidential Detour *(centered around Martha Custis Dr.)* The Metropolitan Life Insurance Company developed the 285-acre community of Parkfairfax from 1941 to 1943 to appeal to the new commuter. With the housing shortage brought on by the Depression, increased size of the federal work force, and World War II mobilizations, the suburb offered an attractive home setting and easy access to Washington, D.C. You could rent a three-bedroom unit in 1943 for $90 a month (including utilities). The first tenants were military officers, lawyers, economists, engineers, secretaries and accountants.

This is a mid-20th century example of a planned garden-style suburb, with streets winding amid the gently sloping hillside. Its asymmetrical plan distinguishes it from the grid plan used in the colonial town (see Site 11) and earlier streetcar suburbs (see D-7 Rosemont Historic District Detour and D-8 Town of Potomac Historic District Detour).

Colonial Revival–style architecture was chosen for the lush, park-like development, named after the Fairfax family, wealthy landowners who had befriended young George Washington after his father's death. All the street names are associated with the Washingtons and colonial history. Numerous design techniques were used to create a sense of neighborhood—houses face away from the streets, toward one another, or are set around squares.

Many public figures have lived in Parkfairfax, including two of Alexandria's American presidents. The Richard Nixon family *(in a rare Parkfairfax photo, right)* resided at *3538 Gunston Rd.* (1947–51). The Gerald Fords lived at *1521 Mt. Eagle Pl.* (1951–55), before building their own home (see Site 42 B). Other residents have included astronaut Edward White, Secretary of State Dean Rusk, and nearly 20 members of Congress.

REPRINTED WITH PERMISSION OF THE SATURDAY EVENING POST, CA. 1949, RENEWED-BFL&MS, INC

*To resume the **Campaign Trail**, backtrack to Braddock Rd., turn left onto it and continue 8/10 of a mile down the hill, until you reach the intersection of Braddock and Russell Rds.*

43. Braddock Cannon *(intersection of Russell and Braddock Rds.)* This cast-iron Swedish cannon is thought to have started out with General Braddock *(left)* on his 1755 French and Indian War campaign to defend the western frontiers, but it was abandoned. It now marks the trail taken by his army. The general died returning from the battle of Fort Duquesne, at which George Washington's leadership qualities came to the forefront. Conservators applied ground walnut shells with a pressurized air hose to clean the cannon after removing a heavy build-up of paint. Another cannon was converted into a fountain next to Gadsby's Tavern (see Site 11 E). (ABOVE LEFT) LIBRARY OF CONGRESS; (ABOVE RIGHT) ELIZABETH LUALLEN

If you wish to visit the **North Ridge neighborhood**, *developed in 1890, turn north on Russell Rd.* **Mt. Ida** *(2404 Russell Rd.) was the home of Charles Alexander, Jr., the sixth-generation of the town's namesake (see Site 1).*

TO TAKE THE *Ivy Hill Cemetery Detour, go west uphill on Braddock Rd., and turn left (west) onto W. Alexandria Ave. Continue to Timber Branch Pkwy., turn right, and proceed one block to the entrance to* **Ivy Hill Cemetery**. To CONTINUE ON THE **Campaign Trail**, *continue on Braddock Rd. to the* **D-7 Rosemont Historic District Detour**.

D-6 Ivy Hill Cemetery Detour *(between King St. and Timber Branch Pkwy.; car access at 2823 King St. Please show respect for the cemetery and its visitors, especially during funerals.)* Started as a family burial ground in 1811, the cemetery was dedicated as a community cemetery in 1856 at an event for which "a very large assemblage of ladies and gentlemen was collected"* to sing a hymn and pray. One of the town's largest and best kept cemeteries, non-denominational Ivy Hill has 24 acres of wooded terrain sloping down to Timber Branch, which runs south into Hooff's Run, and then into Cameron Run (see Site 32). Five acres were originally reserved for the poor, "without charge and to be laid out and ornamented in the same manner as the other portion."* A Circle of Honor Memorial near the front gate recognizes the sacrifices of seven firemen killed by the explosion of dynamite in a china shop basement in an 1855 fire started by an arsonist. Two more firefighter memorials are also

64   *"Alexandria Gazette," June 20, 1856, page 3.

here. Many of the families that have owned Alexandria businesses for generations are buried here, including the Bryants, Burkes, Herberts, Janneys, Leadbeaters, Smoots, Stablers and Wheats.

Backtrack to W. Braddock Rd. and turn right (east). Proceed to Commonwealth Ave. To TAKE THE *Rosemont Detour, turn right (south) on Commonwealth Ave. and proceed to its intersection with Rosemont Ave.* To CONTINUE ON THE *Campaign Trail, you can either go north on Commonwealth Ave. to take the **Town of Potomac Detour D-8**, or continue east on Braddock Rd., until you reach Mt. Vernon Ave. (see Site 44)*

D-7 Rosemont Historic District Detour *(centered around Commonwealth and Rosemont Aves.)* This 1908 streetcar suburb was marketed to middle-income families seeking early 20th century amenities—water, gas, sewers, sidewalks, streetlights, police protection and trolley station—as well as green lawns, big lots and fine views. Note the wide median that contained the streetcar tracks of the Alexandria and Fairfax Electric Railway, chartered in 1892. New homeowners could board the trolley at Commonwealth Ave. station at the foot of Rosemont Ave. and arrive in Washington, D.C. in only 18 minutes for 5 cents.

Backtrack on Commonwealth Ave. until you reach W. Braddock Rd. To TAKE THE *Town of Potomac Detour, cross Braddock Rd., and continue north on Commonwealth Ave. Turn right on Bellefonte Ave., then turn left on Mt. Vernon Ave. Proceed 2 blocks to Windsor Ave.* To CONTINUE ON THE *Campaign Trail, turn right (east) on Braddock Rd., and proceed until you reach Mt. Vernon Ave. (see Site 44)*

D-8 Town of Potomac Historic District Detour *(centered on Mt. Vernon and Windsor Aves.)* The **Town of Potomac** (1908) included two subdivisions—Del Ray and St. Elmo—which were laid out in 1894. You could buy a lot for $1 down and $1 a week mortgage. Residents commuted by electric railway to D.C. or worked at Potomac Yards, one of the largest railroad switching facilities in the region. The area also included the St. Asaph's Race Track *(located between Mt. Ida and Stewart Aves.)*, which opened in 1888 as the Gentlemen's Driving Club, but it was closed in 1904 due to the new suburbanites' desire to improve morality. The St. Asaph's Track attracted so many gamblers that the Good Citizens League was formed to eliminate the establishment. With changes in voting laws, a new Commonwealth Attorney tried to close the business, even leading a group to chop down the gambling house doors with axes! The historic district is a fine "streetcar suburb" representing the 1890s. Architectural styles include Queen Anne, bungalow and Colonial Revival houses, and commercial buildings of Art Deco and Art Moderne styles. Visit the **Town Hall** at 2113 E. Windsor St.

To resume the Campaign Trail, go south on Mt. Vernon Ave., turn left onto Glendale Ave., then turn right to enter the school grounds.

44. George Washington School *(1005 Mt. Vernon Ave.)* and **Alexandria 200th Anniversary Time Capsule** *(north end of football field; access from Glendale Ave.)*   The school opened in 1935 as a high school. African Americans attended Parker-Gray High School east of the railroad tracks. In 1949, Alexandrians celebrated the 200th birthday of the town by filling a time capsule (manufactured by the Torpedo Factory) with memorabilia and burying it here. The forgotten capsule was rediscovered by students, and its location is now marked at the north end of the football field.

1961, ALEXANDRIA LIBRARY, SPECIAL COLLECTIONS

BIOfact: George Washington Rock & Rolls!

Two popular musicians of the 1960s attended George Washington High School. Jim Morrison of the *Doors*, an icon of the rock scene, lived on Woodland Terrace and graduated in 1961. Known for his rendition of "Light my Fire," biographers note that Morrison's teachers viewed him as a smart but troubled student. He read voraciously and wrote poetry journals, but also played pranks at school.

Another GW student, Ellen Cohen, went to New York after high school. By 1964 she had changed her name and was singing with Zal Yanovsky (later with the *Lovin' Spoonful*) as *Cass Elliot and the Big Three* in D.C. clubs. A year later, "Mama Cass" became a co-founder of *The Mamas and the Papas*. Her lyrical voice is remembered for "California Dreamin" and "Dream a Little Dream of Me."

HENRY DILTZ; WWW.ANGELFIRE.COM/ MA2/MAMASANDPAPAS/CASSPHOTO.HTML

Continue south on Mt. Vernon Ave. to Braddock Rd., and turn left. Pass the Braddock Road Metro Station on your left, then veer right onto N. West St. Take an immediate left onto Pendleton St., and continue for five blocks back into Old Town until you reach N. Alfred St. You enter the local **Parker-Gray Historic District** *at N. Patrick St., and the* **Alexandria Old & Historic National Landmark District** *at N. Washington St. To begin the* **Sugar House Trail***, turn left onto N. Alfred St. and proceed to Wythe St.* ∎

 ## Sugar House Trail

9

Length:

0.74 miles

Terrain:

Flat trail along
Old Town streets; street and
pedestrian traffic

Highlights:

● Lee Family and
George Washington Treks

● Alexandria Black History
Resource Center

● The Lloyd House

● Friendship Firehouse

*The sugar
house interior above
(also see back cover)
shows the process
of boiling raw
sugar (muscavado)
from the West Indies,
which was
later refined here
using sugar-
cone molds (left) and
syrup jars.
Alexandria was
one of the country's
largest producers of
refined sugar
in the early 1800s.*

(ABOVE TOP)
THE BRITISH LIBRARY

(ABOVE LEFT)
ANNA FRAME

Sugar House Trail

45. Alexandria Black History Resource Center and **Watson Reading Room:** Museum and library focused on African American life.

46. Lee Family Trek: Cotton mill and four houses occupied by noteworthy Lees:

(A) *428 S. Washington St.*, Edmund Jennings Lee.

(B) *614 Oronoco St.*, Lee Fendall House, Henry "Lighthorse Harry" Lee.

(C) *609 Oronoco St.*, Cornelia Lee Hopkins.

(D) *607 Oronoco St.*, Robert E. Lee.

(E) **Mt. Vernon Cotton Mill**, *515 N. Washington St.*

47. Friends Burying Ground: Quaker cemetery and City library.

48. Lloyd House and Hoffman Sugar House: A mayor's home, it was sold to pay debts and used as a Quaker school.

49. George WashingtonTrek: Three blocks with buildings related to George Washington.

50. Moore-McLean Sugar House: Loaf and lump sugar were produced here by African Americans.

51. Friendship Firehouse: Earliest fire company operated with volunteers.

To begin the trail, go to the intersection of N. Alfred and Wythe Sts.

* **45. Alexandria Black History Resource Center** and **Watson Reading Room** *(638 N. Alfred St.)* One room of the museum was built in 1940 as the Robinson Library. Construction of the African American community's first public library was prompted by the 1939 sit-in at the City Library (see Site 47). Abandoned in the 1960s following desegregation, the Robinson Library became the focus of citizens' efforts to create a center for African American heritage in the 1980s. This area is in the Parker-Gray Historic District, a local preservation zone in the historic "Uptown" black neighborhood. *Open to the public.*

Backtrack south on N. Alfred St., cross Pendleton St., then turn left on Oronoco St. and proceed to N. Columbus St. To TAKE THE *Lee Family Trek, continue east on Oronoco St. to its intersection with N. Washington St.* To CONTINUE ON THE *Sugar House Trail, turn right (south) on N. Columbus St. and proceed to Queen St. (see Site 47).*

46. Lee Family Trek *(begins at N. Washington and Oronoco Sts.)*
Members of two Lee family branches moved to Alexandria from their rural

*For information on symbols used in this book, turn to page 13.

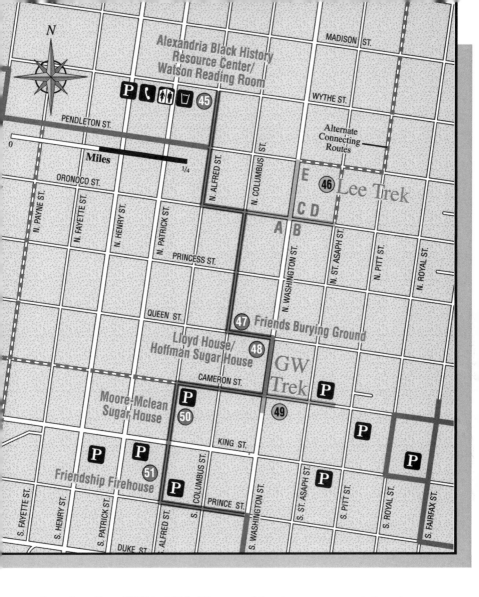

plantations from 1784 to 1815. They sought a stronger economic base in the city as agricultural trade with England declined after the Revolution. Eventually 30 Lees, predominately the fifth generation since the first Lee arrived in Jamestown, lived here. The Lee family bought and sold properties to one another, cared for each other's children and widows, and built a 100-year tradition at **Lee Corner** *(Washington and Oronoco Sts.).*

(A) SW Corner *(428 S. Washington St.)* Edmund Jennings Lee bought the lot in 1801 and then moved across the street in 1836. He served as mayor and court executor, was president of the Alexandria Canal (see Site 4) and a founder of the Episcopal Seminary (see Site 42). Edmund became the guardian for his 11-year-old nephew, Robert E. Lee, after his father died. Edmund's son Cassius, Robert's cousin and best friend, lived here until he moved to Canada during the Civil War.

(B) SE corner—**Lee Fendall House** *(614 Oronoco St.)* The lot was originally purchased by Henry "Lighthorse Harry" Lee, Robert E. Lee's father. Philip Fendall, lawyer and a founder of Bank of Alexandria (see Site 11), built the house in 1785 and later married Henry's sister, Mary Lee. Although the property was seized by the Union for a hospital during the Civil War, the Lee family returned and stayed in the house until 1903. Artifacts excavated from the well include many Victorian women's objects, including a curling iron and a cupid-decorated pipe.

John L. Lewis, president of the United Mine Workers Union, lived here from 1937 until 1969. *Open to the public.*

(C) NE corner *(609 Oronoco St.)* Constructed in 1795, the house became a Lee residence in 1814 when Cornelia Lee Hopkins moved here. Her sister, Portia Lee Hodgson, lived at Bellevue (see Site 2). Anne Harriotte Lee, Edmund's daughter, moved here from across the street when she married John Lloyd in 1820 (see Site 48). Cornelia's stepdaughter resided here and raised Cassius Lee's son after his wife died in child-birth. In 1873, the property was bought by Richard Bland Lee II, whose father had been the guardian of Portia and Cornelia in their youth.

(D) The Boyhood Home of Robert E. Lee **(607 Oronoco St.)**, a twin to its neighbor at 609, was built by John Potts, Jr. With George Washington, Potts established the Potomac Company, an early effort to build a canal next to the upper Potomac River to facilitate river trade. Robert E. Lee *(right)* moved here with his family at age three; his injured father left when Lee was six years old and died five years later. Lee left home to attend West Point in 1825 and became commander of the Confederate Army in 1861 out of loy-alty to his home state of Virginia.

Backtrack to N. Washington St. Go one block north to Pendleton St.
(E) The **Mt. Vernon Cotton Mill** *(515 N. Washington St.)* is the only Old Town mill to survive. Women worked here, weaving 5,000 yards of sheeting per 11-hour day. The old mill and the four blocks to the north were later occupied by **Portner's Brewery**, from 1868–1916. It was one of the largest breweries in the South and exported lager beer on a fleet of rail cars packed with ice.

*To resume the **Sugar House Trail**, backtrack on N. Washington St., and make a right on Oronoco St. Turn left on N. Columbus St. Go two blocks, and make a left onto Queen St.*

47. Friends Burying Ground (grounds of **Barrett Branch Library** at *717 Queen St.*)   The cemetery was established by the Alexandria Monthly Meeting of the Religious Society of Friends (Quakers) in 1785. They leased the land to the City for a library in 1937. A 1994 addition necessitated archaeological identification of 159 graves; of these, the remains of 64 burials were carefully excavated and reburied. Visit the exhibit on Quakers inside. African Americans staged a sit-in at the Library in 1939 to protest their exclusion. In response, a separate one-room library (see Site 45) was constructed for black patrons.

Follow Queen St. east, and turn right (south) onto N. Washington St.

48. Lloyd House *(220 N. Washington St.)* and **Hoffman Sugar House** *(NOT VISIBLE)*   In 1810, Jacob Hoffman bought the home and established a large sugar refinery next door. It was held by the Lloyd family from about 1832 into the early 20th century.

Continue south on N. Washington St. to its intersection with Cameron St. To TAKE THE George Washington Trek, turn left (east) on Cameron St. To CONTINUE ON THE Sugar House Trail, turn right (west) on Cameron St. and proceed to its intersection with N. Alfred St. (see Site 50)

49. George Washington Trek *(the 700, 600, and 500 blocks of Cameron St.)*   Townspeople considered Washington their greatest citizen. Although the Washingtons did not reside here, they often traveled from their Mt. Vernon plantation to Alexandria. He was seen frequently in Christ Church, taverns and shops, and at friends' homes, political gatherings and debates leading to the American Revolution.

"Lighthorse Harry" Lee, father of Robert E. Lee, brought his family to **611 Cameron St.** when they arrived in 1810. A Revolutionary War hero, he delivered the famous eulogy calling Washington "first in war, first in peace, and first in the hearts of his countrymen."

The **Yeaton Fairfax House** *(607 Cameron St.),* built by William Yeaton (the architect of the Washington family tomb at Mt. Vernon) in 1800, was owned by Thomas Lord Fairfax, 9th Baron of Cameron, the son of one of Washington's closest friends, Bryan Fairfax of Mt. Eagle. It has been called Alexandria's finest Federal-style building.

The **George Washington Townhouse lot** *(508 Cameron St.)*, was purchased by Washington in 1763, and by 1769 a small house, stable and outbuildings had been erected. The house was often rented or lent to friends and family; records also show that Washington used this house while in Alexandria. The structure was demolished in 1855 and was reconstructed in 1960 .

Backtrack on Cameron St., and cross to the west side of N. Washington St.

Christ Church *(118 N. Washington St.)* was completed in 1773. Cameron St. deviated from the standard city grid because the church was built before the town's expansion. Both George Washington and Robert E. Lee attended church here and silver plates mark their pews. Burials began at the **Christ Church Cemetery** by 1766 and ended about 1809 (though a number of Confederate soldiers were reinterred here from National Cemetery (see Site 26) in 1879). City archaeologists discovered 52 unmarked graves with historic hexagonally shaped coffins prior to construction of an addition. Graves continue under the sidewalk beyond the cemetery walls. *Open to the public.*

*To resume the **Sugar House Trail**, take exit onto N. Columbus St. and cross it. Continue straight (west) onto Cameron St. and proceed to N. Alfred St.*

50. Moore-McLean Sugar House *(NOT VISIBLE; at Cameron and N. Alfred Sts.)*

In the early 19th century, Alexandria was one of the largest producers of refined sugar in the United States. With muscavado (raw sugar) shipped from Cuba, the refinery (1804–28) produced lump and loaf sugar, syrup and candy. Alexandria Archaeology excavated here and found numerous structures related to the sugar refining process, including a huge brick cistern, as well as thousands of earthenware sugar molds and syrup jar fragments. Seven enslaved African Americans, two of them children, provided the refinery's labor. A portion of 111 N. Alfred St. once formed part of the refinery complex.

Turn left (south) onto N. Alfred St. and cross King St., after which it becomes S. Alfred St.

51. Friendship Firehouse *(107 S. Alfred St.)*

The Friendship Fire Company, established in 1774 on Market Square, was the first volunteer fire company in Alexandria. The current firehouse was built in 1855; the museum displays early hand-drawn fire engines and other historic fire-fighting apparatus. *Open to the public.*

*Proceed south on S. Alfred St., and make a left onto Prince St. Go two blocks to S. Washington St. to begin the **Friends Trail**.* ■

*The Society of Friends, or Quakers, were a sizable economic
and social force in antebellum Alexandria. Robert and Anna Miller's
50th anniversary (above, top) assembled their large family.
Edward Stabler (left), apothecary, quietly emancipated many enslaved
people. Mary Hartshorne Stabler (right), Edward's second wife, raised
15 children and was a proponent of female education.*

 # Friends Trail

Length:
0.72 miles

Terrain:
Flat trail along Old Town streets;
street and pedestrian traffic

Highlights:
● The Lyceum, Alexandria's
History Museum

● Old Town Architecture

● The Alexandria Academy

73

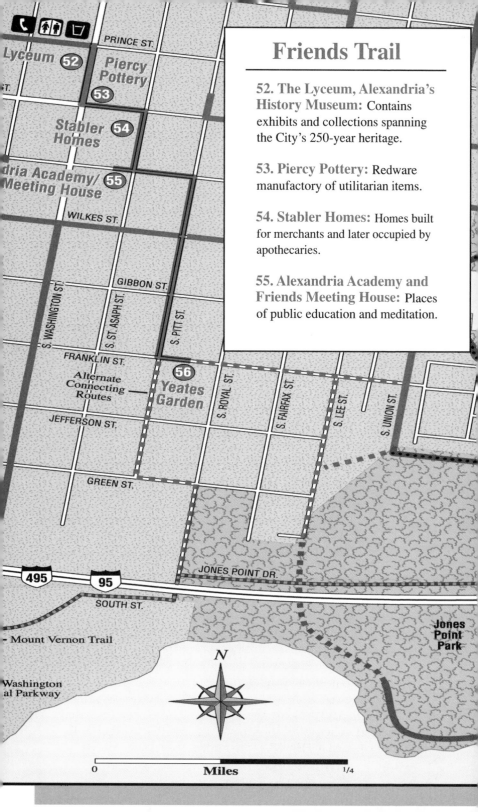

PRINCE ST.

Lyceum 52

Piercy Pottery

53

Stabler Homes 54

dria Academy/ 55
Meeting House

WILKES ST.

GIBBON ST.

S. WASHINGTON ST.

S. ST. ASAPH ST.

S. PITT ST.

FRANKLIN ST.

Alternate
Connecting
Routes

56
Yeates Garden

S. ROYAL ST.

S. FAIRFAX ST.

S. LEE ST.

S. UNION ST.

JEFFERSON ST.

GREEN ST.

495   95

JONES POINT DR.

SOUTH ST.

Mount Vernon Trail

Washington
al Parkway

Jones
Point
Park

N

0   Miles   1/4

Friends Trail

52. The Lyceum, Alexandria's History Museum: Contains exhibits and collections spanning the City's 250-year heritage.

53. Piercy Pottery: Redware manufactory of utilitarian items.

54. Stabler Homes: Homes built for merchants and later occupied by apothecaries.

55. Alexandria Academy and Friends Meeting House: Places of public education and meditation.

The trail begins at the intersection of S.Washington and Prince Sts.

52. The Lyceum, Alexandria's History Museum

(201 S. Washington St.)   Quakers helped build the Greek Revival style Lyceum in 1839. It functioned as the city's first cultural center. Today, it serves as a museum which collects, preserves and interprets the history and material culture of Alexandria and Northern Virginia. *Open to the Public.*

Continue south on S. Washington St. to Duke St., and cross the street.

53. Piercy Pottery *(NOT VISIBLE; between 220 S. Washington St. and its intersection with Duke St.)*   A Revolutionary War veteran, Henry Piercy brought his German tradition of redware ceramic manufacture here from Philadelphia. Although disabled during the war, Piercy produced his distinctive yellow-slip combed- and trailed-design wares here from 1792 until 1811. His retail shop was located on the 400 block of King St. Archaeological excavations at both the pottery and the shop have yielded thousands of fragments of pots, jars, pans, chargers and milk pans that were used in kitchens before they were replaced by grey stonewares (see Site 22).

From S. Washington St., turn left (east) onto Duke St, and go one block. Turn right onto S. St. Asaph St. and cross the street.

54. Stabler Homes *(305 and 307 S. St. Asaph St.)*   Merchant partners, James Lawrason and Benjamin Shreve, built adjoining houses between 1783 and 1785 (see Sites 12 and 24). The houses shared a large brick ice well that straddled the property line. It was probably used by both households to keep foods from spoiling. Son and father, William and Edward Stabler, both Society of Friends members, apothecaries and abolitionists, lived here later (see Site 11 F).

Continue south one block on S. St. Asaph St., then turn left (east) onto Wolfe St., and cross the street.

55. Alexandria Academy and Friends Meeting House

(600 block of Wolfe St., south side)   Founded in 1785, the Academy included the Free School, which was endowed by George Washington and provided education for those unable to pay tuition. (No public education was available at that time). The Quaker Meeting House, now the site of the Little Theater, stood to the left of the Academy. The Friends, often called Quakers, were a major force in the town's economic, cultural and humanitarian development before the Civil War.

Backtrack east on Wolfe St. and go one block. Make a right (south) onto S. Pitt St. and proceed for three blocks. Turn left (east) onto Franklin St.

56. Yeates Garden *(house at 414 Franklin St.)*   In 1813, William Yeates, an English member of the Society of Friends, began planting a large plot with flowering trees. By 1850, it was a pleasure garden where ice cream was served and which functioned as a "promenade for ladies and gentlemen," a place which presented a "splendid water scene on the Potomac."*

*The intersection of S. Pitt and Franklin Sts. marks the end of the **Friends Trail** and of the **Alexandria Heritage Trail**.*

*FROM HERE, YOU MAY RETURN TO **Old Town Alexandria** and to **Daingerfield Island**, by following Franklin St. east to S. Union St. and turning left (north).   OR YOU MAY CONTINUE SOUTH TO THE **Mount Vernon Estate** (home of George and Martha Washington) by continuing south on S. Pitt St. and turning left (east) on Green St. Proceed one block, then turn right (south) on S. Royal St. and pick up the **Mount Vernon Trail** going south. Follow this nine miles until you reach the **Mount Vernon Estate**. ∎*

Additional Reading

Alexandria in The Civil War by J.G. Barber. H.E. Howard, Inc., 1988.

A Guide to Historic Alexandria by W. Seale. The City of Alexandria, 2000.

"A Remarkable and Courageous Journey, A Guide to Alexandria's African American History." Alexandria Convention and Visitors Association, 2001 (free).

A Seaport Saga, Portrait of Old Alexandria, Virginia by W.F. Smith and M.T. Miller. The Donning Company, 2001.

Alexandria, A Town in Transition, 1800-1900 edited by J.D. Macoll. Alexandria Bicentennial Commission and Alexandria Historical Society, 1977.

Col. John Carlyle, Gent. A True and Just Account of the Man and His House, 1720-1780 by J.D. Muson, Northern Virginia Regional Park Authority, 1986.

Historic Alexandria, Street by Street by Ethelyn Cox. Historic Alexandria Foundation 1976

Mr. Lincoln's Forts, A Guide to the Civil War Defenses of Washington by B.F. Cooling III and W.H. Owen II. White Mane Publishing Company, 1988.

"Recreation Facilities and Trails Map," Alexandria, Virginia (free).

The Alexandria Canal: Its History and Preservation by T. S. Hahn and E. L. Kemp. West Virginia University Press, 1992

Index

Italic indicates illustrations.

Places Open
to the Public

*This symbol
means wheelchair
accessible.*

*Contact each place for hours of
operation and other information.*

Alexandria Archaeology Museum
The Torpedo Factory Art Center
105 North Union Street,
Room # 327
(703) 838-4399
www.AlexandriaArchaeology.org

**Alexandria Black History
    Resource Center and Watson
    Reading Room**
638 North Alfred Street
(703) 838-4356
www.AlexBlackHistory.org

Alexandria City Hall
301 King Street
(703) 838-4000
ci.alexandria.va.us

**Alexandria Library,
    Barrett Branch**
717 Queen Street
(Entrance on Wythe St.)
(703) 838-4577
www.alexandria.lib.va.us/
branches/barrett.html

Alexandria Seaport Center
Alexandria Waterfront,
south of Founders Park
(703) 549-7078
www.alexandriaseaport.org

The Athenaeum
201 Prince Street
(703) 548-0035

Carlyle House Historic Park
121 North Fairfax Street
(703) 549-2997
www.carlylehouse.org

Charles E. Beatley, Jr.
  Central Library
5005 Duke Street
(703) 519-5900
www.alexandria.lib.va.us/branches/
  beatley.html

Chinquapin Park Recreation
  Center
3210 King Street
(703) 931-1127
ci.alexandria.va.us/rpca/
  rpca_chinq_home.html

Christ Church
118 North Washington Street
(703) 549-1450
www.historicchristchurch.org

Department of Recreation, Parks
  & Cultural Activities
1108 Jefferson Street
(703) 838-4343/4344
ci.alexandria.va.us/rpca

Fort Ward Museum & Historic Site
4301 West Braddock Road
(703) 838-4848
www.FortWard.org

Freedmen's Cemetery
1001 S. Washington Street
The Friends of Freedmen's Cemetery
638 N. Alfred St.
www.freedmenscemetery.org

Friendship Firehouse Museum
107 S. Alfred Street
(703) 838-3891
www.ci.alexandria.va.us/oha/
  friendship

Gadsby's Tavern Museum
134 North Royal Street
(703) 838-4242
www.GadsbysTavernMuseum.org

The George Washington Memorial
  Parkway Headquarters
Turkey Run Park
McLean, VA 22101
(703) 289-2500
www.nps.gov/gwmp/

The George Washington National
  Masonic Memorial
101 Callahan Drive
(703) 683-2007
www.gwmemorial.org

Jerome "Buddy" Ford Nature Center
  and Dora Kelley Nature Park and
  Wildlife Sanctuary
5700-5900 Sanger Avenue
(703) 838-4829
ci.alexandria.va.us/rpca/
  rpca_rc_buddy_home.html

Lee-Fendall House Museum
  and Garden
614 Oronoco Street
(703) 548-1789
www.leefendallhouse.org

The Lyceum, Alexandria's
  History Museum
201 South Washington Street
(703) 838-4994
www.AlexandriaHistory.org

Old Presbyterian Meeting House
321 South Fairfax Street
(703) 549-6670
www.opmh.org

The Protestant Episcopal
  Theological Seminary
  in Virginia
3737 Seminary Road
(703) 370-6600
www.vts.edu

Ramsay House Visitors Center
221 King Street
(703) 838-4200; 800/388-9119
www.funside.com

Stabler-Leadbeater Apothecary
  Museum
105 - 107 South Fairfax Street
(703) 836-3713
www.apothecary.org

Torpedo Factory Art Center
105 North Union Street
(703) 838-4565
www.torpedofactory.org

Winkler Botanical Preserve
5400 Roanoke Avenue
(703) 578-7888